FORM,
FIT,
AND FASHION

First published in the United States of America by
Rockport Publishers, a member of
Quayside Publishing Group
100 Cummings Center
Suite 406-L
Beverly, Massachusetts 01915
Telephone: (978) 282-9590
Fax: (978) 283-2742
www.rockpub.com

Library of Congress Cataloging-in-Publication Data

Calderin, Jay.
  Form, fit, and fashion : all the details fashion designers need to know but can
never find / Jay Calderin.
        p. cm.
  Includes index.
  ISBN-13: 978-1-59253-541-5
  ISBN-10: 1-59253-541-0
  1. Clothing and dress. 2. Fashion design. 3. Fashion. I. Title.
  TT507.C3154 2009
  746.9'2–dc22

                                                           2009028314
                                                           CIP

ISBN-13: 978-1-59253-541-5
ISBN-10: 1-59253-541-0

Editorial and Art Direction: Alicia Kennedy

Cover and Graphic Design: Kelly Smith and Chris Grimley for over,under
Illustrations: Jay Calderin

Printed in China

FORM,

FIT,

AND FASHION

**ALL THE DETAILS FASHION DESIGNERS
NEED TO KNOW BUT CAN NEVER FIND**

JAY CALDERIN

CONTENTS

i.

INTRODUCTION

The premise behind this handbook for fashion designers is that the art and business of fashion is ultimately a body of symbols and systems—a language. To communicate effectively within the industry and with the consumer, the designer must have access to an array of relevant information and resources. Since by definition fashion is ever changing, the focus here is on developing strategies that provide a competitive edge, no matter what the prevailing trends of the moment might be. These formulas also afford the creative side of fashion a fertile environment for growth.

Importantly, *Form, Fit, and Fashion* approaches its subject through an entrepreneurial lens. Even within large corporate fashion houses, designers often consider themselves independent entities—free agents. Their career arcs are frequently defined not only by the positions they have held, but also by the strategies they have employed. Whether their reputations have been meticulously planned or have developed organically, these histories are in the end a commodity, requiring polished packaging and integrated delivery systems to have the greatest impact. Contemporary fashion designers face the job of designing a career path as well as a collection.

The dialects of style are as varied as the cultures that cultivate them. Regardless of the vernacular, successful long-term design influences are based on a closed circuit, one that conveys the designer's message clearly. Designers can tap into this circular pathway at any point, but they must complete the course. This book serves as a primer for newcomers and a reference guide for professionals engaged with the daily demands of this art form/business. Each section represents a connection that fashion designers make between their original idea and the audience they wish to reach. As this volume is designed to be concise, convenient, and portable, the material is intended to act as a catalyst for further study and experimentation.

Section 1, **RESEARCH**, is about fashion intelligence—gathering information to identify skill sets and lay the groundwork for building a cohesive collection. Careful self-examination, vocabulary development, an understanding of fashion history and of forecasting techniques all contribute to the acquisition of project-specific data. Section 2, **EDIT**, takes the next step: refining concepts through a process that collects, reviews, prepares, and arranges the research. Constructing a mood board, fixing on a specialization, studying consumer profiles, and establishing a budget help to narrow the designer's focus. Section 3, **DESIGN**, establishes a blueprint, using color, textiles, silhouette, and accessory design. Each endeavor must be backed by a deliberate intention—a detailed, purposeful plan and an inventive approach to integrating the components that will result in a successful prototype. Section 4, **CONSTRUCT**, examines how the concept developed within the design process is implemented, employing techniques from rendering to patternmaking, stitching, and finishing. During this period, the designer will also resolve issues with production and determine quality-control standards. Section 5, **CONNECT**, explores how the designer prepares the work for public consumption, concentrating on the power of words and images and experiences in communication. Generating a portfolio, building a brand, working with the market, and producing shows identify and amplify the designer's vision. Section 6, **EVOLVE**, addresses the designer's challenge to create meaning while embracing change. Celebrity, art, technology, and global cultural shifts, as well as personal experience and education, all influence fashion design. Designers must understand their part in what a collection or label or company represents. Adding to the mix, a series of interviews with prominent industry leaders provides insights into the phases described throughout *Form, Fit, and Fashion*.

1.

RESEARCH

Good design is based on a clear understanding of the end user. At the core of customer comprehension is information, and research is the way to get it. The intuitive designer internalizes the hunt-and-gather process, while the deliberate designer makes a conscious decision to target, collect, and filter through various data.

The mindset with which fashion designers approach their research correlates directly with how they have been hardwired to learn and to interpret information. So which avenue—the intuitive or the deliberate—comes easier to a designer is not of great importance: More valuable is the ability to employ both strategies. A command of history, for example, can be earned through the diligent study of books, but it can also be mastered by immersing oneself in the art and music of a period or even be absorbed through the eyes of others who have interpreted a period for television or film.

Observation and experience are vital to the development of a fashion designer. A hunger for and curiosity about the world around them will fertilize designers' imaginations and hone their critical-thinking skills. As designers cultivate good instincts, they will give the appearance of having an effortless grasp of the design process. Traditional research techniques will allow designers to continue to access and explore uncharted territory. New frontiers will always present themselves when content is constantly replenished and refreshed.

Chapter 1: Evaluation

To say that the field of fashion design is highly competitive is a tremendous understatement. The fashion centers of New York, Paris, and Milan lead the industry, but are by no means the only places where a designer can pursue a career. Every major city now seems to have a regional pool of style makers, fashion design schools, and local fashion weeks. Do-it-yourself programs, classes, books, and magazines provide just enough of what someone might need to feel like an authentic fashionista. Reality television shows and unlimited access to information on the Internet also add to the mix of aspiring designers.

In the celebrity-driven culture that the fashion industry feeds, any inkling of talent will often be blown out of proportion. This exposure affords new designers with their coveted fifteen minutes of fame, but also robs them of the opportunity to fully develop their message and their craft. They are immediately tested by demanding consumers and media outlets moving at lightning speed. To survive depends on an understanding of how the system works and a healthy skepticism of their own press. In the long term, building a successful career as a fashion designer requires much more than making beautiful, well-constructed clothes. That's merely the price to play.

A good designer can create anything with sufficient research and a clear awareness of the design challenge being undertaken. A great designer does more. The Pareto principle describes a law of the vital few, where 80 percent of the effects result from 20 percent of the causes. In fashion, this small but essential core is the spark that sets things into motion. Visionary, unique, inspired, ahead of their time: Theirs are big shoes to fill, even when designers feel that they, too, have something to contribute.

The bad news is that when it comes to clothing the human body most everything has been done before. The good news is that it hasn't been done by each new designer. Why this should matter to anyone else is a tough question that demands a response full of meaning, purpose, and confidence; otherwise it just gets lost in the sea of options that flood the fashion marketplace every year. To truly grasp what one stands for both personally and as a designer will infuse one's work with passion and one's message with clarity.

THE INDIVIDUAL DESIGNER

The first step is for designers to establish—with absolute honesty—what they bring to the table.

Natural Talents

Everyone has gifts. Having a flair for fashion or an instinct for design is not always an indicator of a good fashion designer, nor is it a prerequisite. An inherent affinity for any number of other disciplines, such as math, science, or sports, may provide as good a base to build on as an art-related foundation. With or without an innate aptitude for fashion, curiosity, dedication, and the occasional leap of faith are markers of the potential for success in the field.

Learned Skills

Anyone can acquire proficiency in an activity, given enough time and effort. Fashion encompasses a vast range of specialties, each with its own techniques and set of skills. By honing these skills, designers establish a fluency and immediate recall in the workplace. Nothing beats actual experience. Through classes, workshops, and internships designers can build hand-to-eye coordination, learn to anticipate problems, and address the particular challenges of executing their ideas.

Interpersonal Intelligence

As designers gain a clear picture of what they want to accomplish, they must be actively listening and observing the nonverbal cues to the needs and desires of others. Such attention will better equip designers to manage relationships within a design team or with vendors, say, and to persuade others to make concessions in the name of collaboration.

Defining Success

Like any creative endeavor, fashion is demanding and regularly tests the resolve. Designers must understand their primary motivation for pursuing a career in fashion, whether fame, financial reward, critical success, or to fill a void in the market. A venture that needs to generate a profit as well as acclaim presents certain realities. A designer may want to be respected for artistic contributions to the field but can't avoid the bottom line. Prioritizing goals early on creates a touchstone for every stage of the design process.

STARTER QUESTIONS

Well-crafted questions will help fashion designers identify and quantify their existing talents and skills, as well as determine how they work with people, how they define success, and how they tap into their creativity. These questions can be exciting, thought provoking, and sometimes intimidating. Designers should approach their answers as baselines rather than as judgments of the validity of their path.

Why do I want to be a fashion designer?

What inspires me?

Do I have a grasp on fashion history?

What training do I have?

Do I know how garments are constructed?

Do I have an understanding of textiles?

What is my industry experience?

What specialized area of fashion interests me?

Have I committed to a professional career path?

What are my business skills?

Am I comfortable with technology?

Can I adhere to timelines?

Am I good with people?

Where do I plan on working?

Who are my industry role models?

When will I start my next project?

How will I maintain fit and quality standards?

How large a body of work have I built?

How do I plan to continue learning?

Armed with a better idea of the areas in which they are competent, fall short, or excel, designers must next take action to protect the environments that allow their innate gifts to flourish and expose themselves to a wide variety of places and situations that inspire and afford them opportunity. At each step, designers' understanding of who they are within the field of fashion will broaden.

THE DESIGN TEAM

Designers must decide which skills will become an integral part of their own design process and which will be better handled by individuals for whom it is second nature. In building a design team, designers should seek out and surround themselves with people whose skills complement their own, whether in the category of sewing techniques or business models, say. Always strive to attract the very best talent available. Good designers are also leaders who will not hesitate to hire someone who is better than they are in a particular arena. Well-balanced teams allow individual members to concentrate their efforts on their part of the process.

Designers should regularly update the biographies and/or résumés of the entire team. A good understanding not only of their backgrounds, but also both their professional and personal interests, allows designers to engage team members creatively in their vision. Individuals who function as an extension of the designer's skill set can be focused on specific components of any project, enabling them to take it further on behalf of the designer.

Classes, workshops, lectures, and special fashion events provide designers with numerous opportunities for connecting with experts and peers from whom to build a team. Designers must be prepared for each encounter: Know how to present an identity with enough detail to entice, and yet concisely so as not to bore. Observe behavior and listen carefully for valuable content. Discreetly and casually collect contact information and follow up once the encounter has been processed.

MENTOR MATCHING

Designers can benefit enormously from finding a mentor. Learning can come from both established fashion professionals and from peers who are making strides in areas the designer wishes to engage. For anyone going to the trouble of reaching out for this kind of support, a level of humility and active listening are essential. Situations might arise in which the designer disagrees with the advice being shared. But competing to make one's point negates the full benefit of what a mentor may provide.

Hero worship is a different thing all together, because it is based on the myth surrounding a person rather than the facts. Those facts are simple: What decisions has a designer made, what were the results, and how have they stood the test of time? Historical and contemporary visionaries often become bigger than life within the context of one's daily experience. In fact, it is sum of their choices to which the designer responds and aspires.

TOOLS AND MATERIALS

Photographs by Tracy Aiguier.

Especially when starting out, designers must determine the tools and materials needed for their work. This inventory has a monetary value; but more important, it has a direct effect on how a designer will choose to execute an idea.

Money obviously allows for smoother and more seamless operations. The level of access to funding for any project can pose different types of challenges, yet a creative approach can find ways to stretch the effectiveness of any budget. Designers must constantly decide where they will make sacrifices and where they will not compromise.

The tools and materials required for all facets of any fashion challenge, from concept through construction and delivery, must be taken into account. Some are project specific, while others are a part of the overall needs of running a business. The list can be extensive and will continue to grow along with the scale of the business, but it begins with some fundamentals. Materials and tools should serve the needs of the overall design goal and the project in hand. A designer must avoid falling into the trap of acquiring tools without having a well-defined purpose for them. The right tool for the right job, however, is a smart investment, as it will often save time in the long run and will usually produce a polished result.

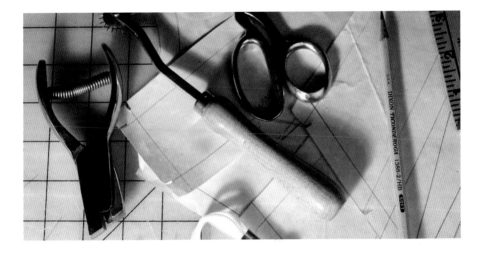

INVENTORY OF FUNDAMENTAL TOOLS FOR THE FASHION DESIGNER

Art	Patternmaking	Construction
Markers	Dress Form	Sewing Machine
Paints	Muslin	Overlock Machine
Brushes	Pins	Buttonhole Machine
Colored Pencils	Pencils	Hand Needles
Bristol Board	Dotted Paper	Fabrics
Tracing Paper	Oaktag Paper	Threads
	Paper Scissors	
Lap Board	Weights	Linings
	Pattern Hooks	Interfacing
Art Software	Hole Punch	
(Adobe Photoshop	Notcher	Notions
Adobe Illustrator)	Awl	Trim
Scanner	Tracing Wheel	Fabric Scissors
		Rotary Cutter
Presentation Folios	Tape Measure	Cutting Mat
	C-Thru Ruler	
	Yardstick	
	Hip Curve	
	French Curve	

THE CUSTOMER

At every point, fashion designers must ask themselves who they are serving. Many new designers are misled by the fact that large fashion companies are often diversified and offer products to multiple audiences. This broad designer presence in the market is usually the result of a long period in business and the carefully planned development of individual off-shoots. These branches of the business depend heavily on the success of the parent company. The Donna Karan brand is a good example of a company that worked diligently for many years to perfect the way it served its female customer before it began to offer menswear collections.

Packaging	Promotion	Documentation
Hangers	Business Cards	Digital Camera
Garment Bags	Stationery	Digital Video Recorder
Shopping Bags	Web Authoring Software	Video Editing Software
Tissue Paper	(Adobe Dreamweaver,	(Adobe Premiere, Avid,
	Panic Software's Coda)	Apple Final Cut Studio)
Boxes	Website	
Address Labels	Website Host	
Shipping Service		
	Unique URL Address	
Hang Tags	Email Address	
Designer Labels	Logo Merchandise	
Size Labels		
Care Labels	Social and Professional	
	Networking Services	

Designers must narrow the customer field or run the risk of not appealing to anyone. Instead of declaring their customer to be twenty to fifty years old, a designer might place the emphasis on the need and desires of the thirty-five-year-old woman. Serve that woman well and younger women who connect with the significance associated with the thirty-something lifestyle will be attracted, as will an older consumer who wishes to infuse her image with a younger message.

Once designers have identified the customers they want to address, they need to figure out how to reach them. The direction of research and development now turns outward. Designers must form a clear and detailed understanding of their target. Observations will be drawn from both demographic and behavioral patterns.

Demographics

Demographic research produces raw data, including such details as age, location, income, profession, ethnicity, marital status, and number of children. This kind of information can be purchased from large companies that specialize in such research, but will come at a high price. The information can also be acquired on a smaller scale through more grassroots efforts that survey the designer's immediate community.

Psychographics

Although demographics generate a picture of the customer, it is merely an outline. For a more nuanced understanding of the designer's ideal target, the research needs to dig deeper. The designer should want to know what a woman does for fun, whether she prefers to cook or eat out, and any number of personal likes and dislikes that make her real in the designer's mind. No longer reduced to mere statistics, the customer can now be imagined as living in the designer's creations. All these considerations will be reflected in the designer's work, which will connect with the client in a meaningful way.

CULTURAL CLIMATE

What is happening at any given moment at the city, national, and global levels plays a role in how a designer's work is received. Politics, the economy, and world events become factors in the perceived value of what a designer produces. Wartime and national tragedy have historically been powerful influences on the attitudes of those with purchasing power, both during and after hard times. Following both World Wars, society responded with a celebration of youth, as is evident in the flapper culture of the 1920s and the mod and hippie cultures of the 1960s. More recently, after 9/11 a strong focus on family and home life pervaded all sectors of design. The current downturn in the economy has led some designers to forgo opulence and excess, and others to embrace more optimistic neon colors.

Fashion designers must ask themselves whether they anticipate their ideas being accepted or rejected because of current events and the influence of these events on public opinion. Customers are only part of the equation. Also in play are how the designer's employees are affected and how the media will interpret a collection as it relates to the news of the day. Designers might even ask what kind of entertainment is being successfully served to the public. For instance, are they looking to escape into fantasy, the way audiences in the 1930s turned to Hollywood for a respite from the Great Depression?

Pop references and celebrity obsessions have also become a part of the cultural mix. Elinor Glyn coined the use of the word *It* as a euphemism for sex appeal and sass in her 1923 novel *The Man and the Moment*. Four years later, when the actress Clara Bow appeared in the film based on Glyn's novel, the author dubbed her the "It Girl." Since then every generation has had its It Girl. Today, It Girls, It Boys, and It Products come and go at a much faster rate. A fashion designer who gravitates toward popular culture now needs to ensure that the "it" factor of their designs is not "so five minutes ago."

THE MEDIA

A strong understanding of media outlets and their missions can lead to very fruitful relationships for the fashion designer. Every successful newspaper, magazine, television show, and website has carefully researched their audiences to present them with the message they want in the style they want it. Designers who wish to be a part of that message must often tailor their content to create a natural fit. They must also find the correct language to best capture the essence of their work.

Great attention must be paid to the documentation of the designer's body of work, both past and present. Storytellers in the media will be looking for ways to weave tales relevant to their readers or viewers. Personal histories also play an important role in the process. A family photograph of the designer as a child seated with his mother at a sewing machine might speak to the inevitability of this career path, but equally an image could reflect the odds the designer had to overcome to pursue her passion. Furthermore, any images, still or moving, that are associated with the work must not only be on message but also reflect the aesthetic standards of the media outlet.

LOCATION

Just as in the world of real estate, location is one of the most important factors to influence how successful an endeavor will be. When it comes to fashion, designers must display an understanding of the place (or the differences among the various locales) where they do business. Urban settings often produce a taste for dark, somber palettes and professional silhouettes. By the same token, customers living in an urban environment might also buy into more provocative, even experimental designs when expressing themselves in social settings. Weather, as it relates to certain regions, can help an aesthetic evolve. In warm tropical climates, bright colors and large-scale prints are integral to the culture influencing fashion trends.

Chapter 2: Collection Theory

With a little creativity and a basic grasp of how a garment is constructed, many people will dabble in fashion and fancy themselves designers. With enough time, they might even accumulate a collection of garments. Certainly, their work might be an artistic accomplishment, but it does not address what the industry expects from the fashion designer each season. Designers are asked, above all, to translate a design philosophy into an evolving series of collections that speaks to their customers during every fashion cycle.

ACCESSING INSPIRATION

An artist may spend time courting the muse, but a fashion designer seldom has the luxury of waiting for inspiration to strike. Accessing the creative mind is simple if one fuels the source on a regular basis. Designers must train themselves to collect tear sheets from magazines and printouts from websites, as well as swatches of colors and textiles, and to keep notebooks of written ideas and sketches. Whatever form they take, these resource files should be maintained and organized for easy retrieval when trying to stimulate the imagination. Beyond fashion images, they should include material drawn from art, technology, science, graphics, architecture, advertisements—in other words, anything that triggers a response.

RESOURCE FILES

Category	Subcategories
Fashion	Daywear, eveningwear, menswear, outerwear, athletic apparel
Accessories	Shoes, bags, jewelry, hats, eyewear, hosiery, belts, gloves
Beauty	Models, hair, makeup, tattoos, piercing, fitness
Swatches	Color, texture, pattern, decoration, fastenings
Silhouette	Architecture, furniture, plant life, animals, science
Art	Painting, drawing, photography, sculpture, dance, theater
Culture	Folk art, television, film, animation, music, celebrity
Technology	Internet, communication devices, music players, hardware
Transportation	Cars, motorcycles, bicycles, boats, trains, airplanes
... and much more.	

Mood Boards

A useful way to assemble the many inspirational components of a collection is a mood board. If space allows, a designer can place all the elements of the resource file—fabric swatches, sketches, photographs, buttons, trim, tear sheets, and printouts—on a bulletin board. In some studios, the assemblage can take over an entire wall. Smaller versions are easy to compile as collages and flip books.

THEMES

Themes provide fashion designers with a lens through which they can focus on a particular design challenge. Continuing the metaphor, a camera will do the job it was created to do, so long as the person holding it can meet the minimum requirements of pointing it in the direction of the subject and releasing the shutter by pressing down on a button. More times than not the result will be exactly what one would expect: an acceptable image. Similarly, someone with a fundamental understanding of how a sewing machine works can put together a garment.

But simply addressing the basic needs that a particular garment must satisfy is not design. A fashion designer is called to take the creation of an article of clothing to another level. Once research has led to inspiration, the designer develops and tests formulas in the design room. The result is a unique theme that bears the signature of how that designer has chosen to solve the design equation. And this is what a customer ultimately buys into.

Referencing Periods

When embracing any theme, the designer must take special care not to risk duplication. A concept may incorporate Victorian design elements, but should not translate these details literally if the designer is truly looking to innovate. Doing so results in the re-creation of historical garments that may still be relevant today, keeping in mind that the business of fashion does have a large percentage of "stylist" designers. This type of designer reproduces tried-and-true garments with modifications that relate to current trends and tastes. The work usually involves a certain amount of interpretation that allows it to go beyond mere replication. Without interpretation, the outcome speaks more to costume design than to fashion.

The Hollywood Pitch

To communicate the idea behind a new movie project Hollywood executives might pitch their projects using well-established references that are both familiar and have a successful track record. These associations provide a level of comfort and accessibility. Referencing multiple sources of inspiration becomes a way to infuse the idea with a fresh perspective.

A fashion designer faced with the prospect of developing a collection for teens could look to popular cultural associations. An X-meets-Y approach can get things started. For one designer, "*Harry Potter* meets *High School Musical*" might conjure up images of British kids in school uniforms and mythical winged creatures, all set to perky teen music. Add a twist like *Star Wars: The Clone Wars*, and the mix now encompasses space travel references and anime-inspired style lines. The combination of recognizable components and an unpredictable path will be fertile ground for novelty, if not invention.

COLLECTION DEVELOPMENT

The Menu

In the process of developing a collection, the designer must turn to a checklist of design building blocks to ask what silhouette, line, patterns, texture, colors, and decoration will be employed. The answers become the fixed menu of options for the project, and a designer's choices will directly influence how harmonious (or intentionally discordant) each component appears in any ensemble. Beyond pulling from this bill of fare for individual ensembles, the designer must clearly visualize how these elements will all work together as a collection.

Scale

Aspects of core themes should be explored at various scales to uncover every possible application. By finding multiple ways to deliver their message, designers can reach a wider range of consumers likely to identify with a particular facet of the concept. Not everyone would be immediately receptive to a "rose" theme, for example; a narrow definition might constitute a barrier to interest. The diligent designer will consider different modes of interpreting the flower.

Detail (mini)

Small buttons embossed with the shape of a rose are used as a functional detail.

Three dimensional (midi)

A silk rose manufactured as a literal expression of the theme is used as decoration.

Overscale (maxi)

Fabric is printed with an image of roses so big that it becomes abstract when wrapped around the body.

Center of Interest Detailing

A well-defined center of interest is the first place on a garment where one connects with a designer's message. How the center of interest is handled sets the tone for the collection. A small detail like decorative buttons on an otherwise plain suit can provide a subtle center of interest. Designs that feature busy patterns and heavy ornamentation are apt to melt into a collage of details, making the overall silhouette the focus.

Expected: A blouse whose V-shaped opening is trimmed with a double row of ruffles to accentuate the neckline.

Unexpected: A little black dress with a high neck and long fitted sleeves that turns to reveal a plunging back neckline.

Camouflage: An A-line tunic with high side slits worn over narrow trousers to create fluid unrestricted movement at the hip.

The Reveal: A classic tailored tweed suit that opens at the wearer's discretion to reveal a wildly colored print lining.

More than one focal point will tend to overwhelm the garment, distracting from rather than enhancing the design. A single center of interest can have a positive and powerful effect even on simple shapes.

Entry-Level Pieces

When fashion designers do a good job of relating to their target audience, they also attract those who aspire to the same aesthetic but with fewer means. Designers should put careful thought into products that allow these consumers to invest in the look. The entry-level buy-in should never be an afterthought or a watered-down version of the designer's high-end products. They should have a "cool factor" that is attractive to both the target customer and the aspirational one. These products include but are not limited to T-shirts, accessories, beauty products, and fragrances.

Show Time

Mixed into a collection will be a selection of showpieces, items that are newsworthy for their innovation or their shock value. Although a designer's bread and butter might be in more traditional items, the attention-getters will make it onto the printed page or website. Runway shows are the theatrical forum that serve up these pieces for consideration by the press, the buyers, and the public imagination.

Loyalty

Building loyalty is also by design. Once designers have defined their place in the market, they face the challenge of developing new ideas while remaining true to the established principles behind the brand that struck a chord with their customers in the first place. Finding that balance every season will underlie the design process for each new collection.

Chapter 3: Fashion History

Fashion designers have a wealth of information to turn to when they look to the historical archives of clothing. A student of history can spend a lifetime delving into such a fascinating subject, and even the most avid fans will merely scratch the surface. Any good designer, however, should make a habit of two things: First, cultivate an understanding and an appreciation for the cycles of history and the ways that they allow one to anticipate how society might respond to ideas. Second, continue to seek out, collect, and assimilate the historical references that speak to them as a designer.

No abridgement of an era could do it justice for the true scholar. Volumes upon volumes of detailed treatises have been dedicated to the study of almost every historical period. The goal here is to begin a simple outline that will serve as a roadmap, encouraging many side trips into the vast and varied periods of fashion that are so well documented in books, on the Internet, and in museum collections (many of which are available to industry professionals and students by appointment). This simplification is intentional, for it serves to clarify a larger picture as well as the stimuli behind changes in fashion.

The evolution of fashion runs in cycles, each with peaks and valleys symbolic of their corresponding socioeconomic impacts. In recent history, this can be illustrated by the rise and fall of hemlines. Fashion icons also play an important role in every era, as they breathe life into clothing and often put their unique stamp on the fashions of their day. With a broad perspective on all these aspects of fashion history, designers are better equipped to recognize how trends develop and can both deliver what their customers desire today as well as anticipate future demand.

COSTUME HISTORY

The origins of clothing falls into the category of what is now considered regional or folk costume. Much of it can often be pinpointed to a country, a region, or even a town because customs and traditions in any particular area were so insulated from the rest of the world. As communication and transportation technologies expanded over time, information and products would reach farther and farther, and fashion cycles would speed up.

In the Beginning

The first garments fashioned by man were made from the hides of animals. Initially, worn over the shoulders with no way to secure them, these skins were cumbersome and left parts of the body unprotected. The Paleolithic Age is distinguished by evidence of the use of stone tools. From a fashion perspective, the truly significant discovery of this period is the invention of the eyed needle. Needles made of bone and wood allowed cut pieces of hides to be assembled to conform to the body.

Felt and bark cloth were developed from animal and vegetable fibers, respectively. Layers of these fibers were put through a matting process until they bonded, producing a workable cloth. Eventually, people learned to spin these fibers into thread. The threads were then woven into cloth, usually small rectangles that were wrapped around the body like a sarong. Over time the skill and scale of weaving advanced, yielding fabrics that inspired more elaborate draping schemes. Roman culture saw draped garments as the mark of civilization and considered any kind of fitted garment to be barbaric.

The evolution of these types of garments can be tracked from Egyptian through to Roman culture. The Egyptians had the *schenti*, a man's loincloth or kilt in white linen, and the *kalasiris*, a women's sheath dress. In Crete during the Minoan Bronze Age, one of the first European civilizations, garments begin to be cut to fit the body. Basic garments with minimal cutting and simple sewing were the staple of wardrobes in ancient Greece. Both men and women wore the *chiton*, a tunic fastened at the shoulder by a *fibula* pin; women also wore a wider version of the chiton called the Doric *pelpos*. In ancient Rome the tunic and the cloak were central. Women wore a *stola*, an ankle-length garment with sleeves that was girdled at the waist by the *cingulum* and at the hip by the *succincta*.

The Byzantine Period, roughly from the fifth to twelfth centuries, incorporated both Greek and Roman concepts with a rich Asian opulence. The influence of this mix continues to be found during the Middle Ages and Renaissance. An important element of the look involved the concealment of body shape, often achieved through layering.

European Style

Clothing throughout the thirteenth century was very simple and varied very little between men and women. A loose-fitting full-length gown with fitted sleeves worn with a narrow belt and a sleeveless coat called the *cyclas* was the norm. Until this point, very little diverted from Roman influence.

The fourteenth century inaugurated the Renaissance and brought the first major transition from simple draped shapes to fitted garments. Contoured seams and the start of tailoring techniques now enabled clothing to become more of a sheath around the body. Buttons and lacing allowed for an even closer fit. Women of the time wore an ankle- or floor-length chemise called a *cotte*, or kirtle. The fitted version of the gown worn on top, called a *cotehardie*, often featured long hanging sleeves. In Europe throughout this period, fashion began to change at an unprecedented pace.

During the fifteenth century Europe experienced an abundant prosperity, the growth of the middle classes, and the development of a skilled workforce. This created an appetite for extravagances. Voluminous gowns called *houppelandes* featured floor-length sleeves and were worn with doublets, high collars, and hose. Headwear became more important and was trimmed with all manner of feathers and jewels. Everything became more complex and varied by region.

The sixteenth century was characterized by an increased opulence in fashion, most especially in England under Elizabeth I. Some of the atypical fashion details included the lace Tudor ruff, a hoop skirt called a farthingale, and rich surface ornamentation. In sharp contrast to the sloping narrow shoulders of the early 1500s, the Elizabethan court adopted shoulders that were high and wide with narrow sleeves reflecting French and Spanish styles. The shoulders were further enhanced by padded and jeweled shoulder rolls and accentuated by deep V-shaped waistlines. The V shape was mirrored by skirts that opened at the front to display petticoats or heavily decorated foreparts.

Fashion of the seventeenth-century baroque reveals a strong Puritan influence, evidenced in the natural, dark, somber colors and modest designs. Excessive ornamentation was discarded in favor of simpler broad lace and linen collars. Full slashed sleeves became very fashionable. Waistlines rose to create shorter bodices that were worn with contrasting stomachers. The period also witnessed the change from hose to breeches for men. A desire for uniformity became evident with the popularity of matching ensembles that speak to the contemporary suit. Under Louis XIV, the French began to focus on becoming leaders in the production of luxury products and fashionable clothing began to reflect the demands of the season and comfort.

Eighteenth Century

The eighteenth century saw fashion celebrated as culture. One popular garment was the contouche, a loose robe with large back pleats so often painted by Antoine Watteau that they came to be called Wattaeu pleats. Fashion icon of the day Madame de Pompadour popularized the lavish rococo style. At this point, by mid-century, the women's torso was encased in an inverted conical corset with sleeves becoming bell- or trumpet-shaped, and the full-skirted silhouette widened further. Hoop skirts worn in the 1730s and 1740s give way to panniers, or side hoops. By 1790, although skirts remained full, the exaggerated form had disappeared, and a fashion developed for the pouter-pigeon front, with many layers of fabric pinned to a bodice.

Riding habits and men's tailoring found their way into women's fashion in the second half of the century by way of the popular German traveling suit called a Brunswick gown, a two-piece ensemble that featured a hooded jacket with split sleeves and a matching petticoat; the caraco, a jacket-like bodice worn over a petticoat and based on the dress of servants and country women; and the joseph, a coatdress styled after the riding coat (adopted by the French as a redingote). After the French and American Revolutions fashion became politicized and austerity came to equal democracy. The end of the century gave way to an unconfined long silhouette categorized as directoire, empire or regency, with a high waistline located under the bust. Deriving its inspiration from the Greeks and Romans, this neoclassical style took Europe into the early 1800s.

One figure of special note in the eighteenth century was the dressmaker and stylist Rose Bertin. Bertin, who would later became known as the Ministre de la Mode, was instrumental in generating a passion for the latest fashions thanks to her work for the French queen Marie Antoinette, whom she dressed from 1770 until she was dethroned in 1792. Through her clever self-promotion, business acumen, and transnational reach, Bertin helped to turn dressmaking toward a modern model of the fashion business. Contributing, too, to the wide dissemination of fashion trends by the end of the century was the rise in popularity of fashion plates and journals.

Nineteenth Century

The 1800s were a time of modernity. The needle trade grew exponentially due to technological advances. Mass production was possible because of inventions like Elias Howe's sewing machine in 1846. Machines that specialized in sewing buttons, making button holes, and knitting made large production runs a reality. Isaac Singer patented the first home-scaled sewing machine and distributed it widely. At the same time, standard paper patterns became available through mail order. Of great significance, the first modern department store, the Magasin au Bon Marché, opened in Paris as early as 1852; across the Atlantic, Wanamaker's opened in Philadelphia in 1861.

By the 1820s women's fashion had moved away from the classically influenced empire style and returned to the corseting and full skirts of the previous era. In the last quarter of the nineteenth century, however, it was the bustle that defined fashion. The conservative Victorian era is known for a prudish societal focus on moral values, especially female purity. Ironically, the fashionable silhouette of the day, although covering most of a woman's body, amplified the hourglass proportions of the bust, waist, and buttocks, eroticizing and idealizing an extreme version of the feminine form. Some likened the allure of this extreme silhouette to the interest in a woman known as Saartjie "Sarah" Baartman, who was exploited as a sideshow attraction called the Hottentot Venus. Baartman was considered an exotic curiosity because of the exaggerated scale of her posterior in relationship to the rest of her frame, a genetic characteristic of the Khoisan people of South Africa, in particular the women. Thus, a fascination with novelty and the uneasy suppression of sexuality could be seen to come together in the Victorian bustle.

The early bustle of 1870s can be described in terms of the lightness of material and lack of decoration. It was often created through the manipulation of the fabric that was draped in the rear, using pleats, flounces, and bows. The front of the silhouette had the appearance of an apron. For a short time, from 1878 to 1883, the bustle disappeared in lieu of a more natural, flat-backed dress. The cuirass bodice, a long-waisted bodice that extended below the hips, and the polonaise, a princess sheath dress, achieved this slim shape. The period from 1883 to 1893 constituted the revival of the bustle. This new bustle had the look of an upholstered shelf, due to its large, almost horizontal protrusion. It was further accentuated with heavier fabrics and more ornate decoration. By the end of the 1800s, though, the bustle had been reduced to a small pad that carried into the Edwardian era.

Parallel to mainstream fashion, a movement emerged in the 1860s and 1870s known as artistic and, later, aesthetic dress. In protest against crinolines and restrictive corsets, as well as the idea of mass-produced clothing, a group of artists, writers, and actors, most famously associated with Dante Gabriel Rossetti and William Morris, promoted this looser, distinctly bohemian style that embraced many medieval and Renaissance sensibilities.

With the decline of the bustle, sleeves gained more prominence, culminating in the mid-1890s with gigantic leg-o'-muttons offset by a tiny waist. The American artist Charles Dana Gibson captured the ideal in his satirical illustrations of the modern woman. Although she became an icon of the era, the "Gibson Girl" was meant to caricature the sense of competition, independence, and athleticism that defined this new woman—not necessarily traits that were encouraged for genteel ladies. The embellished blouse became a signature of the Gibson Girl, featuring details like lace inserts and trim, embroidery, appliqués, faggoting, tucks, and pleats. She also sported shirt collars with ties, bows or cravats. She wore these tops over skirts shaped like a bell or an inverted tulip. Tailored traveling suits were a fashionable and practical variation of the new look.

When Edward VII ascended to the throne of England in 1901 fashion favored the mature figure with ample curves and rounded bust line. The silhouette, called the S-bend or S-curve, was achieved by tight-lacing the corset, which pushed the hips back and thrust the bust forward to form a monobosom. Clothing, however, was about to give way to a new streamlined silhouette, and the Edwardian era marks the last moment in fashion history that, by today's standards, could be regarded as costume.

FASHION DESIGN

Many of the precepts that we accept today as defining haute couture can be traced back to Charles Frederick Worth, an Englishman who opened his first fashion house in Paris in 1858. Often called the "father of haute couture" (history being written by and for the winners), Worth was highly successful as a designer of lavishly decorated gowns of luxurious fabrics and meticulous fit. More lasting, however, was his impact on the industry as a businessman, a promoter, and a celebrity in his own right. Thanks to his mastery of self-promotion, he and the House of Worth are remembered for being the first to show a complete collection of designs on live models. After the showing, clients would make their selections, place orders, and have custom-fitted garments created for them—the very business model still practiced for haute couture, but an innovation in its day.

Also a technical innovator, Worth accelerated the patternmaking process by developing standardized interchangeable components—sleeves, bodices, collars, skirts, and so on—that could be reused in different combinations when designing new garments. He took advantage, too, of the newly invented sewing machine for most of the production process, saving hand-work for fine finishing. In another pioneering move at the dawn of the department store, Worth disseminated high fashion by selling his dress designs to other dressmakers and clothing maunfacturers for distribution worldwide.

Although many of his contemporaries may have had similar business practices and most certainly contributed to the fashion of the period, Worth stands apart as a fashion leader for his embrace of a thoroughly modern way of doing business, both behind the scenes and in the public eye. In 1868 he and his sons founded the Chambre de la Couture Parisienne, forerunner of today's Chambre Syndicale de la Haute Couture, to establish the criteria a fashion house had to meet to be labeled couterier.

Photograph by Hulton Archive/Getty Images.

Costumier and dress designer
Charles Frederick Worth

Haute Couture and the Chambre Syndicale

Haute couture constitutes made-to-order, custom-fitted garments constructed of high-quality fabrics and sewn with extreme attention to detail and finish. In France, the Chambre Syndicale de la Haute Couture is the regulating commission responsible for bestowing on designers the highly prized classification as an official haute couture house. The organization has demanding standards: A fashion house must create fifty new and original designs of day and evening wear to be shown as collections twice a year in Paris. It must also employ a minimum of twenty full-time technical workers. The number of houses that can boast the label of haute couturier changes every year and has dwindled over time, it but remains the highest benchmark of quality and artistry in the industry.

Prêt-à-Porter

Prêt-à-porter constitutes any off-the-rack garment, regardless of quality. These garments are available in standard sizes and even at the luxury level are considerably more affordable than the couture clothing that often inspires them. Most couture houses offer one, if not a number of, ready-to-wear collections. These collections generate greater profits as they are manufactured using factory equipment and techniques, and are thus produced more quickly, in larger numbers, and at lower cost.

The Belle Époque, as the French term the period between 1890 and 1914, saw the advent of clothing design recognizable today as fashion rather than costume. One prominent designer was Jacques Doucet, who flourished during the 1890s. He was known for using fur in the manner of fabric, seen in his designs for fur-lined coats. His tailored suits and fluid tea gowns were also coveted items. An extension of aesthetic dress, these tea gowns were worn uncorseted at home throughout Europe and America. The trend would have a direct influence on two of Doucet's in-house designers, Paul Poiret and Madeleine Vionnet, whose own designs later contributed to freeing women's bodies from the corset.

Charles Frederick Worth, court gown and train, 1888

1910s
ORIENTALISM
PAUL POIRET

1920s
THE FLAPPER
GABRIELLE "COCO" CHANEL

1930s
THE BIAS CUT
MADELEINE VIONNET

1930s
HOLLYWOOD GLAMOUR
EDITH HEAD

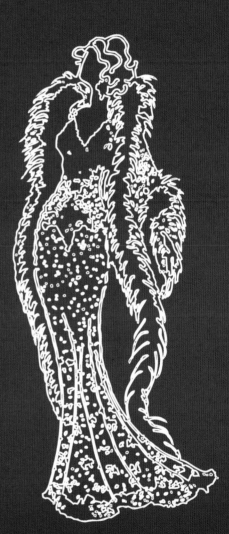

1940s
MILITARY-INSPIRED SHOULDER PAD
GILBERT ADRIAN

1940s
COROLLE, THE NEW LOOK
CHRISTIAN DIOR

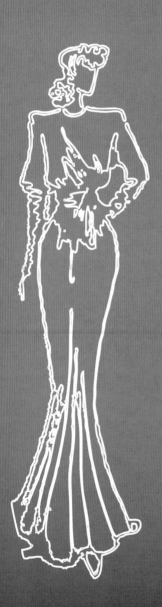

1950s
THE DESIGNER'S DESIGNER
CRISTÓBAL BALENCIAGA

1950s
POODLE SKIRTS
THE BOBBY SOXER

1960s
FIRST LADY OF CAMELOT
OLEG CASSINI

1960s
MINI MOD
ANDRÉ COURRÈGES AND MARY QUAN

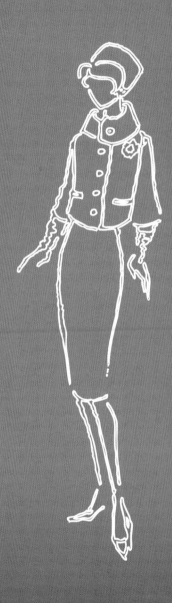

1970s
MASCULINE TAILORING
YVES SAINT LAURENT

1970s
THE ANNIE HALL LOOK
RALPH LAUREN

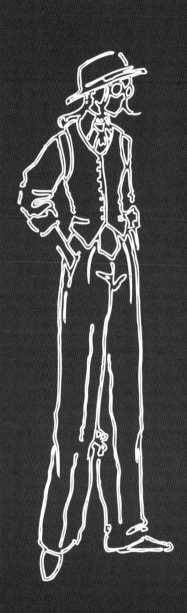

1980s
POWER DRESSING REINVENTED
DONNA KARAN

1980s
THE JAPANESE SCHOOL
YOHJI YAMAMOTO

1990s
GRUNGE
MARC JACOBS FOR PERRY ELLIS

1990s
MINIMALISM
CALVIN KLEIN

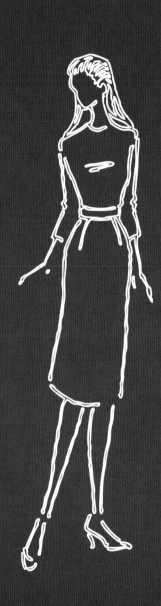

1910s

In a sharp departure from the elaborate tailoring and patternmaking that had ruled fashion, Paul Poiret based his designs on simplicity of structure and draping. Influenced by the Ballets Russes and drawing on his experience with fur at the House of Doucet, he became famous for his homages to orientalism, including the harem and lampshade looks he launched in 1913. Although remembered for his flowing unstructured garments, Poiret was also the creator of the hobble, a skirt so narrow it required a knee-long corset or belting that restricted a woman's legs below the knee to keep her from taking wide strides. Despite its constraint, the hobble skirt proved popular among fashionable women.

The tea gowns of artist/inventor Mariano Fortuny emphasized the female figure in motion. He, too, looked to the cultures of the Orient for his experiments in textile design. For the Greek sculpture–inspired Delphos gown of 1907, Fortuny's unique fine-pleating technique secured one of many patents that his innovations would earn. His long body-conforming gowns were worn by famous women of the time, such as dancer Isadora Duncan and actress Lillian Gish, as well as society ladies.

Both the suffrage movement and World War I, during which women successfully filled roles usually occupied by men, redefined a woman's capabilities. Clothing design had to respond to women's desire to imagine a more active part in their own lives and society at large. The war also had a major effect on women's fashion by way of the adoption of garments, like sweaters and trench coats, that were traditionally worn by military men.

1920s

Celebrating youth after the devastation of the Great War, the Jazz Age was a time of bright young things. Women bobbed their hair into boyish styles such as the eton and the shingle, topping them off with newsboy caps and cloche hats. Silhouettes suppressed the bust, hid the waist, and favored narrow hips. Hemlines rose but not until 1927 did they reach above the knee, only to come crashing down with the Stock Market in 1929. Women embraced public behavior designed to shock. Applying makeup, smoking, driving, and patronizing saloons, cabarets, and speakeasies in the face of Prohibition accentuated the rebellious nature of the period. In 1920 Frances Marion's movie *The Flapper*, starring Olive Thomas, defined the icon of the Roaring Twenties. Later, actress Clara Bow built her career on the scandalous Flapper image. The excavation of Tutankhamun's tomb in 1922 also influenced fashion and accessory design.

Helping to set the new tone in France, Coco Chanel eschewed the corset for a relaxed, modern style. She became renowned for both her beaded dresses and her simple jersey suits and knitwear, including her signature cardigan jacket, which endure today. Another leading designer to free women from the corset in the 1920s was Madeleine Vionnet, who achieved fame for her bias-cut clothing that accentuated the natural curves of the female form. Her sensual and easy-to-wear designs would remain a force throughout the following decade.

Clara Bow in *Get Your Man*, 1927

1930s

In response to the Great Depression, fashion embraced escapism. In the 1930s people in the long lines wrapping around city blocks might as easily be waiting for bread as for a movie. Hollywood became the reliable source of fantasy and hope for a better tomorrow, and movie fashion became the epitome of glamour and grace. Consider Jean Harlow's ethereal glow—the result of double-processed blonde hair, powdered skin, and flowing silk satin gowns.

Among the most memorable designers of the decade was Elsa Schiaparelli. She had a taste for theatrical design, and her signature color was a hot "shocking" pink. (Her designer fragrance was actually named Shocking.) The dada and surrealist movements not only influenced her fashions, they became a part of her design process through collaborations with the likes Marcel Duchamp, Man Ray, and Jean Cocteau. Bigger-than-life lobster prints and shoe-shaped hats were among the fruits of her partnership with her friend the artist Salvador Dalí.

Elsa Schiaparelli in her study

1940s

World War II made fashionable a patriotic "make-do-and-mend" approach. In the United States this attitude prevailed not just at home but within the fashion industry as well. Paris, the fashion capital of the world, was cut off, but American designers rose to the challenge of designing without the benefit of the French perspective. In conjunction with a growing desire for comfort, this wartime necessity ushered in the age of American sportswear. Chief among designers to promote American ready-to-wear was Claire McCardell. McCardell, who had already turned her back on Paris by 1940, brought imagination and style to a wide range of practical clothing that suited a more relaxed lifestyle.

Shoulder bags became popular during the war, thanks their use as part of the Women's Army Auxiliary Corps (WAAC) uniform, which did not provide the wearer with any pockets. At the war's end, the popularity of the zipper, which Schiaparelli had featured in her gowns in the 1930s, spread around the globe.

Film continued to forge an influential relationship with fashion. Joan Crawford's broad-shouldered figure, rooted in an empowering military silhouette, came out of her loyal relationship with designer Gilbert Adrian. The exaggerated shoulder pads that defined her striking looks for day and evening were widely copied by the ready-to-wear industry.

In 1947 the couturier Christian Dior introduced his Corelle collection, whose soft shoulders, nipped waist, and extravagantly full skirts are often described as a response to wartime austerity and its strict restrictions on fashion. Carmel Snow, then editor of *Harper's Bazaar*, dubbed the generous and hyperfeminine silhouette the New Look, and it would become a prevailing shape for the fashions of the 1950s.

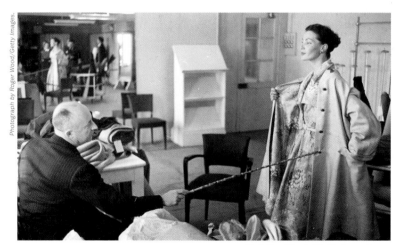

Photograph by Roger Wood/Getty Images.

Christian Dior in his Paris workroom

1950s

The 1950s saw the first effects of the postwar baby boom. The term teenager was coined for the surge of young adults that provided a new market for fashion. In the era of rock 'n' roll, bobby soxers in poodle skirts dancing at the sock hop and greasers in leather jackets driving motorcycles were iconic looks. At the same time, the anticommunist suspicions and fearmongering of McCarthyism took hold, and in models of dress and behavior, social conformity ruled.

Coco Chanel made a successful comeback, reinventing the "Chanel suit" and introducing her signature quilted leather handbag. The boxy suit was the ideal silhouette to serve as an alternative to the corseted waist and full skirt of the New Look. Another symbol of the brand, the Chanel No. 5 fragrance, was immortalized in advertising by spokesperson Marilyn Monroe.

Over the course of the decade, the couturier Cristóbal Balenciaga offered women a radically different silhouette. Already renowned for his vast knowledge of construction and technique, Balenciaga discarded the hourglass to create simple, sleek, fluid designs that formed a new relationship to the body: Innovations that he introduced into fashion included the tunic dress, the chemise dress, the balloon jacket, the baby doll dress, the cocoon coat, and the sack dress.

Photograph by Walter Sanders/Time Life Pictures/Getty Images.

Cristóbal Balenciaga and fashion editor Carmel Snow, 1952

Photograph by Arnold Newman/Getty Images.

Diana Vreeland

1960s

London in the 1960s was at the center of a cultural movement in music and fashion that *Vogue* editor Diana Vreeland in 1963 termed a "youthquake." The teenage model Twiggy, born Leslie Hornby, came to epitomize the mod look in fashion with her short hair and miniskirts. While Mary Quant, famous for her pop aesthetic, also made claim to the innovation, the origin of the miniskirt is generally credited to French designer André Courrèges. Courrèges created ultra-modern clothing based on geometric shapes and incorporating new materials such as vinyl, rubber, and plastic. The white and silver Moon Girl collection of 1964 is typical of his work, reflecting society's fascination with the Space Race. Two other strong influences on fashion were the pop art movement, especially the productions of Andy Warhol, who made stars of underground personalities like Edie Sedgwick, and the hippie counterculture that explored a hedonistic relationship to clothing and grooming.

Photograph by Leon Neal/AFP/Getty Images.

Paco Rabanne, wedding gown

Photograph by Louisa Gouliamaki/AFP/Getty Images.

Andy Warhol, paper "souper dress'"

In the Kennedy White House, aptly dubbed Camelot, Jacqueline Kennedy became the symbol of American style. A true fashion connoisseur, the First Lady drew on influences from the leading couture houses of the day. For her state wardrobe she chose designer Oleg Cassini; her famous pillbox hat was created by Roy Halston, then head milliner at Bergdorf Goodman's in New York. Kennedy's simple but elegant dresses and boxy jackets and coats, characterized by solid colors and ease of movement, were widely copied.

1970s

Marked in the early years by the opposition to the Vietnam War, the oil crisis, Nixon's impeachment, and the rise of the Women's Liberation and Black Power movements, the 1970s were a decade of disillusionment and experimentation. It was a time when the ease and widespread availability of air travel led to a conglomeration of ethnic trends from every corner of the world, among them caftans, kimonos, turbans, peasant blouses, fur vests, and quilted jackets.

Hemlines ran the gamut from mini to maxi and platforms were the shoe of choice. The popularity of disco and glam rock permeated fashion with glitter by way of satin, sequins, rhinestones, Lurex, and lamé in figure-molding styles. By contrast, rejecting glamour or prettiness, the punk scene emerged with ripped and frayed clothing held together by safety pins and chains; body piercings were the preferred adornment. Vivienne Westwood, who would go on to design many influential collections, added bondage gear to the punk fashion mix, in the store she opened with music impresario Malcolm McLauren called Sex.

Diane Keaton and Woody Allen in *Annie Hall*, 1977

Photograph by Brian Hamill/Getty Images.

In the early 1970s Diane von Furstenberg introduced her jersey knit wrap dress, a classic that would be popular for much of the decade (and appear again in the late 1990s). At the same time, trouser suits and three-piece suits became a popular addition to a woman's wardrobe. In 1977 Ralph Lauren's costumes for the movie *Annie Hall* turned Diane Keaton's character into a symbol of the modern women who could adopt and be empowered by the trappings of menswear.

The couture house of Yves Saint Laurent first put women in tuxedos in 1966 and in trouser suits in 1969. In the 1970s Saint Laurent continued to define an ultrafeminine style garnered from men's clothing. He also drew from the global mix to present his groundbreaking Russia collection with its rich colors and opulent fabrics in 1976; the following year he launched the perfume Opium.

1980s

The 1981 wedding of Prince Charles and Lady Diana Spenser greatly influenced bridal and evening wear fashions, producing a glut of frothy ruffled confections with lavish beading. Shoulder pads returned to women's clothing, and designer jeans become a must-have item. Television shows like *Dallas* and *Dynasty* took broad-shouldered power dressing to a new place with vibrant color and sparkle. The cultural excesses of the 1980s were captured in Madonna's "Material Girl." At the same time, the performer Cindy Lauper sparked a growing interest in vintage clothing by creating an eclectic look of her own.

By sharp contrast, the decade also became the setting for an avant-garde Japanese interpretation of fashion, introducing collections by designers such as Issey Miyake, Yohji Yamamoto, and Rei Kawakubo of Comme des Garçons. The aesthetic was simultaneously simple and complex, austere and vibrant, and it addressed the art of crafting garments in a way European and American designers had not yet considered.

Diana Vreeland was firmly established as a consultant to the Costume Institute of the Metropolitan Museum of Art, cultivating a new interest and respect for the historical importance of fashion. The 1980s were also the decade of the supermodel, transforming models such as Linda Evangelista, Christy Turlington, Naomi Campbell, and Cindy Crawford into celebrities. At the same time, designers such as Calvin Klein, Ralph Lauren, and Donna Karan became household names.

Madonna, Like A Virgin tour, 1985   Cyndi Lauper

1990s

In the 1990s antifashion became a way to counteract the indulgences of the previous decade. Marc Jacobs made grunge fashion news in 1992 by sending flannel shirts layered over thermal cashmere tops, crocheted skull caps and Doc Martens down the runway at Perry Ellis. The collection ended his career at Ellis, but also established him as one of the most influential American designers.

Many subcultures became a part of the fabric of fashion during this period. Punk styles, tattoos, and other body modifications extended well into the mainstream. Goth style swaddled almost everything in black, connecting with a tragic romanticism that referenced the Elizabethan and Victorian eras, occasionally eroticized by fetish paraphernalia. Skateboard rats wearing oversized cargo pants were interpreted into everything from cotton camouflage to silk satin. The dot.com speculative bubble made millionaires out of many self-proclaimed computer nerds; embracing their awkwardness and lack of interest in fashion spurred the establishment of geek chic.

Also characteristic of fashion in the 1990s was a strong move toward minimalist styles. The simplicity of form was in part another response to the extravagances of the 1980s. The approach took many forms, from the sleekness and luxurious fabrics of German designer Jil Sander, to the restrained edginess of Austrian designer Helmut Lang, to the commercially safer interpretations of Klein and Karan.

Twenty-First Century

Today fashion cycles run their course at breakneck speeds. Whereas in recent decades one could describe any composition of various styles as a collage, the current assemblage is better compared to a film montage, because it is in perpetual in motion. From year to year, season to season, and even week to week, the fashion industry borrows and blends from all manner of garments and every conceivable historical reference. For some customers, this constant flux of fashion constitutes a never-ending race to keep up with trends. For others, it means adopting a deliberately slower pace that allows them to focus on any number of niche markets that appeal. They pick and choose among designers, all the while building their distinct style. For designers, a keen historical awareness provides an advantage as the twenty-first century tests their facility at producing fashions that serve as a conduit for self-expression in a culture where anything goes.

Chapter 4: Forecasting

Forecasting is a multifaceted exercise. It often involves the accumulation and absorption of massive amounts of information from many different sources. That body of content is then filtered through the eye of the beholder. In other words, it is not an exact science and requires human instincts willing to speculate on what the market will value in the future. Successful predictions are usually founded on project-specific research.

CHANGE

A forecaster needs to be aware of changes in tastes and lifestyles. For example, the threat of global warming has begun to alter a consumer's criteria for purchases. A customer who now wants to know more about what a garment is made of in relation to its impact of the environment reflects a change in attitudes. A forecaster must keep abreast of technological developments as well. Computers have transformed society on the whole, but it is important to know that computer-aided-design has digitized most of the processes that are involved in producing garments, from illustrations to patternmaking.

Trends in movies and music are not only powerful indicators of what the public has an appetite for, but will often initiate trends in fashion. The image of the cool tough guy immediately references James Dean in *Rebel Without a Cause* and Marlon Brando in *The Wild One*. Teenagers to this day integrate elements of this aesthetic into their wardrobes. In recent years, the fashion and music industries have come together for Fashion Rocks, a media event that affords each the opportunity to be associated with the star power of the other. This translates into having the best of both worlds if one buys into the joint presentation of what is hot—rockers, runway, stardom.

Constants are also an important part of the dynamic of change. What items will always be desired or needed? A white shirt seems to be an item that will never be missing from the market. How does a designer interpret a staple like this within the context of all the forecasting information? Designer Anne Fontaine has made her mark in the industry by building a business entirely around the idea of the white shirt. Creating hundreds of variations each year, she balances her customers' desire for new ideas with their need for this essential part of a woman's wardrobe.

Anne Fontaine, white shirt, 2009

HISTORY

Taking both distant and recent history into account is an important part of the forecasting process. Are there precedents for similar products? Will parents react any differently today than they did in the 1960s when miniskirts were introduced and marketed to teenage girls? The delivery model for influencing trends has long been one based on trickle-down theory: Someone at the top of the fashion food chain decides something is worth putting in the spotlight, and in time it makes its way to the masses. This rule held for a long time. Now that information is so readily accessible, however, fashion has become more democratic, and ideas also swim upstream.

Photograph by flashfilm/Getty Images.

Harajuku Girl

STREET

Even the best-crafted intentions of a designer are subject to customers' interpretations once they have adopted a garment. Clocking hours of on-the-street observation will provide insights that cannot be aquired in any other way. Geography is an important factor here. How a target audience wears clothing in an urban setting could differ drastically from what a similar demographic will wear at a suburban mall or in a rural setting. Drawing from the street in her clothing collection, L.A.M.B, as in her music, singer/fashion designer Gwen Stefani has paid homage to the Harajuku Girls from Tokyo's Shibuya Ward. Cosplay (costume play) is a performance art that factors into the mix of looks in the area, where specific characters from anime or manga are translated into fashion. Even the Harajuku categorization can be broken down into more distinctive subcultures, which include Gothic Lolita as well as Ganguro and Kogal, two styles that emulate and update variations on the tanned California Valley Girl.

NEWS

Keeping up with news on a local and international level will ensure that social issues, economic shifts, and political developments are considered. Culture in its broadest definition includes many things, but ethnicity in particular adds to the dynamic based on its prevalence and popularity. A good example is the growth of the Hispanic population in the United States and its influences on the industry on the runway, in advertising, and at the cash register. Data collection must be comprehensive and interpretations tempered to avoid stereotyping. The U.S. Hispanic community, for instance, comprises European, North American, South American, and Caribbean Latinos, representing a kaleidoscope of Latin cultures.

COLOR

The cycle of fashion forecasting usually starts by establishing well in advance the prevalent color schemes for a season. Companies like Pantone set standards for color and work closely with designers to predict color trends. The power of color cannot be underestimated: It connects with people through many channels, from the psychological to the physiological to the aesthetic. Which colors the public embraces serve as a gauge of the society's current mood, and forecasters examine a whole range of influences, not only the economy and politics, but also the environment, sports, technology, and cultural events, to produce a color prognosis. Once a direction for color has been determined, it is the job of clothing manufacturers to turn these choices into raw materials like dyes and yarns.

FABRIC

The textile industry, then, is the next step in the forecasting supply chain. Manufacturers must persue their own specialized research to assist them in deciding on how they will interpret color through fabric. This bridges the gap between color research and the direction designers are poised to move in. Première Vision is a textile trade show that cooperates with weavers and raw materials experts to present not only the fabrications of color and texture that designers can see and touch, but also an expert forecast of their own. Cotton Incorporated, a company that manufactures, markets, and sells cotton products, does research specific to their product and develops trend projections based on that research.

FASHION

Once designers have invested in their choices of color and fabric, they are faced with how to deliver them. The designer often has a vision in mind, but external influences may present interesting deviations from the concept. A designer such as Nicole Miller would undoubtedly have plans for a dress collection in place at any given time, based on the history of her established relationship with her customers. With the announcement that pop icon Madonna was cast as Eva Perón for the 1996 film version of the Broadway musical *Evita*, these plans would be revisited and possibly modified. This would be especially true for the Nicole Miller brand because of the company's reputation for designing feminine dresses, a category of garments that would feature heavily in the film. The female fashion public was hungry for drama and a reason to dress up, and the resulting Evita craze prompted Bloomingdale's to open Evita Shops that featured designers Victor Costa, Elie Tahari, and Nicole Miller.

STYLISTS

Good stylists have a command of fashion and know how to capture a sense of style for the performer, character, or personality they are charged with outfitting. Getting a designer's products on the "right" celebrities or in movies and on television is a big part of how quickly they will be adopted and how successful they will be at the register. Stylists with great forecasting antennae are often responsible for introducing the shoes, bags, and other adornments that achieve "It" status. The popular cable television series *Sex and the City* made shoes a part of character development, and costumer Patricia Field made Carrie's passion for footwear a spotlight for shoe designers. Brands like Manolo Blahnik and Jimmy Choo were respected by the fashion cognoscenti before the series. As the show became evermore a part of the public zeitgeist, they became household names, raising the bar for all other shoemakers.

BEAUTY

Shifts in the popularity of makeup and hairstyles are among the easiest to adapt to and adopt. A designer needs to judge how the swiftness of these changes might reflect on their work. In the mid-1990s, Heroin Chic was a short-lived beauty trend that could undermine even the most fashionable of ensembles, by virtue of its roots in the culture of drug addiction. By contrast, when Alberto De Rossi, the makeup artist responsible for Elizabeth Taylor's look in the 1963 film *Cleopatra*, interpreted the Egyptian extended eyeliner for this period piece, he created what became a decidedly sixties style. More recently, Noriko Watanabe, the makeup artist for 2005's *Memoirs of a Geisha*, successfully updated several geisha looks using Max Factor products for today's woman.

Costumer/stylist Patricia Field, 2009

Where do you start with the design process when developing a new collection? And why that first?

Two things begin the process. One, I start where I left off with a concept from the previous collection, as the first step in a new evolution, or from a curiosity that I haven't explored the idea enough. And, simultaneously, I go back to certain images because they stimulate me in some way—right now, I'm working on concepts and images as varied as Shogun armor to eighteenth-century French chinoiserie reinterpreted, to modern canvases by Adolph Gottlieb. Then there are some solemn images that I always look at.

As I begin my research, I'm thinking constantly, and at the same time choosing fabrics and trying to come up with a base color for the collection that is not colorful. I don't feel comfortable working in color so I have to find a color that's a non-color. Or I'll attack a color like a bright pink or a chartreuse and try to calm it down among all the gray and taupe and black. After the fabrics are ordered, I literally encase myself in a room with images on boards and rough sketches and I begin.

The first step of having a toile made is very difficult for me because it's as if it's a symbolic piece and I have to choose it wisely. Once I see the toile, then I start running with the ideas, sketching, draping, working with the fabric. Often, I will make a painting, have a digital image taken of it, and transfer the screened image onto cloth. I'll paint another canvas and then put the cloth, the chiffon or something, the transparency, on top of that painting. We've done this now every season for a couple of years. Last season I just used an illustration of a planet, which we magnified, but this season the paintings have provided the springboard into the new work, which is very vaporous, mysterious smokelike images.

Do you consider fashion an art form? And why?

Those two words are interrelated. Fashion is not art: It's the couturier who brings the art to the fashion, and it's done through the matching of techniques and the vocabulary coming out of the atelier. So when they say fashion is not art, it's rightly said, but it's the couturier who is the artist. And if you look at the work of Vionnet or Grès or Balenciaga or Courrèges, you undoubtedly cannot say that this is not art. Then there's a whole list of names you can mention that clearly suggests that fashion is not art.

Did you have a mentor in the fashion industry? What did you take away from that relationship that serves you today?

Yes, conceptually, it's clearly been Cristóbal Balenciaga. In the early 1970s when I was in college I discovered a man working in New York who was also from the school of Balenciaga. And I came to New York to work for him. His name was Halston and he was a genius. The third person is a man whom I consider a dear friend; the way he has worked and lived I admire so much, and now he is a mentor in many ways, and that's James Galanos.

Have you assumed the role of mentor for someone else?

You know, that's a good question. So many young people come in here and we start them as interns, we see that they have promise, and they're hired. For example, there's a young man in the studio right now, and I recognize in him so much of myself when I was his age. So I suppose they would say, yes, but it's not a question for me to answer.

How important is the history of fashion to your creative process?

Essential. Essential. I am adamant and almost rude about my expectations that editors and also buyers have an encyclopedic knowledge of our profession to qualify them to judge. How can you possibly talk about satin structure or jersey draping unless you know who Charles James and Madame Grès were? And it's fascinating how many people don't know who these icons were. I have no patience for these people. I approach my profession as an academic also, so I expect everybody around me to know when I make references. My staff is genius, in this respect.

Your work is known for its fine and intricate detail. With an industry that is losing skilled fashion craftspeople with every passing generation, what do you think fashion education programs should include in their curriculum to best prepare designers looking to enter the market?

The question of skill is so important, especially today, because what is being presented as fashion and the prices at which they're established is just so horrifying. Certain critics of my career say I'm from the old school, which I find it terribly insulting because there is no such thing as "old school" when you do it correctly. What's being accepted today as passable is ludicrous. You have $4,000 (£2,500) garments made with merrow machines and plastic buttons and no interfacing or, say, interfacing that's peeling off because it's not been pressed properly. And here's what certain members of the press have said to try to cover up for it: The clothes otherwise have a matronly look. When they throw into play the age game, they immediately frighten all the young people, so rags are now expected. This makes me angry, as you can see it. I am not a stickler, but I believe that quality clothing, clothing with integrity, is made a certain way and there are no shortcuts.

Anybody that wants to be a good designer had better be able to conceive a garment, sketch it, fabricate it, drape it, make the paper pattern, cut it out, sew it, and fit it. Too many designers want to skip to being photographed arriving at a party with a dress on a starlet attached to their arm. There's been a big disintegration.

You are often described as a designer's designer, much like Balenciaga in his day. How does that impact your brand and in what ways does it allow you to connect with your customer?

Those who know who Balenciaga was and what he did—it's a great compliment for me. I'm stunned by it and I'm humbled because I haven't even come close to the body of work that he mastered. Does it impact my brand? No, because most people don't know what he did for the vocabulary of fashion. And when certain journalists draw the comparison I think they're talking about the rigor and the constant seeking of new ways of making clothes and cutting clothes. I have a dear friend, Cathy Horyn, a brilliant journalist from the *New York Times*. When I showed my first couture collection in Paris, it was very, very strict. I thought the collection was beautiful—it was really an homage to the haute couture—and Cathy said, "I know what you're doing, but ease up a little bit." Over the years I've agreed with her, I have taken that in. You can still have the rigor, you can have all the black gazar, black velvet, and black faille that you want, but really you also have to interject the work with enormous sensuality, because everybody wants to be desirable. I've always adored the monastic element that Balenciaga brought to fashion but what I also seek is to bring in the sexual aspect so that the woman feels desirable. Otherwise, very few women will want to walk around in a black gazar tent, which I find the chicest thing in the world.

How does the issue of sustainability affect your design process?

I've always used natural fabrics. I don't use synthetics, never did and don't wish to. I've been ecologically minded just because I like real fabrics.

What advice would you give designers starting their career or a business?

Continue to reinspire yourself. Keep a focus and a clarity and do not let go of your vision, no matter how many people try to tell you that it's not of the moment. Destiny provides the final explanation, I think. And even though we've been in years of homogenized fashion, there are sparks of brilliance all over the place.

It's very difficult for young people now. When I entered the profession, individuality was so respected and admired. You had the building of 550 in New York, you had Pauline Trigère, Norman Norell, Bill Blass, and the great Geoffrey Beene, and you had Galanos on the West Coast, and everyone had their own look. Today individuality is discouraged. We also no longer have an American fashion industry where these kids can seek a job. There are very few design rooms left. Most of these clothes are made in the Orient. The samples are not made with artistry, they're done with measurements and no life. I find that very disappointing and just depressing for students.

Have you diversified your design work? If so, how? And if not, why?

We do have a store in Korea. Although we've done some pieces that we sell out of the show-room, I haven't yet created a full-fledged home collection. It's something I look forward to get-ting into, because I'm obsessed with things for the home.

It's essential to have global distribution, today more than ever, because economically we can't depend on our own markets to carry a business. All of the most important retailers in the country are in a state of fright and panic and have cut their budgets. Everyone is waiting for this year to unfold to see what kind of losses we're going to experience. The problem for my clothes is that they're very expensive, and by the time you distribute them in Europe, the price is three times higher.

This is one of the main reasons why about a year ago I eliminated the distinction between haute couture and prêt-à-porter. I have the spring collection or the fall collection and they're filled with elements of each. If you make a suit, say, and you put it in the couture collection and it's all done by hand and so on, well then that suit is expected to cost $57,000 (£35,350) or something like that. A year ago I was working on vibrations of silk tulle, cashmere, and wool, where we take strips of fabric and stitch them on silk tulle. The technique gives the feeling of utter tailoring with inner structure, but the dresses or jackets or coats are weightless and totally transparent. I said, now this is absurd. If I offer this in couture then perhaps three women will be able to wear the garment. But if I put it in the ready-to-wear, it retails at $17,000 (£10,550) and you sell thirty of them. And you make a difference in apparel. Because I have my own workrooms, I was able to evolve the vibration technique, to do it in a new way, to do it bit faster so I could lower the price and have greater distribution. The concept remains couture. The essence, the approach is still couture, but the accessibility makes the collection a little more alive, more aware.

How do you strike a balance between the theater of the runway and the reality of retail?

I don't show anything on the runway that I don't produce. There isn't a separate collection house that buyers are going to see for sales. What I show is what I sell. And I will not put things in the collection that are necessary commercially, because we don't sell them. A notched collar jacket with a set-in sleeve is not something that anybody desires from me. What I am working on for the fall presentation is very conceptual. It has to do with, I suppose, eccentricity. No one needs anything. Our clients certainly don't need anything. The element of creating desire, to be desired, is what I'm working on. And here's the test, you could spend hundreds of thousands of dollars on clothes, but if you look good in a white Hanes T-shirt and a pair of jeans, that's it. Everything else is superfluous.

Overleaf Paintings, left to right: *Peering into the Void, Glimpse, Intentio,* and *Chado,* 2007.
Spring 2008 Collection. Photographs courtesy of Chado Ralph Rucci.

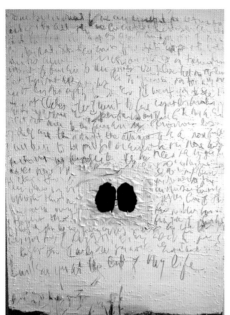

2.

EDIT

For the fashion designer, the editing process requires a clearly defined goal and knowledge of the distinct methods for how to correct, condense, and organize information. The designer modifies ideas by working with language—written, spoken, and most important, visual. The "images" a designer creates are not simply of garments though. They are also made up of each interaction and transaction surrounding the offered products and services. Therefore designers must at all times be able to dissect, discard, and recompose any facet of the work to properly reflect their message.

A critical mind will collect data through many channels. Fashion designers will find their senses—whether of sight, smell, sound, taste, or touch—fruitful filters for gathering and analyzing information. Built-in tools for asking nonverbal questions, these instinctual pathways automatically cut out what is not needed or wanted to narrow in on what matters.

Editing also involves reflection—the time for information to be absorbed; observation—the act of taking in the behavior of individuals, groups, and environments; experience—the collection of activities where participation builds knowledge; and reasoning—the thoughts that make sense of information as it applies in any given situation.

Chapter 5: Crafting Questions

Among the first questions a designer might ask is Why ask questions? The answer goes to the heart of design, because good design speaks to ideas potent with meaningful content. Crafting good questions can precipitate a windfall of information and ideas. When questions hit the mark, they yield more refined questions that reach into the core of an idea. This path of inquiry helps to extend a concept as far and as wide as it can go.

Asking questions, well-crafted or otherwise, is a worthless exercise without active engagement. Designers have to avoid trying to impress with how much they know about a subject, instead, inviting others to share their perspectives and preferences. Listening quietly, with earnest curiosity, and leaving personal opinion out of the mix are prerequisites. Designers will have plenty of time to interpret and make a mark on the information once they have collected it and applied it to their fashion goal.

SOCRATIC METHOD

The Socratic style of questioning calls for the responses to be accurate and for the thought process behind them to be complete. It offers the fashion designer a good model with which to begin. If the answers meet the challenge of this type of inquiry, they move the dialogue in the direction of actions that will benefit the designer's goal. Open-ended questions elicit detailed responses. They also generate subtle insights beyond the basic information being addressed. This technique is especially good for project development because it provides in-depth understanding.

Questions that Clarify	Questions that Challenge Perspectives
How much more can you tell me?	Why is one viewpoint more valid than another?
Why is this the right direction at this time?	Why have others been successful with similar and dissimilar products?
How does this idea relate to the company brand?	How would your customers respond to this collection and how would they benefit?
What do you already know about your audience?	What are the strengths and weaknesses of this plan?

Questions that Probe Assumptions	Questions that Investigate Implications and Consequences
What are you taking for granted?	Is the projection or forecast valid?
Why would you assume a customer would buy your product versus a competitor's?	Why will this be your best work to date?
How can you verify or prove that there is a need or desire for this style?	How does this collection affect the development of your brand?
What would happen if the market changed dramatically?	What happens once you are in the marketplace?

Questions that Scrutinize Reasoning	Questions that Examine the Question
Is the evidence there?	Why ask why?
Why is this trend happening now and are those reasons enough to make you follow?	Why bother to explore the idea for this project?
How can you be sure that your resources are accurate?	How does this concept apply to everyday life?
What evidence do you have to back up your proposed project?	What was the point of all the research?

OTHER MODELS

Fashion designers, like other creative people, have many different models for asking questions, depending on the particular subject of their investigation. They must then discern which body of answers is applicable and analyze their meanings to evaluate how to best use the information. The models on these pages are useful, respectively, when establishing the basics associated with an idea; when building a well-structured, engaging story around a brand; when building a talent and resource inventory of the designer's team and associates; and when exploring the big picture.

THE FACTS JOURNALISM

Who?	Who is your audience?
What?	What are their needs?
Where?	Where are they located?
Why?	Why would they choose your product or service over another?
When?	When will you be engaging your target audience?
How?	How will you deliver your idea?

STORY TELLING LITERATURE

Cover	What would establish the appropriate first impression?
Jacket Flaps	How would you pique the interest of your audience?
Contents	What would be the structure of your story or project?
Introduction	How would you set the tone with meaning?
Forward	Who would be a spokesperson to endorse your product or service?
Act 1	Beginning: How would the beginning capture an audience's imagination?
Act 2	Middle: What struggles could you anticipate and how would you resolve them?
Act 3	End: What would success look like in the end?
Summary	How do you reinforce the connection with your audience?
Bibliography	What information could you freely share that would add value?

HUMAN RESOURCES THE RÉSUMÉ

Cover Letter	How do you introduce yourself to the industry?
Objective	What will be your contribution to the marketplace?
Experience	What do you (and your team) bring to the table?
Education	What have you learned? Where did you learn it? How does that factor in?
References	Who can and will speak on your behalf?
Special Skills	Which related and unrelated skills add value to your enterprise?
Interests	What unique interests color your approach?
Affiliations	What organizations would make good partners?
Contacts	What are the best methods of contacting your peers, staff, and/or customers?

IN DEPTH BUSINESS PLAN

Executive Summary	How would you sum up the best in all areas of your proposal?
History	What is the history of your products/services and what, if any, part have you played?
Objectives	What needs or desires do you fill for your customer?
Products/Services	What will your menu of products/services comprise?
Persuasive Statement	Why would someone be a fan of your work?
Projected Growth	What is your plan for creating and expanding value?
History of Key Team	What are the backgrounds of everyone involved?
Management Team	Who will run things the way that you would?
Funding Requirements	What is the cost for what you need to put in place (staff, equipment, materials)?
Timeline	What is the rollout schedule for your product?
Target Market	Where will you implement the plan?
Marketing Plan	How will you position your brand in the marketplace?
The Competition	Who is doing what you are doing and how are they doing it?
Operations	How will things be carried out?
Personnel	Who will execute your ideas?

BIG QUESTIONS

Art versus Design

What is the difference between art and design? Art answers a self-imposed challenge. Design, on the other hand, must respond to the demands of the consumer. Fashion can indeed rise to the level of art in the hands of a designer who has the vision and the ability to realize the potential of an idea. But the most important thing for designers to consider when wrestling with the kind of approach they want to apply is balance. Is it enough for the arc of a designer's career to serve a need for notoriety or financial reward? What will a designer's legacy be? Heady questions, but the answers will provide designers with a metric with which to measure their success.

The Business of Fashion

Anyone looking to make a living from a career in fashion must contend with the business of fashion. Often creative types will feel at odds with the operational demands of the commercial side of what they do. Business practices will be described as dry, boring, or tedious. How does a designer dispel preconceived notions about day-to-day operations?

Fashion designers are in the unique position of being creative problem solvers. Hence the challenge moves beyond how to get the job done, to how to get the job done in an imaginative way. Some chores simply can't be reinvented, but they can be seen as a part of something more rewarding. In this instance, the most important question is, How can you look at a task differently?

Boundaries

When limits constrain designers' creative flow, they must ask how they can redefine the situation. These limits may present themselves in the form of very tangible points such as budget. In times of financial hardship, for example, where will the cuts be made? Quality? Quantity? Ornamentation? Advertising? Each area of the designer's enterprise needs to be scrutinized with questions that address how integrity survives these realities.

More subjective boundaries may be placed on what designers will produce if they feel the need to respect or rebel against the current restrictions of society and the market. How does censorship become inspiration? The director Alfred Hitchcock was well known for skirting Hollywood's Hay Production Code, which from 1930 to 1968 imposed censorship guidelines on moviemakers. The result was more often than not groundbreaking. The code stipulated that an on-screen kiss could not last longer than three seconds. Hitchcock created memorable screen kisses in *Notorious* (1946) and *To Catch a Thief* (1955) by using a very clever cutting style. Technically, each segment of the kiss clocked in at three seconds. In *Notorious* the kiss was intercut with conversation and in *To Catch a Thief* with images of fireworks bursting in air.

In the final scene in *North by Northwest* (1959), a kiss cuts to a shot of a train entering a tunnel. Fashion history is replete with cases of turning what seems like a compromise into an opportunity, another design challenge. The hemlines of the 1920s have been stereotyped as scandalous because they landed above the knee. In fact, that length lasted for only two years. Yet designers had geared up to the short-lived trend with long sheer skirts over shorter linings, uneven, asymmetrical, scalloped, and handkerchief hems, which exposed the knees through movement. How can contemporary designers speak to the age they live in and still push the envelope?

Think Tank

One of the most powerful questions designers can ask of themselves or their team is, What if? This is a trigger for free association that can churn up some great ideas. Brainstorming sessions can be exciting opportunities for exploring ideas, no matter how fanciful. Not every idea that comes out of these discussions will be a gem. So it is important not to weigh down the process with the expectation of a specific result. Some of the best brainstorming sessions will serve as a spark for bigger, better, and broader outcomes. A designer might want to assemble, either formally or informally, a group of people who have a track record of being able to think out loud. The group should represent an assortment of strengths: good judges of behavior, skilled wordsmiths, talented visual artists, and, of course, the business minded.

This process is not the same as making decisions by committee, where each opinion must be factored into the result and which, more often than not, produces watered-down concepts. A little dissent among members of the group who don't agree with the direction or don't see its potential can really help force others to hone their vision as well as their delivery. Someone should always be at the helm to help facilitate a productive and safe environment for these meetings of the mind and to make the final call. If a designer is lucky, the last question will come in the shape of a challenge to choose from many good ideas.

This collaborative effort of gathering information can also be seen in the design room as part of the fitting process of a sample garment. A designer will work with the patternmaker and the stitcher to fine-tune the math and the sewing techniques, affecting the overall look. Even the cutter can contribute by making suggestions that will influence the design and fit and will affect the cost of the garment. Designers should also ask for feedback from the fit model, to ensure that their experience of the garment achieves what was intended.

Casting a wider net by bringing in objective parties that represent the target customer will furnish more data. This method of testing prototypes is called a focus group. The term conjures up images of people behind two-way mirrors giving their opinions about cereal. Although this kind of testing still takes place, it is not as fruitfully applied to fashion. Researchers now remove the focus group from sterile environments, bringing the model right to the public in the form of experience stations. The product gets into the hands of end-users where they can be observed in a less clinical way.

Chapter 6: Mood Boards and Library

Mood or inspiration boards can be described as posters that map out the fashion designer's mental process in developing a collection. They help to direct and explain style, allowing anyone to imagine the effect that the designer is attempting to create. Assembling mood boards digitally is efficient, but must be weighed against the benefits of displaying tactile, three-dimensional components with which people can interact. The physical sensation of seeing how a fabric drapes, reflects light, and feels to the touch has much greater impact than looking at it as a flat picture. The organic visual format allows the eye to scan at length or in brief, or to jump around the board at will. Moreover, the combination of photographs, sketches, texts, and color and textile swatches becomes a design in itself.

Fashion designers use the board both to develop concepts and to communicate with colleagues and clients. Just as magazine editors will often dedicate a wall to planning the flow and big picture of an issue, designers will post all their sources of inspiration on a board to look for connections and contradictions and to step back and see how it reads as an overall message.

To generate their mood boards, designers often start with the resource files they will have already been compiling. Most designers will find that they require additional reconnaissance work specific to the collection or project at hand. This is not an area where designers should skimp or simply make do with what they have. A sense of freshness cannot be faked, at least not for any length of time. Designers will only achieve that latest, greatest version of their style by bringing in a constant flow of new stimuli.

Tonal Theme

Black-and-White Theme

Vibrant Mood Theme

Photographs by Tracy Aiguier.

FUNCTIONS

Abstract

Boards often take the shape of a free-form collage. This helps to liberate ideas into an abstract form and makes it easier to discuss content.

Common Ground

Everyone with whom the designer works can tap into a board at a different point and in a different way that is meaningful to them. This builds a consensus around the board's core concept.

Teamwork

Developing a board can be a group effort, with each individual adding to the process by collecting and contributing images, texts, and swatches. The board thus becomes an excellent tool for team building.

Rough Sketch

Boards enable designers to create a quick mock-up of their concept. This prototype skirts the need for perfection at the initial design stage.

Dialogue

Boards generate the language that will surround the work. Conversation about the boards provides common reference points. This helps to avoid misleading or misinterpreted messages as the project develops and decisions need to be made.

DESIGN LIBRARY

In addition to collecting inspiration items for their resource files, designers will also want to build a fashion library. A reference library should be diverse and include both physical and digital formats. Increasingly, books and magazines relevant to a designer are being produced for distribution on the web and for electronic devices such as the Sony's Reader or Amazon's Kindle.

The pages of printed books hold a world of information and beauty. A design library should cover everything from fashion history to designer biographies to explorations of color and textiles. With an exquisite selection of coffee-table books the designer can experience the next best thing to being in the room with the subject. Exhibition catalogues are especially useful, since in many cases garments or accessories from museum archives might be on display for only a limited period.

Many designers collect complete editions of important fashion magazines such as *Vogue* and *Harper's Bazaar* and have them bound. Some newer publications also merit collectable status. *Visionaire*, launched in 1991, is a good example. The publication is a multiformat album of fashion and art produced in numbered limited editions, elevating its value and its desirability. Unlike traditional fashion magazines, this type of periodical becomes a more concentrated time capsule of an aesthetic.

Film is also a powerful design resource, and designers might assemble a collection of DVDs that stimulate their creativity. The movie industry has created glamorous and romanticized versions of almost every time period, real or imagined. To take one example, both the 1938 W. S. Van Dyke version and the 2006 Sofia Coppola version of *Marie Antoinette* pay tribute to an important period in fashion history; however, costume designers Adrian and Milena Canonero (who won the Academy Award for Best Costume Design) each took artistic license in interpreting the period for the audiences of their day.

Documentary films and instructional videos provide a wealth of content to pull from. Documentaries in a designer's repository will range from historical to biographical to artistic; they are a great way for new designers to familiarize themselves with their industry and with the lives and careers of a roster of contemporary designers. How-to videos become important when designers want to familiarize themselves with new techniques.

Nothing creates a mood faster or more efficiently than music, and it is one resource that should not be left out of work environments during the design process, not to mention presentations. A design library should contain whatever genres inspire the designer, whether classical, jazz, rock, salsa, country, pop, dance, electronic, R&B, hip-hop, alternative, sound tracks, or world music. For instance, a designer might decide to indulge in musicals while engaged in the creative process because of the familiarity of the melodies and the ease of the lyrics, not to mention the often playful or theatrical nature of the music. Surprisingly, a collection designed in this environment might end up making it down the catwalk to the heavy thump of techno music. Designers will sometimes ask a DJ to remix something from one genre they've been listening to into another to serve the expectations built around a runway presentation.

Chapter 7: Specialization

With so many choices available, fashion designers must define their area of specialization and the niche subcategories within them. Designers might decide to design women's wear. The next step is to get much more specific about the category. If they were to settle on eveningwear, say, they must also determine the age group, size range, (including full figure, petite, and tall) and the price point to which it will be marketed. This all seems pretty straightforward, but even within eveningwear designers have to identify and understand a multitude of subdivisions.

CATEGORIES AND SUBCATEGORIES

Within each subcategory, designers must address the particular social activity and community that the garments serve to engage. Social activities might include work, meetings, and interviews; school; exercise or sports; sports or cultural events (as viewers); eating and/or drinking; socializing or entertaining; dancing; dating; rituals (weddings, bar mitzvahs, proms, funerals); formal events; performance or theater; intimate entertaining and sleep. Communities might be made up of peers, strangers, family, friends, employers, coworkers, team members, dates, intimate partners, the press, or an audience.

SUBCATEGORIES OF WOMEN'S WEAR

Daywear	Eveningwear	Outerwear	Intimate Apparel
Casual Separates	Dance, Club	Casual	Foundation Garments
Dresses	Date	Work	Practical Lingerie
Suiting	Special Occasion	Dress	Show Lingerie
Activewear	Dinner	Weather	Sleepwear
Athletic Sportswear	Cocktail	Athletic	Loungewear
	Black Tie, Red Carpet	Formal	
	Stage		
	Fantasy, Costume		

Categories of Menswear and Children's Wear

For men: Business attire, relaxed suits and sports jackets, casual separates, activewear, athletic sportswear, formalwear, outerwear, sleepwear, and undergarments.

For children: Playwear, dress, sleepwear, outerwear, and costume play.

Women's wear, menswear, and children's wear can be further subdivided as far as the imagination can go and the market will bear. The process has to be comprehensive because today designers must develop not only their product, but also the service built around delivering it, and ultimately, the experience they wish their client to have for the life of the garment.

SCOPE

Another route for classifying a specialization deals with market placement based on price point and the volume of distribution. These channels can be further described as intensive, encompassing the majority of resellers; selective, directed to suitable outlets; and exclusive, limited to select or authorized dealers.

At the high end, a system that used to adhere to a strict order of social class now crosses the boundaries of culture and caste and answers only to the hierarchy of legal tender. This new democratic arrangement brings together the representatives of power and status from every corner of society. The best of client lists are apt to include those who are famous for having money, entertainment value, political influence, revered bloodlines, and at times, no more than infamy—so long as they can pay the price.

Consumer shopping habits now reflect a freedom to tap into the market at different levels. The stigma once associated with discount shopping has transformed into a badge of honor that defines the customer as educated and savvy. Designers who reach into different markets must be sure to make clear distinctions between what they do for a luxury retailer and the work they produce for a discount store.

Collector

The true connoisseur of fashion is in search of rare, one-of-a-kind items. Priceless is often a descriptor in this very elite realm. Haute couture, art pieces, and historically important garments and accessories are treated with reverence as much for their unparalleled excellence as for their scarcity. As of the Fall/Winter 2009/2010 Haute Couture shows in Paris, the Chambre Syndicale de la Haute Couture was represented by only fifteen official members. The importance of this small group stems from how the products of their world-class artistry and workmanship become the seeds of future trends.

CHAMBRE SYNDICALE DE LA HAUTE COUTURE AS OF FALL/WINTER 2009/2010

Official Members	Adeline André, Anne Valérie Hash, Chanel, Christian Dior, Christian Lacroix, Dominique Sirop, Franck Sorbier, Givenchy, Jean-Paul Gaultier, Maurizio Galante, Stéphane Rolland
Correspondent (Foreign) Members	Elie Saab, Giorgio Armani, Maison Martin Margiela, Valentino
Guest Members	Adam Jones, Alexandre Matthieu, Alexis Mabille, Atelier Gustavo Lins, Boudicca, Cathy Pill, Christophe Josse, Felipe Oliveira Baptista, Jean-Paul Knott, Josep Font, Lefranc-Ferrant, Maison Rabih Kayrouz, Marc Le Bihan, Richard René, Udo Edling

Luxury

Luxury is such a popular concept that, in some instances, the word is clearly being overused or misapplied and as a result devalued. Sumptuous affluent living, where abundance and indulgence go hand in hand, is the picture that comes to mind. Designers of luxury clothing apply an almost hedonistic approach to the luxe lifestyle for which they are creating garments. Few people really live this life, but many aspire to it, so these fashions must speak first to the fantasy and second to the reality. Top-of-the-line ready-to-wear collections are developed for freestanding designer-brand stores, exclusive boutiques, and upscale department stores like Barney's New York, Bergdorf Goodman, Harvey Nichols, Harrod's, Neiman Marcus, Nordstrom, and Saks Fifth Avenue.

Mainstream

Mass production requires large runs, produced at a cost that allows for moderate price points in the store. The styles represented by these collections reflect the dominant trends and enjoy a broader appeal. Chain stores asuch as Banana Republic, Anne Taylor, Express, Next, and Uniqlo and department stores such as Dillard's, Kohl's, JCPenney, Macy's, and Debenhams are successful because they can establish a consistent presence in each city where they open a store. Many companies that fall into this bracket reinterpret trends, in essence distilling them for savvy customers who appreciate fashion but also want to strike a balance with their wallet. The widespread influence of these brands also lengthens the life of trends through fashion's own trickle-down economics.

Discount

Discounters such as Kmart, Walmart, and Primark bring fashion down to the bare bones of utilitarianism. But even at this price point consumers want to feel that they are getting fashion, not just clothes. Target has helped to raise the profile of the discount store by partnering with designers to stock affordable designer goods. Off-price companies such as Marshalls, Century 21, and TJ Maxx also embrace this philosophy, attempting to level the playing field when it comes to looking good. Even mainstream brands have recognized the importance of this strategy by opening outlet stores where a bargain hunter can find a higher caliber of merchandise at an often deep discount. Fashion brands such as H&M and Topshop appeal to this mindset, producing what has been termed disposable fashion—it's fun and even if it doesn't survive the season, it's worth the price.

High-Low

Smart and stylish women have long been blending the best of each of these fashion worlds to achieve truly unique styles for themselves. Editing wardrobes in this way has become the norm for the modern consumer, so a designer must have an appreciation for how their work will fit into this picture. Style icon Iris Apfel, known for her adept skill at mixing haute couture, vintage, ethnic jewelry, flea market finds, and even jeans, personifies high-low fashion. This approach to building a wardrobe is not merely a matter of being budget conscious. This customer has prioritized what to invest in for the long term and what is just temporary. It's not about a season, but rather, a way of life: measuring value and maximizing the power of fashion.

Photograph by Evan Agostini/Getty Images

Style Icon Iris Apfel, 2006

SPEED

Fast

New manufacturing methods have made ready-to-wear almost immediate. Fashion can move from the catwalk to the sidewalk at lightening speeds. Although this accelerated process demands trading down from chic to cheap, many designers see its value because of the visibility it affords. Leaders in luxury wear do not always translate into household names, and fast fashion can be a way into almost anyone's closet. The question becomes one of whether the designer has a sufficiently solid foundation to remain first and foremost a high-end brand.

Moderate

Taking the time to "do it yourself" is another route for fashion consumers. When customers place their distinctive mark on an item, infusing it with meaning and memories, the perceived value grows. These fashions can draw on sophisticated skills such as quilting, knitting, or other needlecrafts, or incorporate decorative ornamentation using beads, rhinestones, trims, or even hand painting. It should be no surprise that workshops in millinery, handbag, and jewelry design are among the most popular classes for creative teens and adults. Many big companies have identified the value of inviting customers to have a hand in the design process by letting them create unique, personalized versions of their products. Several of the most prominent sneaker companies, for instance, allow for detailed customization both in-store and on dedicated websites.

Slow

In the spirit of the finest fashion houses, a return to bespoke design serves as an alternative to generic off-the-rack clothing. The customer for slow fashion is willing to wait for quality workmanship and a custom fit. A suit of clothes that is made to order provides the wearer with an authentic sense that these clothes are uniquely theirs. Although the idea is usually applied to fine tailored garments, the ubiquitous pair of denim jeans is now a wardrobe staple that can be special ordered to fit like a glove.

SIZE

Sample Size

The size of designers' samples speaks to both their vision and their priorities. Model dimensions make sense if designers are relying on high-fashion vehicles like runway shows and editorials to promote their collections. Designers must also weigh the importance of prospective customers wanting to visualize themselves in the clothes, literally and figuratively. Can a size 12 woman picture herself in a garment when she sees a size 4 on the model, the mannequin, or the hanger?

Size Range

Designers must decide the size range in which they will make each garment available: XS, S, M, L, XL or 0, 2, 4, 6, 8, 10, 12, 14, 16, 18? This choice again speaks for the designer in terms of what will best express their ideas. Does the cut flatter a woman who is a size 6 as much as it does a woman who is a 16? What do limitations say to the woman who is left out of the size range because she is bigger or smaller?

AESTHETICS

Deconstruction

Deconstruction in fashion design challenges rules and breaks down traditions. The aesthetic includes unfinished, decomposed, and reassembled applications that bring the hidden workings of a garment to the surface. These fashions show construction details that are usually removed, such as basting, or disguised, such as inside-out pockets, zippers, pinked edges, zigzag stitching, and seam work.

Minimalism

Bare and often bold, minimalist fashion simplifies the silhouette and offers a palette of neutral tones. Striking sculptural lines paired with quality fabrics and nominal details serve a modern urban customer's lifestyle. The overall effect is understated and subdued, with an undeniable respect for form, resulting in a sense of timelessness.

Purism

Purist fashion is all about the practicality of a good cut and a basic color scheme, usually in monochromatic shades of white, gray, and beige. It is a quiet style that dispenses with any excessive embellishment in an effort to keep the design uncomplicated and focused on function. Garments that successfully adhere to this design discipline are often reduced to the status of elegant contemporary classics.

SUBCULTURES

Under the current of fashion lies a world replete with subcultures. Each in its own way creates a sense of belonging for those who worship at its alter of style. In some cases, these niche lifestyles stem from the desire to rebel, with or without a cause. This banding together around a common interest like music or politics or cultural identity provides designers with an alternative arena to the mainstream in which to place their designs. The (sometimes overlapping) subcultures described below don't begin to exhaust the possibilities.

Music

Glam Rock
Sexually ambiguous, deliberately artificial, inherently outrageous fashion defines the glam rock image. The source of inspiration is a blend of vintage Hollywood glamour and the glittery sparkle of science fiction imagery.

Grunge
Associated with the Seattle alternative rock scene, this antifashion aesthetic is generally founded in an unapologetically unkempt look. The ubiquitous flannel shirt achieves the right look when it appears to be a thrift-store rescue.

Heavy Metal
The look centers on T-shirts that celebrate heavy metal bands, punctuated by body piercing, cleanly shaved heads, and black face paint.

Hip-hop
Hip-hop traces back to African-American youth culture in the Bronx of the 1970s and reached the mainstream in the 1980s. Brightly colored track suits, sheepskin jackets, and Adidas sneakers are a few symbols of a look that is now considered old school (old skool: old is kool/old's kool). A subculture of hip-hop, gangsta style is identified by baggy pants, tattoos, and bandanas; prison life also influenced the look with shirt tails worn outside with baggy pants worn low without a belt and often with one leg rolled up. Hip-hop's later mainstream version is much flashier, with jewelry, or bling, becoming a measure of status and central to the look. Hipsters today wear a slimmer silhouette, with overscale ornamental belt buckles, biker chains, trucker caps, skull and skeleton imagery, loud patterned hoodies, and snow gear.

Psychobilly
Women's psychobilly fashion of day dresses and skirts mixes 1950s rockabilly with 1970s punk and a adds a dash of Indie flavor. B-movies, especially horror films, and hot-rod culture are recurrent inspirations. Tattoos are a prominent detail of the style.

Punk
Punk fashions are meant to be confrontational, shocking, and intentionally offensive. Rebellion is at the heart of a style that borrows the boldest images from many other subcultures.

Hip-hop Influence   Punk Influence

Photograph by DreamPictures/Getty Images.

Photograph by Katja Buchholz/Getty Images.

Trappings of the B&D (bondage and discipline) and S&M (sadomasochism) lifestyles find their way into the look. Female punk style is a deliberate combination of the stereotypically masculine and feminine: Pairing combat boots with a girly tutu is just one recognizable expression. Heavy eyeliner, mohawks and liberty spikes, safety pins (holding ripped clothing together or worn as jewelry or piercings), torn fishnet stockings, and studded or spiked jewelry have become punk trademarks. Leather, rubber, vinyl, chains, and duct tape also play a part in punk antifashion. The modern punk has come to stand for many things, with new sartorial interpretations by the anarchopunk (anarchist), the crust punk (extreme political/military), the deathrock punk (goth), the hardcore punk (working class), the pop punk (emo), the skate punk (skater), and the Suicidals (punk-cholo gangs).

Rockabilly

A hybrid of rock 'n' roll and hillbilly or country music, 1950s rockabilly was also influenced by western swing, boogie-woogie, and rhythm and blues. Teenagers emulated the style of music idols like Elvis Presley and Jerry Lee Lewis. The fashions meld looks from teddy and greaser cultures, typically slim trousers coupled with short-sleeved Daddy-O or Sir Guy shirts and crepe-soled brothel creepers.

Rock

A grittier evolution of rock 'n' roll style, rock's rebellious attitude is often expressed in leatherwear, skintight clothing, and wild hair, intensified by sweat on skin. The rough and raucous rock scene has also subscribed to the power of fashion, and many performers work in close collaboration with designers.

Techno

A style that emerged from the electronic dance scene, techno fashions include funky street wear, like V-neck T-shirts and tight pants in neon and fluorescent colors (anything that looks good under a UV black light), accessorized by record bags, canvas sneakers, and horn-rimmed glasses.

Trance, Ambient, or Chillout

Baggy pants and tight tops in vibrant, happy colors form the basis for another look coming out of the electronic dance scene. Dark settings, artificial fog, projected imagery, LEDs, strobes, and black lights all invite the use of light, bright colors and reflective garments. Elaborate costumes are also common at raves, where, under the influence of club drugs, the ultimate accessory is a glow stick.

Social Rebellion

Beatnik

Beat was slang for beat down and beatniks were underground nonconformists express-ing themselves through poetry readings in coffeehouses—a bohemian culture of the 1950s depicted in the literary output of Allen Ginsberg, William S. Burroughs, and Jack Kerouac. The fashion cliché of the Beat Generation builds on a foundation of all black. Turtlenecks and tapered pants offer a neutral base for trademark beatnik accessories like sunglasses, berets, and cigarettes. Grooming includes flat-ironed hair for women and goatees for men.

Casuals

This style arose with rowdy and often riotous football (soccer) fans dressing in designer labels as a way to blend in, avoiding their own team colors. This is fashion as camouflage, leaving the wearers free to stir things up.

Cyberpunk

Projected scientific and technological advances, cybernetics in particular, are grafted onto a radical attitude in a look that rebels against the established social order. High tech and low life are the terms that best describe the fusion of machine and man that is central to this aesthetic. The fashions incorporate dark imagery that is meant to capture a sense of hyper-reality. Although the clothing is often gritty and well worn, glowing shocks of colors appear among pieces that emulate computer components.

Eco

Whether one calls it global warming or climate change, the threat of an endangered planet has spurred on a movement of sustainable fashion designs and practices. The ecofashion consumer reads labels and wants to know a garment's fiber content and how it was made and where. For a long time, the look was defined by earthy crunchy, hippie gear, but technological advances have transformed organic fabrics. No longer is this customer limited to a wardrobe of roughly woven hemp garments. Bamboo, for example, the new star player in the textile industry, can produce some of the softest and most comfortable fashion fabrics available.

Photograph by Danny Martindale/Wireimage.

Cyberpunk at Manish Arora, 2007

New Age

The essence of new age style taps into a conglomerate of spiritual and religious traditions to provide a feeling of calm, stress-free well-being. Natural pigments, stones, crystals, precious metals, wood, and shell are incorporated into designs to help the wearers connect with their surroundings, the planet, and universal forces. The spectrum of chakra (energy center) colors in clothing and jewelry is often meant to prompt a holistic, healing response.

Psychedelic

Altered states of consciousness, perhaps induced by psychotropic drugs, provide the inspiration for the psychedelic imagery in the music and visual arts of the late 1960s. The fashions center around kaleidoscopic patterns and swirling fluid shapes in colors translated by a mind that's free from conventions.

Rocker Biker

Essential to this tough bad boy look built around motorcycle culture is a leather jacket, usually enhanced by pins, patches, and studs. Life on the road is met head-on with an open face helmet, aviator glasses, and a white silk scarf. A leather biker cap, Levi's or leather pants, and motorcycle or engineer boots add to the biker wardrobe.

Skinhead

T-shirts and traditional brands of jeans—Levi's, Wrangler, and Lee—are the foundation of the skinhead style. A common accessory is a pair of narrow suspenders (braces). Outerwear includes denim jackets and flight jackets, as well as Harrington jackets (short lightweight zippered jackets with a tartan or checked lining) and donkey jackets (wool work coats that feature a protective shoulder yoke made of plastic, leather, or vinyl). Skinheads might also sport an iridescent tonic suit with sleeves and pant legs altered to be shorter. Heavy-duty footwear—army surplus boots and Doc Martens—gain further power through a shoelace color code whose meanings depend on who adopts it.

Zoots

The zoot (or zuit) suit of the late 1930s and 1940s was an exaggerated garment that became an expression of rebellion and self-determination. Zoot suits were luxury items that allowed marginalized groups—Mexican-, African-, Filipino-, and Italian-American youth—to define themselves. Central to the look are the *tramas*, high-waisted, pegged trousers with a cuff, and the *carlango*, a long coat with wide lapels and broad padded shoulders. Completing the style would be a chain reaching as low as the knee, a pair of *calcos*, French-style pointy shoes, and a *tapa* or *tanda*, a wide-brimmed felt hat adorned with a long feather.

Culture

Afrocentric

The Afrocentric style marks a connection to traditional African culture as well as more recent movements such as Rastafari. The afro and other natural hairstyles, braids, and dreadlocks celebrate black pride. The fashion embraces culturally specific color schemes, such as red, green, and gold in Africa and red, green, and black in the United States, and garments such as the caftan; the dashiki, a brightly printed and/or embroidered top; and the *agbada* or *grand boubou*, an embroidered wide-sleeved robe. African textiles are fundamental to the style: African lace, kente cloth, *aso oke* or prestige cloth, *bògòlanfini* or mudcloth, Kuba cloth, gold-embroidered George fabric, bazin or Guinea brocade, and wax prints in colorful dynamic patterns. Ethnic jewelry also plays an important role, with items made of wood, cowrie shells, cow bone, glass beads, and lucky eye pendants.

Cowboy

The western cowboy is a uniquely American symbol that has captured the imagination of the world. Highly romanticized lore surrounds the masculine ideal that has inspired a range of iconic figures from John Wayne to the Marlboro Man. Each of the core items—chaps, jeans, cowboy hat, bandana, cowboy boots, and gloves—is a functional part of the actual cowboy life, and much of it has made its way into mainstream wardrobes. Decorative piping, fringe, leather, embroidery, and even rhinestones push the look into the arena of country western fashion.

Fetish Influence

Goth Influence

Fetish

Fetish wear is about extreme provocation. Leather, latex, nylon, PVC, spandex, and fishnet are worked into body-conscious and often restrictive garments. Stiletto shoes and ballet boots with at least seven-inch heels transform the overall silhouette dramatically. Hobble skirts, corsets, collars, and latex cat suits redefine the shape and movement of the body; eroticized items such as body stockings, miniskirts, and garters are designed to elicit a titillating experience for the wearer as well as the observer. Stylized costumes based on traditional stereotypes of garments, for instance, the wedding dress or the French maid's uniform, might be made over completely in sheers, lace, or leather.

Gay

When fashion is described as gay, it usually refers to retro camp, trend-conscious, ostentatious, or effeminate styles. The interpretations of the stereotypical macho men of the Village People provided a perfect image of the hyper-masculinized gay clone of 1970s: black leather chaps over faded blue jeans, a vest with no shirt or an often white T-shirt, and black boots. Circuit boys are the most recent version of the gay clone: Devotees of an ongoing series of themed parties, they can be identified by their tanned gym bodies, buzzed haircuts, and tattoos, cargo pants, tight tank tops, and visible designer underwear. The metrosexual label applies to the straight man who pays the kind of attention to his grooming and wardrobe usually associated with a homosexual lifestyle. Drag or cross-dressing can apply to both men and women who adopt a style that incorporates elements from the wardrobes of the opposite sex or flat out reproduces it.

Goth

Originating in the United Kingdom, goth style is prevalent around the world. Founded on a blend of nineteenth-century gothic literature and horror movies, the look can be adapted and translated in various ways. Black clothing is a mainstay. Heavily applied makeup that uses thick eyeliner, red lips, and dark shadows can be harsh against an almost white complexion, but can also be executed to emulate the beautiful porcelain-like perfection of a doll's face. Style details are pulled from many sources, including deathrock, punk, BDSM, and Victorian, Renaissance, and medieval images. Androgynous and mystical styles are also popular.

Greaser

In the 1950s a group of working class youth, often associated with jobs at gas stations and garages, were dubbed greasers because of their slicked-back hairstyles. Cuffed jeans and baggy cotton twill pants worn with chain wallets are the norm for the look. Tops vary from classic T-shirts in black or white with rolled-up sleeves and A-shirts (athletic shirts) to more fashionable Italian knit shirts, Sir Guy shirts, and Daddy-O bowling shirts. Outerwear includes work jackets, dark trench coats, denim jackets, and leather motorcycle jackets. Harness, engineer, army, or cowboy boots and Converse Chuck Taylor All-Stars basketball shoes are common footwear for this tough guy look, while Italian pointed-toe shoes provide a dressier option.

Hippie

Hippie culture embraced the multi-ethnic clothing from China, Tibet, India, Russia, Africa, Mexico, and the Mediterranean that became more readily available during the late 1960s and early 1970s. The aesthetic was also a collage of many different elements that speak to nature and self-expression: hemp, cheesecloth, patchwork, tie dye, love beads, flowers, crochet, macramé, knits, headbands, long hair, bell-bottoms, granny glasses, bare feet, and sandals. The essence of the hippie was reincarnated for the new millennium as bo-ho chic. Beads, embroidered fabrics, and velvet trim are just a few of the crossovers.

Lolita

Baby dolls and Victorian children's clothing influence the Lolita look that originally took hold in Japan. Fashion connoisseurs of the style add rococo and gothic elements and personal touches to make the look their own. Lolitas can be sweet and innocent or provocative and sexual. Dresses are predominantly knee length and worn with petticoats and knee-high socks or opaque tights. Platform shoes give the look a decidedly contemporary edge. Teddy bears and dolls are carried as accessories to achieve the little girl look.

Mod

The mod 1960s style is marked by an obsession with fashion and an ultra-cool aesthetic. Boutiques on Carnaby Street and Kings Road in London were at the center of a youth-targeted market. The androgynous look for women comprises short haircuts, trousers, men's shirting, flat shoes, and very little makeup. Ever shorter miniskirts offer an alternative to the man-tailored fashions.

Preppy
Preppy style emulates the moneyed clothing of prep school life: a neat coordinated look punctuated by sweaters tied around the neck, with standing collars, pearls, headbands, ribbon belts, and penny loafers. Other signatures of this status look are khakis, plaids, corduroys embroidered with whales, lobsters, or palm trees, polo shirts, oxford cloth button-down shirts, and tote bags. Colors tend toward lime greens, yellows, and pinks. Monograms are ubiquitous.

Skater
Skateboard fashion trends mix punk, metal, and urban fashion styles. It includes the sneakers, baggy pants, hoodies, loose T-shirts, and funky hats worn by skateboarders. The punk skater wears jeans and old rock band T-shirts, skull jewelry, and classic Vans or Chuck Taylors. The fresh or hip-hop skater wears more sports apparel, incorporating gel or air sneakers and baseball caps. The artsy or jazzy skater wears a skinnier silhouette and sports thrift-store chic and black Vans sneakers. The rasta skater adds Bob Marley T-shirts, yellow, red, and green colors, and traditional skater sneakers to their interpretation.

Steampunk
Steampunk is a perspective on style that merges Victorian and Edwardian aesthetics and modern technology. Gowns, corsets, petticoats, and bustles are paired with both period accessories, such as pocket watches and parasols, and contemporary accessories, for example, cell phones or iPods that have been modified to give them a vintage appearance. The menswear influence includes overcoats, suits with vests, and spats. Sometimes the looks are accented by fantasy-inspired items like goggles and ray guns.

Surfer
The laid-back surfer lifestyle is all about riding the waves. Clothes that can make an almost immediate transition from land to water—board shorts, T-shirts with surf motifs, hoodies, bikinis, and flip flops—are the hallmarks of a surfer dude's wardrobe. Hawaiian shirts are a part of an older tradition that has grown to include powerfully graphic patterns. As with many subcultures authenticity is important, so particular labels separate those who surf for recreation and those who have made it the focus of their life.

Teddy Boy
Teddy Boys appeared in the United Kingdom after World War II when youths had access to more disposable income. The clothes had their roots in the refined styling of the Edwardian gentleman and were also identified with American rock 'n' roll. Signature items include made-to-measure suits with long jackets, high-collared white shirts, Slim Jim ties, brocade waistcoats, high-waist narrow drainpipe pants, socks in bright colors, and suede brothel creepers. The feminine version of the Ted was more open to interpretation. A Teddy Girl's wardrobe includes circular skirts with rustling crinolines, hobble skirts, pegged pencil skirts, toreador pants, espadrilles, and pointy-toed shoes called winklepickers. Straw boaters, coolie hats, cameo brooches, and ponytails accessorize the look.

Chapter 8: Profiles

The momentum of the marketplace makes it important for fashion designers not to waste time or resources when targeting the audience for their work. Different types of profiles can help to narrow the field of choices depending on whom the designer has identified as their ideal customer. The customer is, of course, someone whom a designer wants to know very well, as seen through as many different prisms as possible: Statistics, histories, and mindsets are each important indicators. The retail distribution point of the designer's product must also be identified and thoroughly studied. Location is the next consideration, and it will have a direct impact on both the customer and the point of sale. The media's role as gatekeeper and sometime interpreter can be instrumental in both spreading the designer's message and, in the best of relationships, feeding information back to the designer.

CUSTOMER PROFILES

Demographics

The easiest variables to collect and interpret are demographics. Fundamental characteristics such as age, gender, and sexual orientation are the designer's first markers of how consumers might identify themselves. A consumer's educational background, job type, and income bracket are ways to establish their level of compatibility. Whether a consumer owns or rents, lives in a house or an apartment, also plays a part in creating a clearer picture. Marital and parental status, even being a pet owner or not, indicate responsibilities that may place demands and restrictions on income. The ethnic makeup of a consumer group will bring many different cultural considerations into play. This profile will provide designers with a good baseline from which to start, though human experience is complex and always factors into any situation.

What is the age of your customer?

What is their average income?

Do they work? Stay at home? Go to school?

Are they married? Single? Do they have children? Pets?

Do they drive or take public transportation?

What is their level of education?

What is their ethnic background?

Behavior

When studying the behavior of a customer it is important to let time tell. The history of customers' actions is a strong predictor of what they might do next. Keeping a detailed record of their purchases provides a pattern of what they are buying from month to month and year to year, and how often they avail themselves of the designer's products. The rate of return can single out regular customers. Over time, this data will reveal who will buy at full price and who will buy strictly at sale prices. It is also useful to track which magazines and e-newsletters customers have subscribed to and which ads they are reading, as these may be indicators of future value. Loyalty programs are helpful in collecting information to map out patterns. What incentives will prompt a designer's customers to make a purchase is very telling.

How recently did your customer purchase one of your products?

How often do they purchase new products? Are they loyal to your brand?

Which of your products did your repeat customers buy first?

How often do they shop for your products online? How often do they visit your website?

What magazines do they subscribe to? What websites do they follow?

Are they apt to be attracted by an impulse buy?

Psychographics

A designer should know how their customers see themselves. Their perception is important whether or not it corresponds to their actual statistics and behavior. For their mindset, equally, informs their decisions about what and when to buy. Customers' personal preferences can be culled from the type of entertainment they participate in. Reading books, watching movies, listening to music, traveling, pursuing hobbies, and taking classes are at the discretion of the individual and do not necessarily reflect work, family life, or income. Sometimes these activities mirror a guilty pleasure that can provide more insight into their truest interests and desires.

Certain attitudes that affect how a consumer makes buying decisions can come from a combination of personality, class background, and current lifestyle. Personality can be broken down into simple terms such as extraversion and introversion; more meticulous metrics designed to classify personality include openness, conscientiousness, agreeableness, and neuroticism. Social class standings can empower individuals with a sense of self. Nouveau riche versus old money is a perfect example of how economic standing can have very different expressions. Urban, suburban, and rural lifestyles color perspective in terms of how a product will be received; something that will fly in the city may fail in the country.

Value judgments of what is right or wrong will influence consumer decision making on everything from politics to hemlines. Causes generate a frame of mind that affects shoppers. Issues with prominent media attention can bring about a shift in the collective social consciousness and prompt individuals to buy accordingly. The issue of fair trade, for instance, will mobilize the public to boycott a company if they are found to employ sweatshop labor in abusive conditions. During times of war or fiscal downturns, another phenomenon affects the temperament of the buyer: "Luxury shame" is an example of how conspicuous consumption can feel like an embarrassment rather than a pleasure during an economic recession. If designers serve an affluent clientele, doing business in this kind of environment requires a delicate touch, otherwise they risk being perceived as vulgar rather than luxe.

What hobbies interest your customer?

Do they travel for work? For pleasure?

Do they prefer to go out for dinner or cook at home?

Do they live in an urban, suburban, or rural setting?

Is your customer outgoing? Or reserved?

What books, movies, or music do they enjoy?

What is their relationship to money?

Are environmental and fair trade issues important to your customer?

What are their political views?

RETAIL PROFILE

Any environment that sells designers' clothing or accessories, whether it is their own domain or a store that carries their merchandise, merits thorough examination. Carefully crafted retail environs that pay attention to lighting, music, floor plan, and staff attitude are more conducive to achieving a designer's goals. Average price point will establish where a designer is positioned in the hierarchy. The intended customer of a store is not always the actual customer: Observation over time can help to establish who frequents the location, but more important, who leaves with a purchase and how often. Many of the same considerations can be translated to the online shopping environment, which similarly demands a consistent baseline of customer service, aesthetics, and ease of shopping. There should be defined advantages to both in-store and online transactions.

How does the building exterior reflect the brand?

What kinds of displays are used? What style of mannequins, if any?

What kind of mood does the lighting and music set?

Is the product displayed in a crowded or open manner?

What overall impression does the staff make?

Is the environment about creating an experience or making a sale?

What is the environment for online sales?

LOCATION PROFILE

The location of a brick-and-mortar operation should be studied in relation to visibility, foot traffic, and accessibility. Relevance in a neighborhood can be a driving force in the success of any retail endeavor. If the location is out of the way and meant to be a destination in itself, then drive time from major population centers should be calculated. Basic needs such as the availability of parking or public transportation seem obvious, but are often overlooked. Designers must ascertain whether the demographic composite of a locale works for or against a venture. They also need to determine whether the neighborhood embraces or rejects the designer presence, and in the bigger picture, whether the city has a population large enough to sustain it. Year-round weather patterns will determine business practices, as well. A city's approach to building tourism can offer a model for strategy.

How visible is the retail operation?

How heavy is foot traffic in the area?

Is the location handicap accessible? Does it have stairs or an elevator?

How does natural light affect the store's interior at different times of the day?

Where and when can deliveries be made?

Is customer parking available? Is there public transportation nearby?

What complementary businesses are in the area? What competitors?

MEDIA PROFILE

The contemporary designer must be, at a minimum, conversant with and, at best, earnestly engaged in all forms of media distribution. The vehicles are not as important as who they serve and how they are used to engage them. Studying each publication and program before attempting to establish a line of communication will allow designers to customize a story for the reader or viewer in the appropriate style, making it an easy editorial choice. In the world of print, the high cost of production has placed an exorbitant premium on space on the glossy page. This is especially true of newspapers, which, though considered to be on their way to obsolescence, still have the power to deliver a message. The publishing timetables for dailies, weeklies, monthlies, quarterlies, and special editions are all different, and designers need to adhere to their schedules if they want to improve their chances of getting coverage. Broadcast and online outlets have similar structures. Television, cable, and radio programming usually follow magazine, talk, or news formats. Websites bring the blog world into the equation, where opinion is king. Professional and social online networks can also be a great way to spread a designer's message in the hope that it becomes as viral as possible.

Who is the reader or viewer?

What is the manner and extent of distribution of the publication or show?

What is the editorial calendar for the publication or show?

What do specific writers and editors focus on? News? Human interest?

How do they prefer to receive unsolicited materials? What visual material do they require?

What is their lead time for stories?

What professional and social networks are relevant?

BRACKETING

Once designers have pinpointed their customer, they receive the added benefit of automatic bracketing. The segment of the population who constitute the next generation or those who have aspirations to the lifestyle associated with it form one side of the bracket. Teens have historically been very receptive to clothing that might afford them the illusion of the privileges of adulthood. The other side of the bracket is made up of that part of the population inter-ested in recapturing an aspect of the target's lifestyle that they have already experienced, or perhaps missed. Boomers who dedicated their youth to raising families might have developed an appetite for fashion that is infused with the vitality and vibrancy normally associated with a younger customer. If designers remain constant to their ideal client, their work will project authenticity, something that will be attractive across a wide spectrum.

ANALYSIS

After all the data mining has taken place, designers have two primary methods of assessment. They can learn to predict how their target audience will respond to their work based on cus-tomer histories gathered over time, or they can segment their audience based on the combined profile data. Well-executed research will provide a wealth of information, allowing designers to create an in-depth, well-rounded customer model. Designers will then want to learn how to manage the relationships they have with their customers, figuring out how and when to engage them and with what product or service.

In the midst of all this intelligence gathering, it is easy to forget that the dynamic between the designer and the client is not a straight line. Collecting feedback to make course corrections and manage expectations is an ongoing process. The eagerness of the aspirational customer should not be underestimated and should be a component of the evaluation. These customers may not be the designer's primary objective, but they will often go far out of their way to buy into a particular aesthetic if the designer provides them with a point of entry.

In the end, when making decisions based on research about human beings, designers need to remember that, no matter how sophisticated the model, they are only making educated guesses. The moment a final conclusion is drawn about any person or any group is exactly the same moment the lock on it begins to lose its grip. A designer must never assume definitively to know what's best. Designers that evolve with their client base succeed. Designers that anticipate the transformational curve excel.

Chapter 9: Budget, Time, and Money

A budget is a communication tool that makes it possible to translate creative ideas into numbers. Numbers are the language of business. Investors and lenders are more apt to take any idea seriously if it is viable when evaluated in financial terms and if it can be built into a strategic timeline. Budgets allow the fashion designer to estimate costs and predict profits. To make the most of a budget, a designer must be an educated consumer and will want to get multiple quotes on services and products to compare the value and impact that these transactions will have. Simple math will calculate the pluses and minuses when expenses are compared with revenue. Many services and software programs are available to help the designer keep up with the management of dollars and cents, not to mention hours and minutes. In essence, these tools are about formatting tables or keeping ledgers into which data can be plugged and be accounted for. As the process progresses, designers should regularly revisit their budget to be sure they are meeting their bottom line.

TIME

Time plays into a budget as much as, if not more than, money does because well-established deadlines are designed to coordinate with many other systems. Many billing cycles are structured on a monthly schedule, which makes it a sensible time pattern to emulate. In planning the long-term flow of operations, a designer wants to start with the end goal and work backward, determining how pockets of time will be allocated and whether or not there will be sufficient time to accomplish any given task. Moreover, the amount of time involved in the production of a garment figures prominently in the equation a designer would develop to price the product at a level where a profit can be made without pricing it out of the game.

COSTS

Breaking down the cost of doing business into line items helps designers review their data, decide on priorities, and target where they need to edit. The start-up budget must involve the cost of organization (legal and accounting fees, remodeling costs) and acquisition of capital (tools, machinery, furniture, and signage). Both areas are investments in the future of the endeavor. An operations budget comprises regularly scheduled expenses such as rent or mortgage, payroll (salaries and freelance fees), utilities, maintenance, office supplies, telephone, travel, transportation, insurance, interest, and taxes. A block of the budget should allow for promotional efforts (advertising), as well as the unexpected (repairs). Production costs may be grouped under this category to cover the expense of raw materials such as fabrics, thread, trims, and notions. Additionally, a combined total of overhead costs must be applied to the number of units that can be produced within the same time frame for pricing.

MULTILEVEL STRATEGIES

Part of any spending plan should take into account multiple strategies for the allocation of both time and money.

Small

Grassroots efforts, including social and professional networking, require a commitment of each of these resources. Modern political campaigns offer a successful prototype for this sort of grassroots strategy that is worth imitating.

Medium

Fundamentals such as overhead expenses are more about maintenance, but still figure in the bigger strategic picture. For without diligent planning and management, the designer's operational structure will crumble.

Large

Big-ticket purchases, which might arguably be unnecessary, can be justified if they adhere to a level of excellence associated with the brand's mission: whether in the form of product, customer experience, or standard of living.

BUSINESS PLAN

A business plan is a blueprint that includes all pertinent information about an initiative. The objective of the endeavor is carefully laid out and the rationale behind it is explained. The plan for putting it all into motion completes the proposal. If designers also define the criteria for the dialogue that will help others make a decision about participation, then they can set the tone and not be misunderstood.

Although the executive summary will be read first, it should be written after the rest of the business plan has been composed. It is meant to highlight the best points of each section and prompt the reader to continue. The overarching message in the summary should reflect the company's mission, its objectives, and the keys to unlocking its success.

Background

A company description should paint a complete picture of the business, including its legal identity (sole proprietorship, partnership or joint venture, publicly traded corporation, private corporation, or LLC [limited liability company]), the history of its development (or intent to develop), its design workspace and locales, as well as its plan for moving forward.

A detailed description of the product and/or service that a designer is entering into the marketplace should center on the consumer's perspective. The designer should address how sourcing and technology will affect development, and how fulfillment will affect the customer. For consistency's sake, the language and imagery used for sales should be crafted to complement the brand. The designer should also speak to how the product might be parlayed into new ones in the future.

The management team should be identified by way of biographies, résumés, and other supporting materials that attest to their merit as part of the endeavor. This information will outline the hierarchy, pinpoint missing members, and put a human face on the project. Alliances and partnerships also factor into this area of human resources.

Marketing

A comprehensive market study must be backed up with generous amounts of data detailing how customers will be engaged and how their needs will be met. Market segments, trends, and growth patterns must be identified. The designer must describe how the project relates to the industry as a whole and who the other players are in the marketplace. Finally, the distribution of the merchandise needs to be outlined.

Operations

The business plan also needs to offer a specific plan of action that describes how the management team will implement their strategies. The plan must note the team's responsibilities and explain how their results will be measured with regard to meeting deadlines and budgets. This must include how day-to-day sales will be designed, cultivated, executed, and assessed.

Web

An online presence is essential in today's fashion market. Designers must assess how they will avail themselves of all the advantages of the medium. A summary of plans for the Web, including organizational and operational expenses, must be generated. The look of the designer's website and the function it will serve must be explained: Is it informational only or will sales be generated through it? The plan must show how the website will be marketed.

Financials

The plan's financial analysis does not have to be intimidating or full of jargon. A few common-sense business concerns can be understood in terms of indicators and ratios that make it clear how the company plans to break even. Key financial indicators are profitability (earnings and sustained growth), solvency (creditor obligations), liquidity (cash flow), and stability (long-term projections). Financial ratios compare current business health with past performance, projected performance, and the results that competitors are showing. Much of this information can be condensed into clear visual statements in the form of easy-to-read tables and charts. Designers should let the data speak for itself, with a minimum of ornamentation and avoiding visuals that muddy comprehension.

SAMPLE DATA CHARTS

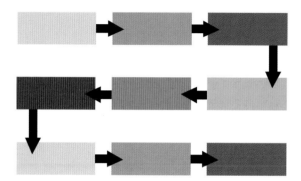

Flow Chart

A flow chart displays the sequence of events in a particular process and can be used to visualize the steps involved in the launch of a product.

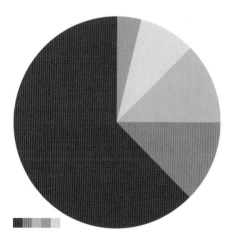

Pie Chart

A pie chart shows how the whole is divided into parts. In a budget, each segment represents the percentage of money being allocated to different areas of a company or project.

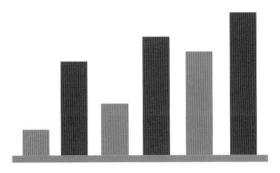

Bar Chart

A bar chart, also called a histogram, is a way to summarize data, allowing multiple comparisons to be made using bars of varying length. It can graphically map out the correlations between the revenue and expenses of a business.

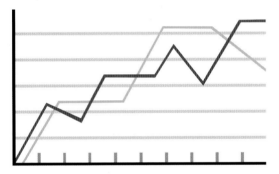

Line Chart

A line chart illustrates relationships and comparisons through time. It can be used to analyze the differences and similarities in sales from one year to another.

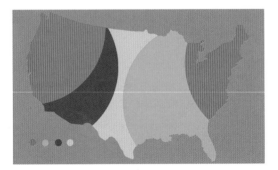

Cartogram

A cartogram uses a map form to display values by area, with regard to the proportion of customers, sales, and so forth, in a specific geographical region.

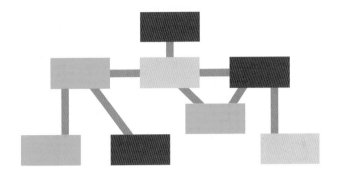

Organization Chart

An organization chart is useful when showing a chain of command within an organization and how departments within it relate to each other.

Venn Diagram

A Venn diagram, also called a set diagram, displays relationships among select groups (of people, places, or things), specifically where they overlap. It can distinguish the common ground among different customer groups.

Where do you start with the design process when developing a new collection? And why that first?

I've created men's collections and women's collections and home furnishings collections over the years, and I've always thought the first thing was spirit of the collection. You know the image and the overarching strategy. Within that, you must be consistent with everything you do. All good designers have their own DNA. A lot of people want to be designers, but it's more than just picking nice fabrics—you really have to have a point of view. You start with a concept, then every other aspect has to fit your DNA to be on message.

Key for me this season is that the clothes have to be real, they have to be acceptable, and they have to be invested in somebody's life. Whatever creative ideas I have, they must interface with how the clothes work for people—that's very important for me. If I had wanted to be an artist, I would have just painted on canvas. A designer is obliged to create relevant clothes, especially in this climate and this environment.

Where do you go from there?

The mental sketch pad. The next stage is to envision what the collection looks like, maybe the shape of the jacket. My signature has always been texture and pattern. Very often, I let the fabric tell me what to do. If I see a piece of flannel, in menswear I might say, this wants to be a very dressy suit, or a very elegant dinner jacket, or a great pair of flat-front pants. So I start with the mental sketches, then I think of the fabrics, the looks, and the colors that will fit into that process. And then I begin to make sketches. Before I do professional illustrations, I to do rough croquis and rough sketching.

In women's wear a designer can push the envelope to get attention in big ways, but how do you make a collection stand apart from the rest in menswear?

First of all, women are much more experimental, they're much more intuitive, more ready to accept change, they understand new brands more quickly than men do. So although women's wear seems to be more difficult, it's actually harder to design menswear. If you're just doing runway, you can make silly, absurd clothes, but men shop and buy clothes in very different ways than women do. Women understand how to use their wardrobes; men think of things like whether a jacket is an investment. So how do you turn them on with something new, something innovative, and yet at the same time not so out of their range that they can't stand it? To send an esoteric message to men is very hard because they don't make the connections that women do.

What do you put in menswear to grab a man's attention in this way?

I think that men relate to quality and to beautiful details. They don't respond as quickly to changes in shape. Men have moved to trimmer, leaner silhouettes, because that's sort of the mood. But it's been a slow, evolutionary process. Two words are in contrast here: women's wear is revolutionary and menswear is evolutionary. Male shoppers, fashionable men—even if they're more assertive—can only step out so far before they start looking like they're wearing costumes. Because a guy's range is more limited, it becomes more difficult to be creative and relevant at the same time.

Fashion is definitely a business first and foremost, but do you also consider fashion an art form? A craft?

Fashion absolutely is an art form and a craft. I don't want to be so pragmatic as to say it's only a business; however, the staying power of any designer is gauged by the fact that they can remain in business. So the artistic designer may get critical acclaim, but so many great designers have actually gone by the wayside because in the end they were creating art only, and not art and commerce. The fashion industry is about the marriage of art and commerce, the balance. There is artistry to making people more attractive and more appealing. I love beautiful fabrics because of the messages they send—the luxury of them, the feel and the touch. Really, I consider myself a craftsman, an artisan. So fashion is artistic but it has very, very strong commercial implications.

Did you have a mentor in the fashion industry? What did you take away from that relationship that serves you today? Have you assumed the role of mentor for someone else?

I've had two mentors in my career. One would be Murray Pearlstein, who was the owner and, really, the chief creative force behind the great days of LouisBoston. I was there for twelve years; it was an extraordinary store and I learned so much from him: About having the strength of your convictions, about showing that you believe in it when you do something. Murray is one my true heroes. My other great hero, friend, and mentor is Ralph Lauren. I worked directly with him and one of his directors of design on all the menswear collections. If Louis was my undergraduate education, then I got my MBA at Polo Ralph Lauren.

Over the last fifteen to twenty years it's become increasingly harder for designers to launch new collections. It's extremely difficult today given the current retail climate. The financial pressures on small or young design companies are overwhelming. I feel so bad about that, because the fashion industry and the retail community need new designs and new influences. But I'd like to think that over the years certain designers who have worked for me have learned something, whether they've tried to create their own collections or not.

How important is the history of fashion to your creative process?

Well, it's very interesting. Jump back to menswear. All great modern menswear, from 1900 on, say, has its roots in Great Britain, whether it be tweeds from Scotland, custom-made suits from Savile Row, or the fabulous khakis and military looks of the Empire. For an extraordinary two years I designed all the menswear for Chanel. I spent a lot of time in Paris and I learned a lot about Coco Chanel. As I tried to figure out the brand for the menswear line, I wanted to know what Chanel herself would have done. I really studied her. I read about her, I watched videos of her in the 1960s when she was older. There was a time in her life, referred to as the English period, during which she had an affair with a British lord. She loved his clothes, she loved the big tweeds and the houndstooths and the glen plaids, which still find themselves in the Chanel DNA today. In one great picture she's wearing a man's big tweed jacket—the boyfriend jacket! So, for me, history is in everything, but not to repeat it, because I don't believe in doing costumes. I've always believed that you get a sense or a whiff of something, but you create it for the time you're in. History is what you build off of, and you have to understand history well to change it and to reinvigorate it.

What should a designer understand about the business of fashion? What advice would you give a designer starting their career or a business?

I've taught at Parsons, I've taught at FIT, and I recently taught a course called "The Management of Creativity" at Fordham University at Lincoln Center. I always tell my design students, these young aspiring designers, that they must find a point of view, or what I call the POD factor, the point of difference. When I launched my first collection, why did anybody need to buy something from me? I didn't have a name. I didn't have a reputation. I just had a new collection. So what was going to make some store drop a piece from somebody else and buy my product? As an example, I created a navy blazer in the late 1980s. It wasn't the traditional navy blazer with the gold buttons—you know, the sea captain's blazer. We did it in a softer shape with much drapier fabric and a more interesting silhouette. We didn't use brass buttons, we used dark buttons. So we offered a reason for the stores to buy a new navy blazer that their customers might like. But if I had come out with the same navy blazer that Ralph Lauren or Giorgio Armani was doing, what would the stores have needed me for? I always suggest that young designers find their own viewpoint and speak with it, but also make sure that it's relevant. You can't just say, "Well, I'll be creative and maybe I'll get lucky." You have to touch the nerve of the people that are going to buy your clothes. I think one way to succeed in the fashion world is to balance intellect and aesthetics. Because one alone will not make it happen. If you combine your intelligence and creativity, that's generally a formula for success.

What do you think fashion education programs should include in their curriculum to best prepare designers looking to enter the market?

Most good design schools help their students, the future designers, to understand where the battle is won or lost: not on the pages of *Women's Wear Daily*, but at the retail level. You can get great press—and everyone wants great press, including me—but that's only a very small part of your ability to succeed. I recommend to all of my students to take a job in retail, in order to understand the way things work, to know where their product is going to end up. Believe me, retailers don't necessarily do a great job. Often retailers buy collections the way they want to buy them, not as the designer wants to present them. And that means there's always a little bit of tension. Designers have to learn the dynamics of retail to be truly successful in the fashion business. I know it sounds a little unromantic, but it's the only way to sustain yourself.

What role does celebrity play in your work?

I think my relationship with the sports and broadcasting world has been very strong. In 1988, soon after I launched my first collection, Bryant Gumbel asked me to design his outfits for covering the Seoul Olympics; he was really the first anchor ever to do that. The amount of press we received was amazing. Bob Costas, the host of the Olympics and really the franchise player for all of NBC Sports, is a good friend. He says, "Whenever I've had anybody else make my clothes, I never feel as comfortable, I don't think I look as good, and I want you to continue to work with me." Wynton Marsalis has done events with me and worn my clothes, we've designed for Brad Pitt. But we don't play the game of chasing celebrities. Most of the relationships we've had over the years are genuine, very honest. We do something right that makes the celebrity feel good and they become supportive of the work.

Could you describe the evolution of your brand and how you connect with your customer?

Jaz is my new creation. Just the name "Jaz" speaks to American style, which is classic in its roots but full of innovation and improvisation. And I love how far-reaching that name is; it doesn't need translation anywhere in the world. It's pretty exciting. I'll be honest with you, we've launched in a very strange and difficult climate, where retailers have suffered tremendously with people not shopping. Often men are the first to say, I don't really need a new suit, maybe I'll just buy a couple of shirts and ties. Some men are going to stop depending on clothes. But for the most part, young men still believe that clothes represent who they are. So I think that there's a lot of hope for the line. You have to be smart about making the consumer want to buy the clothes. It'll be interesting to see what happens.

How have you diversified your design work over the years and how has that influenced you?

I've really had a wonderful design career. I've designed cars for General Motors; I did a Joseph Abboud Limited Edition for Buick. I've designed for the Olympics. I've done home furnishings, which is a great extension for me, because they are so textile driven. My fashion collections translate very easily into the home. I've done women's wear, which I miss and would like to do again. I think women's wear made me a better menswear designer because I could push the envelope further. All of these directions have been exciting. I love challenging my aesthetics. That's why designing at General Motors was so fascinating: it was amazing to see how technology and creativity could coexist. And I'm always looking for the next horizon.

Overleaf   Sketches of Jaz Menswear Collection courtesy of Joseph Abboud.

3.
DESIGN

Behind the act of combining raw materials into a finished garment lies the design intent. Like writers who pull from the same lexicon of language to compose expressions of their individual ideas, fashion designers reach their audience because they have processed the same elements of color, textiles, and silhouette through their own sense of style, emphasis, rhythm, and perspective.

Color offers the designer every shade and subtle variation that can be read into by the viewer. Textiles provide a tactile relationship with the garments, as open to interpretation as any other element in the design. Silhouette, the specific shape and scale of a garment, is an essential choice that must be made wisely to create the desired first impression in even the simplest of designs. Accessories that complement or contrast the central concept are a dialect of the design language, a way to personalize the garment.

In the broadest sense, all fashion designers have access to the same tools and materials. They must each also address the basic needs and desires of the person who is to wear their clothes. What distinguishes their work is how their design answers the fundamental questions: What is the message, How will it be delivered, and Why is it important?

Chapter 10: Color

In fashion, color is the domain of chemists who develop pigments and artists who manipulate the full chromatic spectrum. The first are concerned with practical matters affecting the use of color in manufacturing. Is a dye colorfast? How does it respond to heat and moisture? Is it toxic? Does it stain? The latter address the environments in which color will be encountered, taking into account the season, time of day, location, and activity for which a garment is designed.

Once the tangible properties of color have been established, the designer's job is to analyze how it will affect a design when integrated into the mix of silhouette, pattern, texture, and detail. The impact on consumers and their response is the least predictable factor in the equation, due to the complex dynamics of culture, psychology, physiology, and even language.

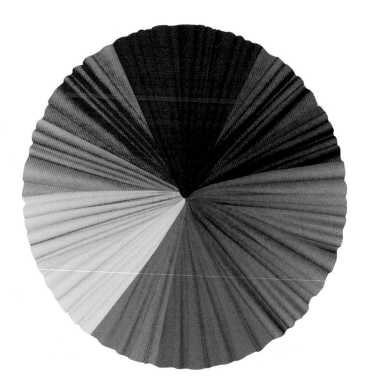

UNDERSTANDING COLOR

Culture

Cultural stereotypes in fashion can be explored through deeply ingrained preconceptions about color. Say the word "red," or display a swatch of the vibrant color, and in relation to fashion it could bring to mind a provocative red dress. One might then associate the image of the dress with a Latin aesthetic, reflecting the passion and sensuality often associated with this culture. Yet in Asian societies an intense vermillion symbolizes prosperity and is also worn by brides. Understanding the connotations that a color carries from culture to culture and for different social groups can clarify and enhance the designer's thinking. In fact, a personal preference for or an aversion to particular colors is the often first cultural stimulus introduced into the design process.

Psychology

The psychology of color can be tricky because of the unpredictability of any individual's associations with a hue. These bonds may have been forged by numerous personal experiences, good or bad. If people believe that they can't wear a particular color, only the most sensitive designer can help them see the role that it might play within their wardrobe palette. Harder still to dispel is the notion that one shouldn't wear a color—perhaps because of hair color, body type, or age. Here the designer has an opportunity to influence how color might be experienced in a new way.

A good example of how perceptions change is the color pink. Present it as a color option for a man today and he might shy away, because modern-day men have been trained to link the color with all things feminine. Less than a century ago, however, many little boys were dressed in pink, while girls wore blue: Pink was held to be a stronger color (akin to red) and blue softer and more delicate. What altered so deeply the gendered affinity or aversion to pink? Did Elsa Schiaparelli's signature shocking pink contribute to the shift in the 1930s and 1940s? What was the impact of the Nazi's association of pink with homosexuality? Did the introduction of Barbie in 1959 tip the scales farther still? Little girls playing with dolls branded in pink could be a powerful image to contend with, even subconsciously.

Physiology

Beyond how people feel about color is how their bodies might respond to it. Many colors have been attributed with the power to induce a physical reaction. Correlations exist between how the human body reacts to colors in nature and how it responds when similar colors are introduced in artificial contexts. A blue the color of a clear sky creates a soothing effect; by contrast, red, the color of blood or fire, is known to stimulate. Designers should keep the physiology of color in mind as they imagine their customer and their customer's audience. When a woman chooses between a pale blue dress and a similar scarlet one, she is aware of what response she might evoke in those who see her wear it.

Nomenclature

The semantics of style are nowhere more important than in a discussion of color. A red by any other name . . . makes all the difference in any dialogue a designer initiates. Unique and descriptive names for color help to paint a picture that more clearly reflects how designers envision the setting for their work. Designers can experiment with the associations suggested by the colors of foods, flora, and fauna. Gemstones are a great source of inspiration for color infused with light. Technology, tools, and transportation may serve as a conduit to a world of terminology attributed to the color of man-made objects.

COLOR NAMES

Primary	Red	Bordeaux, Rose, Crimson, Pomegranate, Fire Engine, Scarlet
	Yellow	Goldenrod, Buttercup, Lemon, Banana, Amber, Mustard, Canary
	Blue	Royal, Navy, Cobalt, Sapphire, Azure, Indigo, Aquamarine, Turquoise
Secondary	Orange	Rust, Pumpkin, Coral, Carrot, Salmon, Tangerine, Sienna, Tomato
	Green	Grass, Avocado, Forest, Mint, Emerald, Kiwi, Chartreuse, Moss, Olive
	Purple	Violet, Grape, Amethyst, Plum, Eggplant, Lilac, Lavender, Magenta
Neutrals	Black	Noir, Jet, Coal, Ebony, Sable, Raven, Caviar, Onyx, Ink, Licorice
	Grey	Charcoal, Slate, Silver, Steel, Stone, Ash, Smoke, Shark, Cement
	White	Old Lace, Magnolia, Seashell, Ivory, Milk, Dove, Pearl, Frost, Cotton

The Senses

In the world of fashion, color is more than just a visual experience. Beyond the observation of color, there is participation. Color is tactile—something that is touched when woven into cloth. Although a fabric might be crafted of the same fibers, color transforms its perception, eliciting different responses. Color also moves. The swing and flow of chiffon versus shantung infuses color with different levels of energy. Color may even have a sound, as when it defines the rustle of crisp papery silk. Designers must consider how the brain processes multisensory information and then attributes many intangible, but often interesting properties to color.

COLOR STORIES

Color is such a subjective consideration, especially as it pertains to fashion, that ideas on color combining are found in many ways: dedicated scholarly research, casual perusal of art books and fashion magazines, or random flashes of inspiration while going about a normal day. The elements of the mix boil down to pure color, shades, and tints. Each term is a way to describe the volume at which a color story is being told and the style or tone in which it is being delivered. Dark color stories might speak with a sense mystery, while pastel stories might speak with a sweet innocent voice. Pure colors are bright, powerful, and sometimes playful. In creating a collection of garments, designers must carefully work the actual colors to understand how they figure in their specific tale.

Monochromatic

Monochromatic color stories for garments can be interpreted in many ways. Fabrics can be dyed with the purest form of a color or with colors that represent different levels of saturation. Multiple levels of the same hue are combined to create a tonal palette. Since fabric can be created with any number of textures, the opacity of a color also comes into play: A sheer fabric such as chiffon can be layered to create the illusion of multiple color tones. Surfaces reflect light in different ways, so a faux fur, a patent leather, and an organza all dyed with the same color will have distinct readings.

Saturation

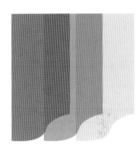

Opacity

Muted

Muted color stories are developed in two distinct ways. Adding black to a color will result in a shade of that color. Shades such as these suggest a darker color story and are often used in fall/winter collections. Adding white will tone down a color to create a tint. The effect is a pastel story, which is usually applied to spring/summer collections. There are no fixed rules, of course, so designers can employ any combination of shades and tints in ways that speak to their vision.

Shades

Tints

FORMULAS

The math of color comprises several basic formulas. These equations explore how an intended color scheme changes based on category, quantity, and combination. The primary colors are red, yellow, and blue. The secondary colors combine two primary colors to produce orange, green, and violet. The tertiary colors combine one primary and one secondary color to produce red-orange, yellow-orange, yellow-green, blue-green, blue-violet, and red-violet. Neutral colors are black, white, and gray, although in terms of fashion beige and brown can considered neutrals, too.

Primary Colors

Secondary Colors

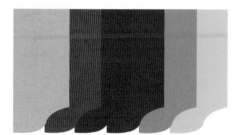

Tertiary Colors

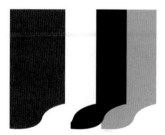

Neutral Colors

PROPORTION

The same colors can have profoundly dissimilar impacts when combined differently in relation to proportion. Once a designer decides on a group of colors, then scale becomes the question. Color collections can very well encompass more than three colors, but they will always fall into three manners of use: foundation, complement, and accent. In relation to clothing, these distinctions can be shown simply in the combination of shirt (foundation), tie (complement), and cufflinks (accent).

Foundation: Red, Complement: Blue, Accent: Yellow

Foundation: Blue, Complement: Yellow, Accent: Red

Foundation: Yellow, Complement: Red, Accent: Blue

PATTERN

Pattern offers another opportunity to explore the relationships among colors. Initially, the designer judges the effect of how each fabric combines colors within its pattern. Once fabrics are chosen, the designer can play with how patterns work with other patterns as well as solids. With even the smallest palette of color, pattern can introduce an infinite variety of interpretations.

Solid Color

Solid Neutral

Stripes

Paisley

Plaid

Dots

Chapter 11: Textiles

The word *textile* can refer to any pliable material made of interlacing filaments, fibers, or yarns. Fabric and fiber are two very different things. Designers cannot simply say that they will be creating a silk dress. By silk, do they mean satin? Brocade? Jacquard? Taffeta? Organza? Chiffon? Crepe de Chine? Velvet? The list could go on, because silk can be woven in any number of ways into any number of fabrics.

FIBER

Fibers can be created from a number of natural sources and have also been produced artificially or synthetically for the last hundred years. Animal-based textiles are made from the fur or hair of animals, or in the case of silk, from the cocoon of a silkworm. Plant-based textiles are made from fibers from different parts of a wide variety of plants. For example, linen is woven from fibers made from the bast of the flax plant. Mineral-based textiles are created from organically derived crystalline solids, which can be composed of pure elements, simple salts, or complex silicates. Man-made, or semisynthetic, textiles are manufactured from naturally occurring polymers; synthetic textiles are manufactured from polymer-based materials.

The industry requires that a fiber content label be sewn into most garments. These labels are the equivalent of the ingredients listing for food products. The fiber content is important because in many cases it will identify how the fabric will perform under specific conditions. For instance, federal flammability standards require children's sleepwear to be flame-resistant, and if the fabric ignites the flame must self-extinguish. Fiber content, finish, trim, and weave all play a factor in whether or not a garment is designated as "machine washable" or "dry clean only."

ANIMAL-BASED FIBERS

Fiber	Source
Cashmere Wool	Indian cashmere goat
Mohair Wool	North African angora goat
Camel Hair	Arabian Dromedary and Northeast Asian Bactrian camels
Alpaca/Vicuña/Llama Wool	South American camelid varieties
Angora Wool	Angora rabbit
Silk	Chinese mulberry silkworm

PLANT-BASED FIBERS

Fiber	Source
Coir	Coconut
Cotton	Shrub
Flax	Herbaceous plant
Jute	Vegetable plant (linden family)
Bamboo	Grass pulp
Hemp	Cannabis
Modal	Beech tree
Piña	Pineapple leaf
Ramie	Flowering plant (nettle family)
Soy Protein	Tofu-manufacturing waste

MINERAL-BASED FIBERS

Fiber	Use
Glass and Fiberglass	Spacesuits
Metals	Fibers, foils, and wires

SYNTHETIC FIBERS

Fiber	Source and Attribute
Rayon	Regenerated cellulose, semisynthetic; high luster and absorbent
Acetate	Cellulose, semisynthetic; high luster and drapes well
Tencel	Wood pulp, semisynthetic; lightweight and retains shape
Polyester	Polymer, polyethylene terephthalate; wrinkle resistant
Aramid	Aromatic polyamide; heat and cut resistant
Acrylic	Acrylonitrile; imitates wools and cashmeres well
Ingeo	Polylactide; hydrophilic, wicks away perspiration
Luminex	Fiber optics; light-emitting
Lurex	Polyamide, polyester; metallic appearance, good for trims
Nylon	Polyamide; imitates silk well
Spandex	Polyurethane; trade name Lycra; stretches easily
Olefin	Polyethylene or polypropylene; hydrophobic, dries quickly

YARN

Fibers are interlocked to create continuous strands of yarn that lend themselves to fabric making. Yarn that is fine enough to use for hand or machine sewing is called thread. In the case of embroidery, it is referred to as floss. Some threads are treated with wax or other finishes to increase their strength. Specialty yarns allow the designer to weave or knit a variety of colors, patterns, and textures into fabric: Chenille yarn's thick lofty finish produces a pile suited to bathrobes. Knickerbocker yarns contain flecks of different colors. Slub yarns vary between thicker looser twists and tighter thinner ones. Heather yarns, made up of strands spun from predyed fibers, create a subtle flecked or mottled effect.

YARN WEIGHTS

Name	Weight Description
Lace	Extra-fine yarn used primarily for laces and other delicate work
Sock, Fingering, Baby, or Superfine	Fine yarn used to make smaller pieces that require great detail
Double Knit, Fine, or Sport	Fine yarn in the midrange of weights
Worsted	Midweight yarn, versatile for many uses
Aran	Less common, bulkier worsted wool, unscoured and usually undyed
Bulky, Chunky, or Craft	Thick yarn used for thicker results
Super Bulky, Super Chunky, or Roving	Thick yarn with the appearance and bulk of rope

Ply

The ply of a yarn or thread refers to how many strands are twisted together to create it. Each strand of yarn has been spun in one direction. Plying involves twisting the strands together in the opposite direction from that in which they were spun. This process results in a balanced yarn that won't twist. When strands are spun in a clockwise or Z-twist, they will be plied together in a counter-clockwise or S-twist. Yarn strength and evenness depends on the number of plies.

Thread Count

In woven cloth, the thread count is established by counting the total number of threads (both warp and weft) per square inch (per square centimeter). Counts that fall between 100 and 180 are classified as percale and are considered to be representative of quality goods, with numbers in the higher range producing a silky touch. Luxury fabrics may reach as high as a 400 thread count. Although some fabrics may boast higher numbers, these quantities provide no discernable difference. The ply and thickness of the thread will determine how many threads will fit into the measurement. Weaving with fine single-ply thread will provide a finer finish and feel, but the cloth will also be more delicate.

FABRIC

Weaving or knitting yarns and filaments creates the pliable material that is fabric. Fabric can also be made by felting, where wool, fur, hair, or synthetic fibers are pressed together using heat and moisture to form a condensed, matted fabric; by tufting, where short loops of yarn are pushed through from the outside of a weave to produce a frayed inner felt pile; or by bonding, where a web of natural or man-made fibers is fused together with adhesives.

Woven Fabrics

In weaving, warp yarns are attached to a loom lengthwise and weft yarns are interwoven crosswise to generate the finished cloth. Where the filling weft yarns loop back onto themselves the fabric is usually woven more tightly; this creates a finished edge that resists fraying and is called the selvage. Looms can be small enough to roll up and carry (backstrap looms), handheld, tabletop, or freestanding. Large-scale automated factory looms can fill a room.

Weaving with different color yarns can produce a variety of patterns, including stripes, checks, ginghams, houndstooths, herringbones, plaids, and tartans. Tartans, affiliated with the Scottish clans, differ from plaids in that the repeat is alike in both directions. Bands of colored threads are distributed in the same order along the warp as along the weft and are woven as a twill.

Freestanding Loom

Industrial Loom

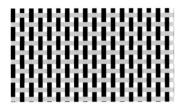

Plain Weave

Simple criss cross pattern made of the same size warp and weft threads crossing over each other in an alternating pattern. Also called tabby weave. Common fabrics are cotton, percale, voile, chiffon, organza, and taffeta.

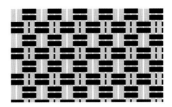

Basket Weave

A variation of the plain weave, it is typically woven with two colors of yarn crossing in an alternating pattern that resembles a basket or checkerboard. Common fabrics are oxford and monk's cloth.

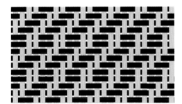

Twill Weave

Weft threads passes over one (or more) warp threads, then passes under two (or more) warp threads. Each consecutive run shifts over slightly; this offset creates parallel diagonal wales on the finished fabric. Common fabrics are gabardine, tweed, serge, and denim.

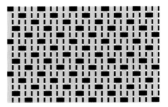

Satin Weave

Four or more weft yarns float over a warp yarn (warp yarns can also float over weft) to create a lustrous appearance. Common fabrics are satin and sateen.

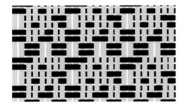

Jacquard Weave

A special loom controls the lifting of warp threads, which allows for fine pattern detail and a more complex design. Common fabrics are brocade and damask. For brocades, an additional layer of decorative weft threads are introduced to produce a raised, embroidered surface.

Loop and Cut Pile Weaves

Warp threads are raised, producing loops that are left in tact for a loop pile. Common fabric is terry cloth. Loops created in the loop pile weave are sheared to create a cut pile. Common fabrics are velvet and corduroy.

KNITTED, CROCHETED, AND KNOTTED FABRICS

Photograph by Jennifer Borton/iStockphoto.

Knits: Fabric is made with needles that facilitate the pulling of yarn loops through each other. The face of the knit structure is represented by knit stitches and the reverse by purl stitches. Alternating between these stitches allows the knitter to create ribs, cables, and numerous patterns.

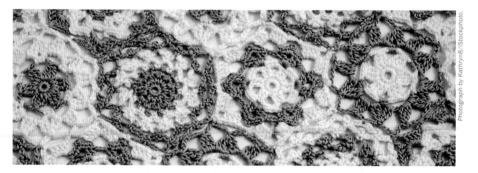

Photograph by Kathryn8/iStockphoto.

Crochet: Fabric is created by pulling yarn loops through each other using a crochet hook. It differs from knitting because only one loop is in play at a time.

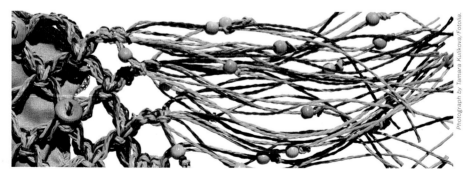

Photograph by Tamara Kulikova/Fotolia.

Macramé: Textiles are formed by hand using square knots and hitching knots.

LACES

Needle Lace: Constructed by using needle and thread to create hundreds of tiny buttonhole or blanket stitches; it is sometimes built on a foundation of paper for control. Styles include Rose Point, Brussels Point, Point d'Alençon, and Point de Gaze.

Cutwork or Whitework: Constructed by removing threads or cutting areas from a woven fabric, which is then finished with embroidery and needle lace. Styles include Broderie Anglaise, Hardanger embroidery, Mountmellick embroidery, and Reticella.

Bobbin Lace: Constructed by braiding and twisting threads attached to wood, bone, or plastic bobbins; the pattern is controlled with pins stuck into a pillow form. In Milanese lace, the design is formed of continuous tape or braid. Other styles include Valenciennes, Chantilly, Brussels, and Genoese.

Tape or Ribbon Lace: Constructed by working textile strips or ribbon into a design by hand or machine; it can be joined with needle or bobbin lace. Styles include Battenberg Point, Branscombe Point, Princess, and Renaissance.

Knotted Lace: Constructed by using a tatting needle or a shuttle to form a pattern of chains and rings from knots and loops. Also macramé style.

Crocheted Lace: Constructed by crocheting motifs separately then assembling them into lace or by employing only chain and double/treble crochet stitches to create a gridlike fabric. The first style is Irish crochet and the second filet crochet.

Knitted Lace: Constructed by knitting with pattern stitches on both the right and wrong sides of the fabric. Shetland knitted lace, famously, can produce a shawl so fine that it can be pulled through a wedding ring.

Machine-Made Lace: Almost any style of lace produced by a machine.

Bobbin Lace   Crochet Lace

PERFORMANCE FABRICS

Technological advances have been instrumental in the development of fabrics categorized as high performance. These fabrics are usually synthetic and are designed to excel in retaining body heat (Polartec, Primaloft, Thermolite, Thinsulate), ventilation/moisture wicking (Coolmax), and resisting bacteria, fungi, and yeast (Biofresh). Fabrics have also been designed to be waterproof (Goretex) and windproof (Supplex, Ventile) and to block ultraviolet rays (SolarWeave), to repel insects (Buzz Off), and to resist abrasions, punctures, and even bullets (ballistic nylon, Cordura). These fabrics are found predominantly in outerwear and active sportswear, but are making their way into many other apparel categories. Microfiber is tightly woven from polyester or nylon filaments half the diameter of a strand of silk. The fabric is so fine and soft to the touch that it is used for evening gowns. The owners of such gowns enjoy the added benefit of wearing a fabric that protects against water and wind.

FABRIC FINISHING

Greige, or gray, goods are unfinished fabrics just removed from a loom or knitting machine. They are usually rough to the touch and require cleaning before they are fit for consumption. These fabrics undergo several processes in the final stages of production to refine them for the marketplace.

Burling: Removes foreign matter, loose threads, knots, and slubs

Scouring: Removes dirt, oils, sizing, and lint

Mercerization (for cotton): Increases luster, improves strength and affinity for dyes

Bleaching: Prepares fabrics for dyeing

Glazing: Enhances appearance

Sizing: Affects surface touch

Preshrinking: Enhances performance

DYEING

Different fabrics require distinct types of dyes, depending on their fiber content. Natural and man-made fabrics include both cellulose (cotton, linen, hemp, ramie, bamboo and rayon) and protein (wool, angora, mohair, cashmere, silk, and soy) forms. Cellulose-based fabrics are successfully colored using fiber-reactive, direct/substantive, and vat dyes (colorless, soluble dyes fixed by light or oxygen). Protein fabrics are best colored by vat, acid, or indirect/mordant dyes that require a bonding agent. Synthetics do not fall into one category; each require its own method: polyester (disperse dyes), nylon (acid, disperse, and pigment dyes), spandex (metal complex acid dyes), rayon acetate (disperse dyes), and acrylic (disperse and basic dyes).

The history of dyes begins with the development of natural pigments derived from animals, plants, and minerals. The first synthetic dye was discovered in 1856. It was aniline purple, also called mauveine or Perkin's mauve (after the scientist who discovered it, William Henry Perkin). Most dyes currently used are in fact synthetic, but the market for natural dyes is growing.

Dyeing can occur at different stages in the development of the fabric. Fibers can be dyed before the yarns or threads are spun. Yarn-dyed goods allow for creative versatility during weaving or knitting. Dyeing fabric yardages is a practical choice when they are meant to be solid colors. In some cases, garments are produced with undyed fabric, allowing color to be the last stage in the process.

TYPES OF DYE

Animal	Mineral
Cochineal insect (red)	Arsenic (green)
Cow urine (Indian yellow)	Brown clay (umber)
Lac insect (red, violet)	Cadmium (green, red, yellow, orange)
Murex snail (purple)	Carbon (black)
Octopus/Cuttlefish (sepia)	Chromium (yellow, green)
Plant	Cinnabar (vermillion)
Catechu or cutch tree (brown)	Cobalt (blue)
Gamboge tree resin (dark mustard yellow)	Copper (green, blue, purple)
Himalayan rubhada root (yellow)	Hydrated iron oxide (ochre)
Indigofera plant (blue)	Iron oxide (orange-red)
Kamala tree (orange-yellow, golden yellow)	Lead (white, yellow-red)
Larkspur plant (yellow)	Limonite clay (sienna)
Madder root (red, pink, orange)	Titanium (white, beige, yellow, black)
Myrabolan fruit (yellow, green, black)	Zinc (white)
Pomegranate peel (yellow)	
Weld herb (yellow)	

Resist and Discharge

A pattern of wax or other dye-resistant substance can also be applied to the fabric before the dyeing process. The uncolored areas create a design. Discharge printing takes place after the fabric has been dyed. A bleaching chemical applied to the fabric removes all or some of the color to create a design.

PRINTING

The printing process uses pigments and dyes to form patterns on fabric. With the exception of roller printing, these techniques can be employed on a small scale for cottage industries or in mass production with machines. Hand-painted fabrics aside, a printed fabric is designed using a motif as a structured repeat. The repeat is a finite block of a pattern that is duplicated and distributed over a surface to create the allover print. Designing prints with repeats can be compared to brickwork: Each brick is laid next the previous one, so that the end of one connects with the beginning of the next. The next level of repeats can line up with the lower one or it can shift over to randomize the pattern. In textile printing, this design technique is called a drop-repeat or a brick repeat and it can be applied both horizontally and vertically. It is important for the design on each panel or section to interlock with the next one, to create the illusion of a seamless pattern.

Common Printing Methods

Hand Block Printing: Blocks of wood are etched with a pattern that is designed to interlock. The block is dipped in the desired color and applied directly to the fabric. The next impression will line up with the last one to achieve the effect that the pattern is continuous. To create more complex designs, the process can be repeated with different colors and block patterns that overlap and interlock with the previous pattern.

Roller Printing: Fabric is passed through engraved pressure cylinders that have been inked. Contemporary machines are synchronized to be able to produce detailed prints with multiple colors. Also called cylinder and machine printing.

Screen Printing: An ink-blocking emulsion is applied to a framed, finely woven mesh in the desired pattern. A squeegee or roller pushes pigment through the unblocked areas, effectively transferring a clear pattern onto the fabric. As with hand blocking, the process can be repeated with new overlapping and interlocking patterns in other colors to create more complexity.

Heat Transfer: Heat and pressure are used to transfer ink on carrier paper onto fabric. In some instances the ink permeates the fabric, while in others the design adheres to the surface. Computer printers and copiers can now print onto carrier paper for iron-on transfers.

Stencil: Cutouts provide the boundaries for painting repeats of a pattern. New stencil patterns and more colors can be overlaid on the first pattern.

SURFACE ORNAMENTATION

Common Embellishments

Appliqué: Fabric cutouts applied for decoration

Beading: Bead embellishment used to create designs

Embossing: Raised design engraved on fabrics using heated rollers and pressure

Embroidery: Thread stitch embellishment used to create designs

Faggoting: Pattern produced by removing weft threads from a section of fabric, while the warp threads are tied in bunches

Rhinestones: Lustrous imitation stones made of glass, paste, or gem quartz

Sequins: Disk-shaped beads, also called spangles or diamantes. (A larger version of the sequin is called a paillette.)

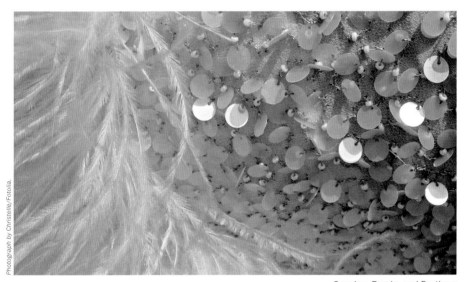

Photograph by Christelle/Fotolia.

Sequins, Beads, and Feathers

Burn-Out

To simulate brocade or eyelet patterns, the burn-out process applies chemicals (most commonly sulfuric acid) to fabric, destroying the fibers they come into contact with. Often the fabric is then overprinted to create the desired effect. Velvet fabrics woven of fiber blends are good candidates for this procedure, because the burn-out chemical only destroys the pile, if it is a cellulose fiber, leaving the synthetic ground intact.

UNDERSTANDING TEXTILES

Although a designer can read through a dictionary of fabric descriptions, there is no substitute for touch. A designer must have direct contact with textiles to learn about them. The weight of a fabric can be measured on a scale, but means something more than a number when it is worn. The drape of a fabric might be described in terms of how much body it has, yet how it moves might inspire the designer in ways that can only be stimulated by interacting with it. Textiles can be studied on many different levels; however, armed with a checklist of fabrics and a good fabric store, designers can truly educate themselves as to how these fabrics might serve their designs.

Fabric Names

A
Acetate
Alpaca
Angora

B
Batik
Batiste
Bedford Cord
Bengaline
Bird's-Eye
Bouclé
Broadcloth
Brocade
Buckram
Burlap

C
Calico
Cambric
Camel's Hair
Canvas
Cashmere
Cavalry Twill
Challis
Chambray
Chantilly Lace
Charmeuse
Cheesecloth
Chenille
Chiffon
Chintz
Corduroy
Crepe
Crepe-Back
  Satin

Crepe de Chine
Crinoline

D
Damask
Delaine Wool
Denim
Dobby
Doeskin
Donegal Tweed
Dotted Swiss
Double Cloth
Double Knit
Double Weave
Duck
Drill

E
Eyelet
Egyptian Cotton

F
Faille
Faux Fur
Felt
Flannel
Flannelette
Fleece
Foulard

G
Gabardine
Gauze
Georgette
Gingham

H
Heather Knit
Herringbone
Holland
Hopsack
Houndstooth
  Check

I
Indian Cotton
Intarsia
Interlock

J
Jacquard
Jacquard Knit
Jersey
Jute

K
Kemp
Kente
Kincob
Knit

L
Lace
Lambswool
Lamé
Lawn
Leather
Leatherette
Linen
Loden
Lycra Knit

M
Madras
Matelassé
Marquisette
Melton
Merino
Mesh
Microfiber
Mohair
Moiré
Monk's Cloth
Moquette
Mousseline
Muslin

N
Nainsook
Net
Ninon
Nylon

O
Organdy
Organza
Osnaburg
Ottoman
Oxford

P
Paisley
Panne Velvet
Peau de Soie
Percale
Pique
Plissé

Pointelle
Pongee
Poplin

Q
Quilting

R
Raschel Knit
Raw Silk
Ribbon Lace
Rib Knit
Rib Weave
Rayon
Rip-Stop Nylon

S
Sailcloth
Sateen
Satin
Seersucker
Sequin
Shantung
Sharkskin
Silk Noil
Silk Dupioni
Spandex
Suede
Surah

T
Taffeta
Tapestry
Tartan
Terry Cloth

Terry Velour
Ticking
Toile
Tricot Knit
Tulle
Tweed
Twill

U
Ultrasuede

V
Velour
Velvet
Velveteen
Venice Lace
Voile

W
Whipcord
Worcester
Worsted Wool

Z
Zephyr
Zibeline

Chapter 12: Silhouette

Silhouette plays a big part in the initial impact of a design. Color, texture, pattern, and detail fill the body of the garment, but it is the form that provides a structural setting for the design concept. The combination of silhouettes is another factor to consider when an ensemble is composed of multiple garments. The contours and dimensions of shapes will influence perceptions of its presence in an environment. Is a dress sleek and fluid? Is a suit bold and angular? Is a blouse billowy and voluminous?

BASIC SILHOUETTES

When combining silhouette shapes, scale will help to accentuate whatever the designer intends to emphasize. A triangular shape creates an A frame, which produces variations such as the A-line, swing, tent, or trapeze. This shape flares out to skim over the body. Inverting the triangle so that it tapers toward the bottom can be described as a V frame. When this shape is paired with a vertical rectangle, it is defined as a Y silhouette. Flipping the Y creates an attractive trumpetlike composite. The hourglass silhouette consists of inverse triangles. Round and oval shapes are effective in adding mass where desired. Stacking the same shapes on top of each other without varying scale or inverting shapes generally results in an overwhelming and unflattering shape. One exception is two rectangles joined as an H frame. This combination will work in narrow proportions for suits and tunics over skirts. Substituting a square for the rectangle can be used to block up and shorten a silhouette. Garments are transformed by silhouette and the ratio of combinations. A fitted bodice paired with a pegged skirt will have an hourglass appearance, while a full shirt or blouse tucked into a straight pant will give the impression of a Y. A dress with padded shoulders and a tapered hemline results in a V-shaped chemise.

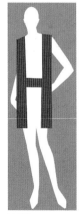  

H Silhouette   A Silhouette   Y Silhouette

GARMENT COMPONENTS

The menu of fundamental garments from which a designer can pull embraces both wovens, which include the fitted bodice, blouse, skirt, pants, jumpsuit, dress, jacket, blazer, coat, vest, bustier, corset, kimono, and halter, and knits, which include the T-shirt, sweater, leggings, bodysuit, unitard, and tank top or camisole.

Many fitted garments are made up of several pieces that can be shortened, lengthened, and sculpted into more specific shapes. A bodice is composed of a front, back, and sleeve. A blouse may also incorporate a collar, cuff, button placket, and shoulder yokes. The particular placement of the darts, seams, armholes, and waistline will customize either. The depth and breadth of a neckline will carve out negative space. Cutting away the top of this garment or extending the front sections can produce a strapless bodice or a wrap top, respectively.

Darts, Seams, and Cuts

Bust Line Darts: Center, waist, French, side seam, armhole, neckline, shoulder, T-dart, inverted T-dart

Princess Line: Side seam, armhole, shoulder, neckline, closed

Seams: Center front, center back, side, armhole, shoulder

Waistline: Empire, high, true, low-rise, dropped

Cuts: Scallops, cut outs, keyholes

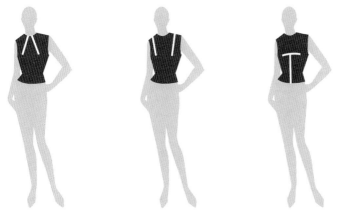
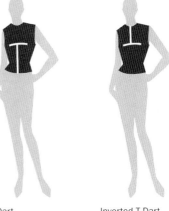

Neckline Dart   Shoulder Dart   T-Dart   Inverted T-Dart

Details

Necklines: Jewel, crew, V-neck, square, sweetheart, asymmetrical, scoop, U-neck, keyhole, boat or bateau, funnel or built-up

Flat Collars: Sailor, Peter Pan, Bertha, convertible, band, mandarin or Nehru, shawl, pilgrim

Built-up Collars: Cutaway, spread, point, rounded club, tab, button-down

Hoods: Gable, French, calash, academic

Lapels: Shawl, peaked, notched, cloverleaf

Armholes: Inset, dropped, raglan, gusset

Cuffs: French, roll back, shirt tailored, barrel

Pockets: Welt, kangaroo, cargo, patch, flap, inseam

Sleeves

Shape: Fitted, straight, bell, full, puff, peasant, leg-o'-mutton, petal or tulip, Juliet, kimono

Length: Cap, short, half, three-quarter, seven-eights, long

Fitted Sleeve   Straight Sleeve   Bell Sleeve   Full Sleeve

Skirts

Shape: Pegged, straight or pencil, A-line, bell or full, tulip

Length: Micro, mini, short, above the knee, below the knee, tea length, maxi or full

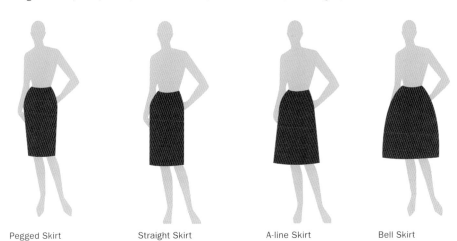

Pegged Skirt   Straight Skirt   A-line Skirt   Bell Skirt

Pants

Shape: Tapered, straight, flared (bell-bottom, boot-cut), full or palazzo, harem

Length: Hot pant or tap pant, short-short, boy short, short, Bermuda, jams, capri, pedal pusher, clam digger, toreador, long

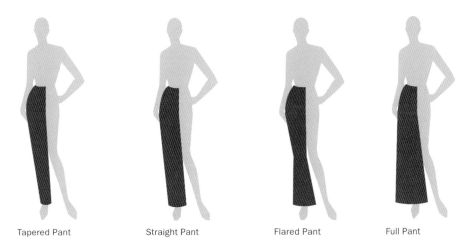

Tapered Pant   Straight Pant   Flared Pant   Full Pant

| Waistline Heights | Sleeve Lengths | Skirt Lengths | Pant Lengths |

Dress

Any combination of top and skirt described above, with or without a seam at the waistline

Popular Full Silhouettes: Chemise or shift, shirtwaist, blouson, tent, trapeze or swing, coat dress

Popular Fitted Silhouettes: Sheath, mermaid, princess, slip, cheongsam or *qípáo*

Jumpsuit

Any combination of top and pant described above, with or without a seam at the waistline

Popular Silhouettes: Coveralls or overalls, ski suit, trouser gown

Suiting, Layering, and Outerwear

Suiting: Jacket, blazer, bolero, waistcoat

Layering: Cardigan, shrug, stole

Outerwear: Coat, cape, cocoon, stadium, trench, wrap

Fabric Manipulation

Flares: Trumpets, flutes

Gathers: Trumpets, flutes, shirring, ruffles, smocking, quilting, puff

Pleats: Knife, box, accordion, tuck, sun or starburst, irregular, primitive, mushroom or broomstick

Drapes: Folds, cascades, cowl, tied, twisted

Flares: Trumpet

Flares: Flute

Gathers: Trumpet

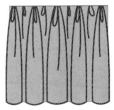

Gathers: Flute

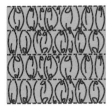

Gathers: Shirring

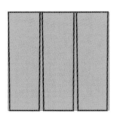

Pleats: Box

Pleats: Accordion

Pleats: Knife

Pleats: Sunburst, Starburst, Fan

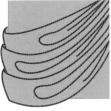

Drapes: Folds

Drapes: Cascades

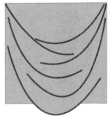

Drapes: Cowls

Chapter 13: Accessories

By definition, accessories are nonessential items. In the fashion industry today, however, the status of accessories often rivals the importance of the garments themselves. Designers have several options when it comes to building accessories into the overall look of a collection. The styling option is to purchase or borrow from companies designing and producing accessory collections that complement their work. The licensing option is to partner with companies that will design and produce accessory collections specifically for their design collections. The in-house option is to design and produce accessory collections themselves.

Milliner hand stitches an Easter bonnet designed by Aage Thaarup, 1940

Photograph by Tim Gidal/Picture Post/Getty Images.

Although accessories are decorative, they can also serve a functional purpose. Practically, hats and scarves can keep the wearers warm, gloves protect their hands, belts hold up their pants, and bags carry their personal belongings. Accessories that boast designer labels, such as handbags and sunglasses, have a prestige factor and provide the status-conscious with a more affordable option for suggesting membership in a particular lifestyle. Accessories can also telegraph an association with a specific religious or cultural body. Religious symbols are incorporated into fashion most often in the form of jewelry or headwear. Accessories, especially footwear and headgear, complete the look of many subcultures and can convey fine distinctions among related groups. Finally, consumers use accessories of every type to express their personal style. For designers, accessories offer another avenue for exploring facets of the story they are telling in their collection.

TYPES OF ACCESSORIES

Shoes: Athletic (sneaker, track shoe), boot, cap toe, wingtip or brogue, clog, dance, flats, thong, flip-flop, heel (high, kitten, stiletto), loafer, moccasin, mule, plain toe, platform, sandal, sling-back, wedge

Mary Janes by Manolo Blahnik

Running Shoes

Bags: Duffel, messenger, satchel, school, tote, purse, shoulder, sling, handbag, framed, clutch, wrislet

Handbags by Shaunt Sarian

Headwear: Baseball, beanie, beret, boater, bonnet, bowler, bucket, cloche, cowboy, deerstalker, fascinator, fedora, fez, headband, helmet, newsboy cap, snood, top hat, toque, turban, visor

Hat by Marie Galvin for GALVIN-ized Headwear

Photograph by Tracy Aiguier.

Photograph by Beau Snyder/iStockphoto.

Belts: Buckle, clip or quick release, utility, web, chain, D-ring, corset style, leather, stretch, tie, obi, skinny

Photograph by Beau Snyder/iStockphoto.

Photograph by Coka/Fotolia.

Scarves: Ascot, bandana, bow tie, cravat, headscarf, hijab or khimar, kerchief, mantilla, necktie, shawl, stole

Eyewear: Eyeglasses, sunglasses, goggles, monocle, eye patch

Jewelry: Bracelet (cuff, bangle, beaded, chain, charm), cufflinks, earrings (studs, hoops, drop), hair clip or pin, tiara, necklace (bead, chain, pendant), pin or brooch, ring, buckle, shoe clip, watch (pocket, pin, pendant, wrist)

Photograph by Alex Mita/AFP/Getty Images.

Photograph by Kristen Johansen./iStockphoto.

Body Modification, Permanent: Tattoos, piercing, scarification, branding, Botox, cosmetic surgery, implants

Body Modification, Temporary: Henna tattoos, beauty marks or bindi, body paint, contact lenses, cosmetics, nail polish

Gloves: Fingerless, full length, gauntlet, knit, leather, mittens, utility

Hosiery: Leg warmers, tights, stockings, pantyhose, nylons, seamed, silk, fishnets, kneesocks, tabi socks, thigh-highs, toe socks

Technology: PDAs, cell phones, iPods and music players, headphones

Sensory: Perfume, cologne, eau de toilette, aromatic oils

Miscellaneous: Fan, flower, organizer or planner, suspender, sleeve garter, hosiery garter, spats, umbrella, walking stick or cane

Photograph by Hola Images/Getty Images.

Tattoo Body Art

Photograph by Danish Khan/iStockphoto.

Hennaed Hand

Photograph by Umbar Shakir/iStockphoto.

Bridal Bindi

Where do you start with the design process when developing a new collection? And why that first?

I have a mobile fashion laboratory called Taller Flora that travels throughout Mexico, visiting indigenous communities and the cooperatives where female artisans create handmade textiles. In these visits, we start the design process by researching a weaving technique or a silhouette traditional to that ethnic group, and from there we develop a new collection. Our unique pedagogy allows workshop participants to communicate through design even in those places where only indigenous dialects are spoken.

How important is the history of fashion to your creative process?

I first studied the history of art to understand the potential of the creative process: The better you know the creative moments in history and their relationship with economics, anthropology, society, and everything around it, the more dimension, the greater richness, you bring to the potential of clothing in all these scenes. Fashion is a very accelerated process and to prevent repeating yourself, it helps a lot to be interested in everything, from history to futurology.

Particularly, I am in love with Mexican history. I live in a country with forty-six different ethnic groups subdivided into hundreds more, plus the urban tribes and the ethnic mixes. Most indigenous women continue to wear traditional garments, and I cannot believe my eyes when I see the wonderful, daring color combinations, the textures and imaginative embroideries of the highest quality. All this creativeness comes from who we were as a people, what we have become, and how we want to be seen in the future.

In your work you balance contemporary design with the preservation of ancient techniques. How does that influence your brand and in what ways does it allow you to connect with your customer?

For a long time, I have been researching, collecting, and cataloguing traditional garment designs that were at risk of extinction. I have used them to prove that, contrary to the kitsch stereotype that Mexico itself exports, ancient patterning is an incredibly elaborate system: Based on the geometry of squares and rectangles only, pieces of cloth are pleated, folded, and seamed (rather than cut) to construct a vast array of garments. This system of dressmaking has been the source of inspiration for my label. Our design method is rooted in these techniques, but also applied to tailored garments. Sometimes with minimal alterations, we can translate traditional garments into the contemporary world of fashion design, both prêt-à-porter and haute couture.

How would you describe the ideology behind your approach to your design work?

A few years ago, I joined PROADA, a government program implemented through the Department of Folk Cultures that is aimed at developing handcraft design. When I started working with groups of indigenous people, I realized that it would be impossible to teach them Western dressmaking techniques. The first obstacle was language: In a co-op of ten women, none or only one of them might speak Spanish, and hence we needed an interpreter. Centimeters and inches were another cultural convention that was sometimes awkward; instead, the artisans used fingers, palms and forearms as measures. At that point, I understood that it was natural to employ the codes that the indigenous people had already mastered. I had to spend an intensive period of time observing their systems to become familiar with them. If I wanted to teach, I first had to learn. In this way, a parallel process arose, an organic pedagogy whose basis is, above all, visual—a hybrid between mimicry and origami.

How does the issue of sustainability and fair trade affect your design process?

Flora's pedagogy has a number of advantages: First, it avoids turning co-ops into sweatshops that manufacture other people's designs. Second, artisans are artists; if they are using a method that is familiar to them, they can initiate changes and invent their own prototypes for new garments. Moreover, creative people who make original designs are also likely to improve their businesses. In turn, they establish ties with other co-ops and strengthen the networks based on fair trade and environmentally friendly materials. Finally, consumers are educated in the process: All the garments bear labels that specify how, where, and by whom they were made.

With an industry that is losing skilled craftspeople with every passing generation, what do you think fashion education programs should include in their curriculum to best prepare designers looking to enter the market?

I think that fashion schools worldwide should map the arts and crafts centers of their country and link them to their design programs. I created a program in Fashion and Textile Design for a university in Mexico, where I established an exchange between the artisanal co-ops around Mexico and the fashion and textile design students. When they know the richness of their country's resources and the exclusiveness of its crafts, young designers are less likely to lose their identity by copying global trends. It can inspire them to propose new trends that will compete better in a fashion industry so eager for novelties and ultimately increase their market.

What should a designer understand about the business of fashion?

Fashion is an industry. If looked at entrepreneurially, designers will see that creativity can be a very good business. And a successful contemporary design practice can help prevent the extinction of craftsmanship. The women artisans with whom I work make their crafts in their community; otherwise, they have to go to the cities, leave behind their families, and lose their craft skills. Nowadays, in countries like mine where a great craft tradition is no longer being passed from parent to child, we have to recognize that we can make good profits with our own creativity and, at the same time, take care of our cultural heritage.

Did you have a mentor in the fashion industry? Have you assumed the role of mentor for someone else?

I've had a number of encounters with personalities on the U.K. fashion scene, such as designer Paul Smith and fashion writer Colin McDowell. In 2008 I received the International Young Fashion Entrepreneur award from the British Council. I really admire the work in the creative industries that they have promoted internationally. We've had a nice engagement since last year. They give us advice in the development of the cultural sector, which we tropicalize to make our own.

As for me being a mentor, I always open my studio to fashion students from around Mexico and the rest of the world. I like to have indigenous interns who have not studied fashion design but have inherited their craft for generations, alongside French or English students who have received the best education in their fashion schools. The exchange that comes out of these different ways of learning and living is very enriching for all and is reflected, in a unique way, in the garments that we make at Taller Flora. We take the best from everyone, always keeping the Mexican design proposal.

How do you strike a balance between the theater of the runway or editorial and the reality of retail?

It is very rare to have in one person the aptitude for being a good creative and also a good business person. Part of a brand's success is creating a strong team: There has to be a person in charge of the theatrical, amusing side of fashion and another that takes care of the business end.

What advice would you give to designers starting their career or a business?

Make whatever clothes you want to make, in any way you want to make them, but go to the people that know how to make them best. There are artisans falling into oblivion all around the world that know how to produce what you want. Traditional crafts and fashion are not mutually exclusive. On the contrary, they can further each other. It is possible to make trendy artisanal pieces.

To efficiently conjugate these two, it is essential to understand the timing of artisanal crafts-manship and the timing of the fashion system. In my case, I have managed to develop two types of collections: those that are fabricated in accordance with the natural rhythm of the artisans and the time they require to make the pieces; and those that respect the demanding rhythm of an ever-accelerating fashion world. In any case, it is indispensable to defy the no-tion that fashion is ephemeral and artisanal tradition immobile. A reconciliation of the two is in order.

How have you diversified your design work?

Indigenous communities are to me a source of inspiration, not only visually, but socially as well. I will go into a community, identify its main problem, and find a way to provide that com-munity with solutions through design. For instance, in San Juan Chamula, Chiapas, a com-munity that makes dolls using ancient handcraft techniques faced an overproduction that was impoverishing them. At the same time, women artisans were too busy making dolls to attend to much else, including health and hygiene. Medical service is scarce in the area and preven-tion is crucial; but occupied by housework, child care, and craft work, it was very difficult for these women to attend health courses. I decided to teach them how to make other types of dolls based on the shapes of the main viruses and bacteria that were jeopardizing the com-munity. Through this initiative the women have learned about the prevention, diagnosis, and treatment of these diseases, and the social bonding that happens while weaving has allowed for instructive conversations. Simultaneously, the doll makers have been able to diversify their production and aspire to new income by offering a unique product in the design market. The project was a way to save these women time, to foster health while working, and to further literacy through design.

Overleaf   Taller Flora, Women's, Men's, and Children's Wear Collections.
          Photographs by Mark Powell.

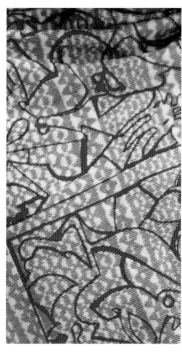

4.

CONSTRUCT

When the fashion designer is ready to execute an idea, it is time to draw up blueprints. Many designers will start by sketching, rendering their ideas on a fashion figure to get a feel for what the garments will look like on the human form. The next step is patternmaking, which can begin with draping or skip right to flat pattern drafting. Once a sound plan is in place, the process of building the garment is underway. Construction might be undertaken by hand, machine, or a combination of the two. The finishing stage is when the designer fits, hems, and presses the garment to give it a polished look. Designers must remember that the first sample garment is a test. Draped muslins, flat patterns, cutting tickets, fittings, and the input of all those who've worked on it will establish a dossier about what went right with the plan, what can be improved about the process, and whether or not the idea is viable.

Chapter 14: Rendering

Anyone can draw. If one can render a conclusion, one can render a drawing. Drawing can be broken down into choices about the assembly of straight lines, curved lines, and the shapes they can create when shortened, extended, or connected. Fashion designers have the advantage that they work with patterns and are familiar with fabric and how it folds and drapes on the body. With this experience, to produce a good croquis, or sketch, is a matter of developing hand-to-eye coordination—which simply takes practice. A recommended method for such training is to use tracing paper for corrections. Being able to see the mistake under a correction allows the brain to process important information. Erasers eliminate this opportunity. They also change the surface of the paper, which can affect the rendering when using paint or markers afterward. Some designers have a natural affinity for rendering; others will find that their skills are stronger in another part of the design process. Regardless, when a fashion drawing is simplified to a kind of schematic, rendering becomes less intimidating. The point is less to draw a pretty picture than to communicate an idea clearly.

TOOLS AND TECHNIQUES

Media

All designers have their preferred media, but any combination of watercolor, marker, or pencil offers them many ways to express their ideas on paper. Watercolors are a great choice for laying down smooth base colors that can be built on; they also offer an infinite amount of color-mixing formulas. Markers fall into two categories: Certain brands will provide the transparent effect of watercolor, keeping in mind that designers must purchase a marker for every shade of color they will need. Other types of markers have an inklike quality that can be useful for making lines pop. Both brushes and markers come in a variety of sizes and shapes that run the gamut from wide, chunky chiseled tips to fine needlelike microtips.

Gel-tip pens can add greater dimension to the finishing process, especially when rendering metallic details. Translucent metallic paints will often require a base color to give the color depth. Gold metallic paint out of the tube can fall a little flat because it is being muted by a white background. Laying down a wash of bright yellow or mustard will each create very distinct types of gold.

Quality of Line

Any combination of tip shapes and sizes will allow the designer to put down both big washes of color and the finest detail in one sketch. The amount pressure with which the drawing instrument is applied will also affect the weight of the line on the page. The movement and release of each stroke creates a sense of energy and movement when it is executed with confidence. Often, knowing when to lift the pencil, marker, or brush off the page is just as important as where to place it initially. Practice and close attention to the intention behind each movement helps not only to create a sense of effortlessness, but also to develop the designer's unique personal rendering style.

Light and Dark

Lighter colors are often easier to manage when rendering because they offer some latitude when it comes to adding color, texture, or detail to make the color rich and realistic. A sketch that is meant to represent a white garment might not require an application of white but simply be about rendering filmy gray shadows, using additional shades of gray for details. Or a designer might choose to use color paper as a contrasting background for a garment that is actually painted white. Darker colors are less forgiving and require a different kind of approach. If a designer applies a deep black pigment, shadows are absorbed by the dark color and accents must indicate where light is being reflected. In this case, using grays or white would help to create detail.

Shadow Mapping

If designers are not drawing from life, they must draft a map of shadows for their sketch. They will need to figure out how shadows will fall on the body, the face, and the garments. Selecting a position for the light source will make it easier to be consistent with the placement of shadows. The transparency of media such as watercolor and marker is helpful, because the illusion of shadows can be created by applying an additional layer rather than mixing a darker color as would be required were an opaque pigment being used.

Shadow-mapped figure

RENDERING THE BODY

The body of a fashion figure is usually elongated to imply grace and movement as well as to provide a greater surface area for details. The average human body is approximately seven to eight heads long. For the fashion figure, the widely used nine-head drawing is a good place to start when it comes to figuring out how to distribute the space from head to toe. Lengthening the hip-to-knee and knee-to-ankle ratio will create that long-legged model look, without distorting the torso's proportions.

Average body proportion versus fashion aesthetic

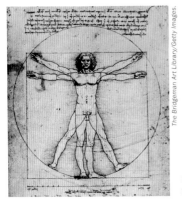

The Bridgeman Art Library/Getty Images.

Leonardo da Vinci, ideal proportions of the human figure, 1492

COMPARATIVE PROPORTIONS

Heads	Average	Fashion
1	Top of head to chin	Top of head to chin
2	Chin to apex of bust	Chin to apex of bust
3	Apex of bust to true waist	Apex of bust to true waist
4	True waist to hip joint	True waist to hip joint
5	Hip joint to mid thigh	Hip joint to knee
6	Mid thigh to mid calf	
7	Mid calf to ankle	Knee to ankle
8	Ankle to toe	
9		Ankle to toe

Some designers take artistic license and render sketches that are even more exaggerated in the name of style. So long as some key points line up this can still give the illusion of being in proportion. The elbow corresponds to the true waistline (at the navel), for instance, and the wrist lines up with the hips. Of course, every designer's preferred aesthetic has a corresponding body. Some designers might lean toward a narrow boyish figure while others prefer a fuller hourglass shape. Choosing between a higher or lower waistline and pairing it with a fuller bust or hip will determine whether the figure has more of an apple or pear shape. Breaking this down into a formula allows designers to make simple alterations to their croquis, customizing it for the demands of the design. It also makes it easier for designers' target customers to imagine themselves in the garments.

Many are of the opinion that designers should take anatomy classes to help improve their sketching. When it comes to the art of fashion, these classes better serve the fashion illustrator. On the other hand, anatomical study will have an impact on designers' patternmaking skills. Anatomy provides them with an understanding of the structure and mechanics of the body, from which they can gain a greater appreciation for how clothing will fit and flow around the human form.

Designers should remember to draw only what they would see from a particular vantage point. For instance, on a front view drawing of a garment the side seams would not be visible. If there is a reason to show the side seams, the figure should be rotated—front, side, three-quarter, and back views—to display the feature in those areas. When a designer chooses to place two or more figures on a page, the poses should reflect the desired dynamic between them. These poses should also create good negative space around and between the figures.

A designer wants the viewer's eye to focus on the clothing, first and foremost. A natural border of space is recommended when determining where to place the figure on the page. Having a figure trail off the page can be distracting. To best serve the clothing in a sketch, poses should not distort the garments, but rather, allow for a clear interpretation of how they are made and how they hang on the body. Keeping arms below the shoulder line, bent knees to a minimum, and arms or long hair from obscuring the design are few general guidelines that will help the croquis retain its value as a communication tool.

RENDERING THE HEAD

Face

Facial structure, like that of the body, is varied. Moreover, different cultures have their own standards of beauty. The "rules" that provide a baseline for the basic proportions of the face, therefore, rely heavily on balance. Designers have the discretion to adjust measurements to capture the essence of their ideal or the customer for whom they are creating a sketch. The face begins with an oval shape, bisected by a centerline, with a corresponding perpendicular line to mark the chin. Half way from the top of the head to the chin would indicate where the eyes are to be positioned. The area below the eyes is then halved to find the position for the nose. The mouth can be placed in the middle of the area between the nose and the chin. The nose and the mouth are centered, while the eyes are distributed in the space of four eyes. Working from the center outward, one eye will represent the space between the eyes. The two actual eyes will be placed on either side, which should allow for the space of half an eye between the eye and the side of the face. The oval can be sculpted on either side by two parallel lines to the face. At the level of the mouth, these lines can bend inward to meet the chin line, defining the jawline. Depending on scale, the ears usually line up on top with the eye and end somewhere between the nose and the mouth.

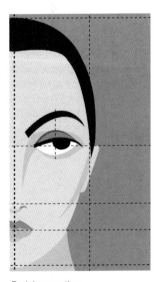

Facial proportions

Eye

The eyes start with an almond shape. The centerline between both tips establishes the tilt of the eye. A third line with less of an arc is drawn from one tip to the other to create the lid. How low the lid is drawn will determine how open the eye seems to be. A circle representing the iris is placed within the original almond shape. The lid line should cut off the top of the circle depicting the iris, which should appear to be perfectly round, although obscured by the eyelid. If the iris is rendered as a complete circle the result will be a wide-eyed, shocked, or frightened expression. When rendering the iris in color, omitting color or adding a white accent in the shape of a small crescent creates the illusion of glistening light.

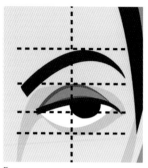

Eye

Lashes can be drawn from the center of each lid outward, with an emphasis on quality of line, so that the drawing tool lifts off the page at the end of each lash. Three to five top lashes are plenty considering the size of the average croquis (obviously, the larger the rendering the more details it can handle). A point above of the eye closest to the center of the face is the starting point for the eyebrow. The arch can follow the angle of the top of the almond and extend as far as three-quarters of the eye before it breaks to level off.

Nose

Rendering the nose is more about shadows than lines. Three circles will define the scale of the tip of the nose and the area over the nostrils. Under the spots where these circle touch are spaces where arcs can be drawn to show the nostrils. In most fashion sketches, these markings alone can be enough to create an impression of the nose.

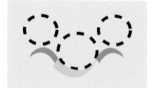

Nose

Mouth

Building the shape of the mouth can be done using three circles stacked into a pyramid. The hill-like space between the circles will determine the opening of the mouth. Cutting a V or U shape out of the top circle establishes the center of the top lip, and drawing sloping lines to connect it with the sides of the mouth will complete the archer's bow silhouette. A straight (or slightly indented) line between the bottom two

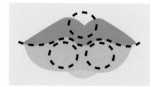

Mouth

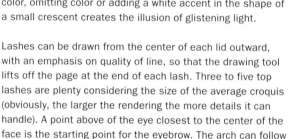

circles creates an area for shadow under the bottom lip. This can also be connected with the sides of the mouth. When rendering the lip in color, making the upper lip a shade darker will create a more three-dimensional look.

Complexion

The complexion of the figure may or may not be a direct reflection of the ethnicity designers are going for. How they combine color with modified features will allow them to develop an international rainbow of models. The place to start is the level of light or dark (very fair, fair, midtone, tanned, dark, very dark) that the designer wants to establish. Once the range is selected, it is a matter of mixing color in the equivalent level of white, cream, tan, or brown with colors that will tint them in the direction the designer desires. For Caucasian skin, pure white will create the appearance of alabaster, but adding red to it can result in a ruddy complexion. Tinting tan with olive can give the impression of swarthy Mediterranean skin, while adding a little black to a darker brown can create a rich African skin tone. Adding the tone-on-tone of freckles to any color makes for a completely new look. Generalizations and stereotypes will be obvious because there are no absolutes. Hispanics, for instance, can be very fair or very dark and every shade in between. As in all things, the choices and customizations designers make will reflect their aesthetics and how their customers see themselves.

Hair

When rendering hair, it should be broken down into sections and locks. Hair stylists use a standard technique for sectioning hair for a haircut, called seven-section parting, which designers can borrow for creating a hairstyle on their croquis. These sections are top, temple/right side, temple/left side, right crown, left crown, right nape, and left nape. Dividing the hairstyle among them helps to plot out what it will do at each point (stand up, curl, lie flat, etc.) as well as how long and at what angle it will be cut. Although a sketch might represent a frontal view, designers should clearly understand what is happening in the back of the head and what part of it will be seen from the front. Once a hairstyle is mapped out, the base shapes can be rendered in a medium tone of the desired

Hair

color. Highlights and lowlights (or shadows) are added as accents for each section. Fine details can be introduced in the form of tufts, wisps, or strands of hair to finish off each section. The texture of hair must also be designed. Will straight hair be blunt, curl under, or flip out? Will curls be large and loose waves or small and tight ringlets? How will sections of hair be swept up to create an updo? How will the scalp be sectioned for braids or dreadlocks? The thickness and length must be determined as well.

Makeup

The application of cosmetics on the croquis should be undertaken with the same kind of planning and artistry with which real makeup is applied. After laying down a base color for the skin, a second layer of the same color can be used to create shadows. Once these shadows have established the contours of bone structure, designers can add eye shadow, rouge, and lip color. A thin wash of color over the skin tone will create a natural look, while a heavier treatment will result in something more theatrical. A light touch is required for eyeliner, lashes, and brows. These details help to define the eye, and it is easier to add than remove.

Makeup

RENDERING FABRIC

Besides having a grasp on the structure of the body and facial details, the designer must, of course, be able to capture textiles, construction, and ornamentation as they relate to the garments they are depicting. Fabric that is manipulated in three dimensions must be translated into two. Flares, for instance, might be trumpetlike when the garment is made out of a crisp, stiff fabric such as taffeta or more flutelike were the same style of garment to be made of chiffon.

The roundness of gathered fabric is subject to the same idea when it comes to ruffles, shirring, smocking, quilting, and puffs. When rendering each pucker and release of a gathered fabric, the designer should remember that each little divot is in fact a shadow and not a line.

Pleats, on the other hand, have a crisp crease in the folds of tuck, box, accordion, and fan pleating. Irregular pleating can take many forms and therefore variations should be studied closely before trying to capture them on the page. This style of pleating, called primitive, mushroom, or broomstick, has been explored by designers from Mariano Fortuny to Mary McFadden to Issey Miyake in his Pleats Please line.

To draw fabric that is draped by folding or tying as well as fabric that falls into cowls or cascades, a designer must be familiar with the nature of the fabric and how it will respond to any of these manipulations.

Another textile issue the designer faces with the creation of a sketch is pattern. Stripes, checks, plaids, and overall patterns each present their own challenges. As in textile design, the fashion designer creates a motif, then decides on its scale and repeats in relation to the body. Grids that represent the direction of grainlines help to plan out how a pattern will wrap around the form. The size of each repeat determines the size of the grid.

To show textiles as texture, the designer's focus is on rendering with color. A sheer becomes a filmy wash of color layered over skin tone and any other fabrics it rests on in the sketch. Lace work is also layered over other colors, but demands strong bias cross-hatching to create the illusion of netting on which the pattern of the lace is built. Feathers and fur require layers and layers of color to create depth at the center and a wispy lightness along the perimeter. Knits are depicted by building up ribs, cables, or twists and stitch details to create the appropriate surface texture for the bulk of the fabric.

Color-on-color surfacing—usually pencil over watercolor—can be used to create different types of weaves—linen, raw silk, denim or twill, and corduroy, for example. The desired level of roughness is influenced by the density of threads, nubs, and slubs in the weave. The viscosity of paint can be applied thickly for velvet, leather, and suede or in thinner wet washes for satin, ombre stripes, dip-dye, or tie-dye.

Adding any type of embellishment or decorative detail (embroidery, sequins, beads, fringe, frogs, bows, piping, decorative stitching, appliqué, passementerie) is the final stage and requires delicate pencil, marker, or even watercolor work. Each type of detail requires individual study, be it the direction of threads, the overlap pattern of sequins, the shape of stitches or beads, or the twist and gauge of cording.

Classic mid-1920s fashion illustration by Georges Barbier

Fine art style illustration by Catherine Abel

Fashion Illustration

A fashion illustrator is not a fashion designer, although a fashion designer can be an illustrator. Fashion illustrations fall under a separate category more closely aligned with advertising. This kind of fashion rendering is the work of artists who are skilled at conveying the messages and fantasies behind the fashion. Everything from fine art techniques to animation-inspired graphics can be used to create a mood around a style. Photography has for a long time overpowered fashion illustration as the method for communicating fashion, but more and more fashion artists are being sought after for their unique interpretations. The line between illustration and photography is also blurring, thanks to computer technology. With a photograph as the foundation, an image can be taken to new heights by a talented computer artist.

Graphic style illustration by Eastnine Inc.

Workroom sketch by Karl Lagerfeld
for the Chanel Haute Couture Fall/Winter
2006/2007 Collection

Sketching Shorthand

Many designers develop a kind of notation for a bare-bones framework that allows them to jot down fashion ideas. This can be akin to a stylized stick figure that they use to create rough pictures of scale, proportion, length, and detail. Whether the idea is captured on a napkin or in a notebook, the fashion scribble is a way to make visual notes. The images might also be accompanied by details and descriptions that allow the designer to revisit them and develop more elaborate renderings.

Techs

Technical fashion sketches can be done by hand, but computer-generated techs have become an industry standard. These sketches are designed to provide more detailed specifications about the actual garments. These simple line drawings are also called flats because they are drawn like clothing lying flat rather than on a figure. This type of fashion drawing is also used on the cutting tickets that accompany a garment during production or on line sheets with information required by buyers.

Draped muslin and draped muslin with computer-generated fabric

Photographs by Tracy Aiguier.

Digital Art

Designers can create digital fashion sketches using computer art software. Adobe Photoshop and Adobe Illustrator are two mainstream programs that serve as excellent digital interpreters of the drawing skills a designer develops in the real world. All of the techniques described for fashion sketches created by hand can be recreated using the on-screen tools, layers, brushes, and filters. Many types of software designed specifically for the needs of a fashion designer are now available. Of course, none of these programs is a substitute for learning how to draw. In the end, a computer and software are just tools like a brush and a pencil. Either discipline must be mastered to produce great images. The advantage of digital art is that it's cleaner and paperless, and it allows the designer to update, correct, and reproduce visual information more easily and quickly.

Designing textiles with software that can communicate with looms and knitting machines is another practical use of technology. This type of program allows the designer to create woven and knit fabrics by coloring each warp and weft thread as well as every knit and purl stitch. Other programs allow the designer to scan in a swatch of a fabric that they may have discovered but that is no longer available. Designers can clean up the scan, then reduce a print to a motif that they can recreate, redesign, or recolor according to how it will best serve their idea.

Draping software makes it possible for designers to create textured surface grids for sketches or photographs of sample garments. They can then assign their digital fabric designs to these surfaces. A picture is worth a thousand words when attempting to describe how a garment will read when fabricated in different textiles. The whole process allows designers to reduce risk by extending a menu of possibilities to a buyer before committing to the production of fabrics and garments.

Chapter 15: Patternmaking

Patterns are as invaluable to the fashion designer as plans are to the architect. Adding volume to a garment or eliminating fullness are the result of decisions about fabric manipulation made during pattern drafting. Every restriction and every bit of ease is built into the pattern. A creative individual armed with a yardage of fabric and a few carefully placed pins can drape themselves into a dress. Transferring this idea onto a flat pattern, with all the information needed to duplicate the process, is where the professional's skill comes in.

Photograph by Popperfoto/Getty Images.

Couturier Hardy Amies in the workroom with Miss Beard, head fitter, 1952

PATTERNMAKING EQUIPMENT

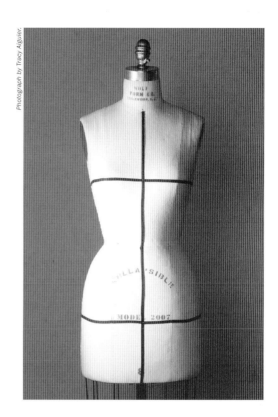

Photograph by Tracy Aiguier.

Dress Forms

Dress forms are not mannequins. They provide a live-model fit but are a lot more forgiving of pin stabs. The base of a dress form is composed of layers of cardboard heat-fused with plaster paste; it is covered in layers of jersey, which are covered, in turn, in linen. A spring mechanism between the shoulders allows the form to collapse, making the removal of garments easier. These body doubles are available in most standard sizes and can also be custom ordered for special clients who cannot always come in for fittings. They are helpful both for fitting a garment and for the original development of a draped pattern.

In the design studio, small variations in a size can be made with wide bias strips of muslin wrapped around the form to generate a gradual increase in the area requiring modification. Adjustable dress forms that change sizes with the twist of a dial might be convenient for home use or in special circumstances, but seldom offer the stability of a professional form.

Tool Kit

For the draping and drafting of patterns, the designer needs a set of tools to facilitate the collection and transfer of measurements, along with cutting and sewing instructions, onto a map that anyone can use to create a sample garment.

Armscye (armhole curve)
Awl
Cloth weights
C-thru ruler
Dotted paper
French curve
Hip curve
Hole punch
Iron and board
Long stapler
L-square
Mechanical pencil
Muslin
Needle point tracing wheel
Notcher
Oak tag paper
Pattern hooks
Pattern punch
Pencils (black, blue, red)
Rotary cutter and cutting mat
Scissors (fabric and paper)
Sewing gauge
Straight pins
Style tape
Tailor's chalk or wax
Tape measure
Yardstick

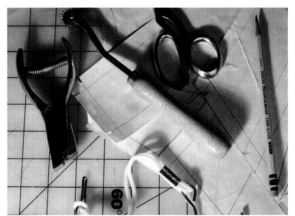

Patternmaking tools

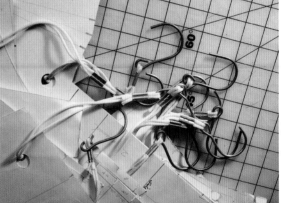

Patterns and Hooks

Photograpshs by Tracy Aiguier.

Slopers

The term *sloper* is commonly misused to describe a fit pattern. As it relates to apparel, a sloper is a pattern blank for a garment that does not include seam allowance or style lines. A sloper has no seam allowance so that it can be used for generating new patterns based on specific dress-form/client/model measurements, or for modifying patterns that are based on a successful model. Creating a sloper for a pair of pants that has been proven to have a great fit at the waist, hips, and rise eliminates the need to return to the drawing board to recreate that particular fit. The sloper can be traced onto paper and altered to create a new style with the assurance of the same great fit. Adding seam allowance at this point makes it a pattern that can be used for the production of the garment. The removal of seam allowance is also an option when generating patterns digitally—as handy a function as the one that reapplies seam allowance to the pattern when modifications are complete.

FLAT PATTERN DRAFTING

Flat pattern drafting can use the information generated from a draped pattern or be developed strictly from measurements. Once the required set of key measurements has been determined, a two-dimensional grid is created on paper to represent a flat version of a three-dimensional form. The process can be compared to the design of a foldable cardboard gift box, where flat board is trimmed and scored in such a way that when folded it will transform into a cube.

The pattern is drafted using a set of measurements and their relationship to one another: how, where, and at what angles they intersect. The more detailed information that is collected the better the fit. Next, ease is introduced to areas that require extra flexibility (across the back, at the armhole, and across the seat are a few practical places), then darts are positioned as fold lines where needed to eliminate fullness, and finally seam allowance is added beyond the stitching lines. A toile, also referred to as a muslin or fit garment, is pinned or basted together for a fitting to make corrections and refine the final pattern.

BODY MEASUREMENTS

Neck circumference (at base)	Waist to hip
Center back neck height	Waist to knee
Chest (above bust, under arm)	Waist to ankle
Bust	Waist height
Bust bridge or span (between apexes)	Hip height
Bra size	Rise (CB waist between legs to natural CF waist)
Bra cup	Crotch length
Bust apex at center front to waist	Crotch height
Natural or true waist	Crotch depth (seated waist to chair)
Abdomen or Diaphragm (fullest point)	Inseam (crotch to ankle)
High hip (approx. 4"–5" [10.2–12.7 cm] below waist)	Inseam to knee
Full hip (approx. 7"–9" [17.8–22.9 cm] below waist)	Thigh circumference
Cross shoulder	Knee circumference
Side shoulder	Knee height
Shoulder slope	Calf circumference
Shoulder to bust apex	Ankle circumference
Cross front (approx. 4" [10.2 cm] down)	Ankle height
Cross back (approx. 6" [15.2 cm] down)	Circumference of the instep
Center front (CF) neck to waist	Height
Center back (CB) neck to waist	Weight
Under arm to waist (approx. 2" [5.1 cm] below pit)	
Armhole	
Arm length from shoulder	
Arm length from center back neck (bent)	
Upper arm length	
Forearm length	
Inside arm length	
Bicep circumference	
Elbow circumference	
Wrist circumference	

Slash, Spread, and Pivot

A pattern piece can be modified employing the slash and spread method. The most common use is to add fullness to an area. If a sleeve pattern is slashed in half lengthwise, it can be kept together at the base and spread at the head of the sleeve to increase the volume of fabric that will be gathered into the cap, creating a puffed sleeve. When the fullness is distributed in the opposite direction, the sleeve will fit smoothly into the cap but flare out into a bell shape at the hem. The pattern pieces can also be spread apart in equal amounts for a sleeve that is full on both ends. Once the pattern is slashed and spread, it is retraced onto paper to include the additional area, creating a new sleeve pattern.

A darted bodice pattern can be slashed to reposition the bust dart with the use of pivoting. A line is drawn and cut from the apex of the original dart to the new location. The apex becomes the pivot point. When the pattern is manipulated to close the original dart at the pivot point, the new dart automatically opens up. The pattern can also be pivoted partially to decrease the size of the original dart, thereby creating two darts. The sum of both darts now eliminates the same amount of fullness in the garment as the original single bust dart. The newly redistributed pattern is traced onto paper, and in both cases the new pattern retains the same fit.

Notches

Small cuts into the seam allowance called notches are used as markers. These notches provide a way to line up sections of a garment meant to be sewn to each other. A front bodice side seam will be notched to sync up with same marking on the back bodice side seam. Because the front and back parts of the cap on a sleeve are different shapes there will usually be one notch on the front section of the cap so that it lines up with a corresponding notch along the front bodice armhole. A double-notch is used to indicate the back part of the cap, which has been drafted to fit into the back bodice armhole.

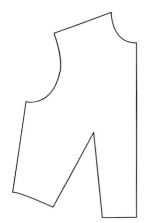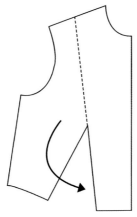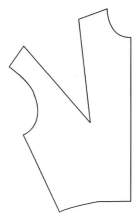

Bodice pattern with
waistline dart

Slash to apex of dart
and pivot to close dart

Bodice with new
shoulder dart

MEASUREMENTS NOT SIZES

Standard Sizing

Anyone who has ever shopped for clothing has confronted the inconsistency of sizing in today's marketplace. From one store to the next, a size 8 will fit in vastly dissimilar ways. The charts on these pages reflect one set of "standards" that have been identified as a baseline for the best fit for the largest audience. They represent sizes as they relate to body dimensions and product dimensions, as well as numbers and codes with no direct correlation to actual measurements. As much as industry standards may provide a designer with a starting point, none exists that is both widely accepted and strictly adhered to in all markets.

MEN Adult Build HEIGHT: 5'10" (1.78 m)											
US	XS		S		M		L		XL		
EU	30	32	34	36	38	40	42	44	46	48	
Chest	30" (76 cm)	32" (81 cm)	34" (87 cm)	36" (92 cm)	38" (97 cm)	40" (102 cm)	42" (107 cm)	44" (112 cm)	46" (117 cm)	48" (122 cm)	
Waist	24" (61 cm)	26" (66 cm)	28" (71 cm)	30" (76 cm)	32" (81 cm)	34" (87 cm)	36" (92 cm)	39" (99 cm)	42" (107 cm)	44" (112 cm)	
Hip/ Seat	31" (79 cm)	33" (84 cm)	35" (89 cm)	37" (94 cm)	39" (99 cm)	41" (104 cm)	43" (109 cm)	45" (114 cm)	47" (119 cm)	49" (124 cm)	
Neck	13" (33 cm)	13.5" (34.5 cm)	14" (35.5 cm)	14.5" (37 cm)	15" (38 cm)	15.5" (39.5 cm)	16" (40.5 cm)	16.5" (42 cm)	17" (43 cm)	17.5" (44.5 cm)	
Sleeve	31" (79 cm)	31" (79 cm)	32" (81 cm)	32" (81 cm)	33" (84 cm)	33" (84 cm)	34" (87 cm)	34" (87 cm)	35" (89 cm)	35" (89 cm)	

Small, Medium, Large

Small, medium, and large come into play when dressing a mass audience that requires a common denominator for size. Society has embraced this formula because it makes the whole process of acquiring and wearing a garment easier and faster. Knits, elastics, and drawstrings have contributed to the flexibility of clothing that serves this functional ease. Another approach that uses S/M/L thinking involves situations in which the scale of a garment relates not to how well it encases the body but rather to how it stands away from the figure. Designers may be tempted to write off this generic metric as a simple, all-purpose fix to the issue of size, but there may be more sophisticated thinking behind these designations. For example, on the artistic side, one might picture conceptual fabric sculptures that test the limits of what can be achieved in clothing and that are judged primarily on aesthetic value. From the position of solving a design problem, one need only consider the caftan: where the space between the wearer and the garment takes on importance as a cooling system.

MISSES Adult Figure HEIGHT: 5'5"–5'6" (1.65–1.68 m) PETITE HEIGHT: 5'2"–5'4" (1.57–1.63 m)

	XS		S		M		L		XL		XXL
US	6	8	10	12	14	16	18	20	22	24
UK	10	12	14	16	18	20	22	24	24	26
EU	36	38	40	42	44	46	48	50	52	54
Chest	28.5" (73 cm)	29.5" (75 cm)	30.5" (78 cm)	32" (81 cm)	34" (87 cm)	36" (92 cm)	38" (97 cm)	40" (102 cm)	42" (107 cm)	44" (112 cm)
Bust	30.5" (78 cm)	31.5" (80 cm)	32.5" (83 cm)	34" (87 cm)	36" (92 cm)	38" (97 cm)	40" (102 cm)	42" (107 cm)	44" (112 cm)	46" (117 cm)
Waist	23" (58 cm)	24" (61 cm)	25" (64 cm)	26.5" (67cm)	28" (71 cm)	30" (76 cm)	32" (81 cm)	34" (87 cm)	36" (92 cm)	38" (97 cm)
Hip	32.5" (83 cm)	33.5" (85 cm)	34.5" (88 cm)	36" (92 cm)	38" (97 cm)	40" (102 cm)	42" (107 cm)	44" (112 cm)	46" (117 cm)	48" (122 cm)
Back/ Waist Length	15.5" (39.5 cm)	15.75" (40 cm)	16" (40.5 cm)	16.25" (41.5 cm)	16.5" (42 cm)	16.75" (42.5 cm)	17" (43 cm)	17.25" (44 cm)	17.38" (44 cm)	17.5" (44.5 cm)

WOMEN Mature Figure HEIGHT: 5'5"–5'6" (1.65–1.68 m) PETITE HEIGHT: 5'2"–5'4" (1.57–1.63 m)

	XS		S		M		L		XL		XXL
US	14	16	18	20	22	24	26	28	30	32
UK	18	20	22	24	26	28	30	32	34	36
EU	32	34	36	38	40	42	44	46	48	50
Bust	36" (92 cm)	38" (97 cm)	40" (102 cm)	42" (107 cm)	44" (112 cm)	46" (117 cm)	48" (122 cm)	50" (127 cm)	52" (132 cm)	54" (137 cm)
Waist	29" (74 cm)	31" (79 cm)	33" (84 cm)	35" (89 cm)	37" (94 cm)	39" (99 cm)	41.5" (105 cm)	44" (112 cm)	46.5" (118 cm)	49" (124 cm)
Hip	38" (97 cm)	40" (102 cm)	42" (107 cm)	44" (112 cm)	46" (117 cm)	48" (122 cm)	50" (127 cm)	52" (132 cm)	54" (137 cm)	56" (142 cm)
Back/ Waist Length	16.5" (42 cm)	16.75" (42.5 cm)	17" (43 cm)	17.25" (44 cm)	17.38" (44 cm)	17.5" (44.5 cm)	17.63" (45 cm)	17.75" (45 cm)	17.88" (45.5 cm)	18" (46 cm)

Of all the debates that ensue when the subject of sizing in the fashion industry is broached perhaps the most heated concerns so-called vanity sizing or size inflation, whereby the designer makes a size intentionally generous. Some would argue that there is no such thing; others that it merely reflects new markets for smaller women, as in Asia. Most recognize that the same nominal clothing size has grown substantially larger since standards began to be applied in the middle of the last century. In the end, although it may serve their psychological need to mirror the current standards of beauty, the elaborate and often contradictory interpretation of sizes does not benefit customers in pursuit of assembling a wardrobe.

Mass Customization

In many high-end workrooms custom-made dress forms can be found. These allow the designer to develop clothing that will perfectly fit the customers whose measurements they possess. With a marketplace that constantly strives to give the consumer more and more choices, customization is an alluring prospect. As early as 1994 Levi Strauss & Company introduced a custom order system that presented shoppers with the opportunity to purchase made-to-order jeans. The manufacturing allowed for an affordable and timely turnaround, but the process of establishing the correct size was more demanding than convenient. Technology is moving quickly to answer the demand for bespoke garments at mainstream prices. Three-dimensional body scans that produce full-body profiles generate all the data necessary to make a garment and promise to be the fast, accurate tailor of the future. As such innovative technology becomes the standard, the sizing systems that consumers are currently at the mercy of could become obsolete.

Determining Fit

A designer can build a reputation on fit—good or bad. In an attempt to illustrate that accurate measurements are the basis for building patterns and attaining the desired fit, some fashion design schools today use dress forms that do not identify size. Designers face many factors. Different women with the same bust, waist, and hip measurements may also have a high or a low waist. Bust measurements themselves must be considered carefully, because a 36-inch (92-centimeter) bustline could be the result of a broad back in combination with a small cup size or the opposite, a narrow back and a large cup size. How proportions change due to the complete length of the torso and overall height will additionally affect fit. Once all the correct measurements have been established, the question of how much ease is added, and where, affects the fit of a garment dramatically. This literally becomes the framework or foundation for the silhouette, style lines, and every other design element that a designer brings to bear. The designer who commits to a particular proportion and serves it well can often count on customer loyalty that builds through word of mouth.

DRAPING

A talented patternmaker is capable of drafting a pattern for any garment armed with only a set of measurements, a pencil, and a ruler. Although this would be a rewarding challenge for its own sake, it does not replace the experience of sculpting with fabric. There are nuances about how the fabric clings to the body that should be felt by human hands. After all, the end user will be a real person responding to the same subtleties once the designer has introduced them into the garment.

Most designers will work with muslin in a weight that reflects the intended fabric. Muslin, being inexpensive, gives designers the freedom to experiment with many variations on an idea and to appreciate the different ways the fabric responds from lengthwise to crosswise grains, as well as along the bias.

Taking the fabric to the dress form is a good way to gauge how the fabric breaks, folds, and drapes. It also provides a better sense of the body and bulk of a fabric, affecting decisions about finishing details. A daring and well-funded designer might drape with the fabric itself. This may make for an extravagant experience, but it's an indulgence that more often than not results in costly waste.

The dictum "less is more" aptly applies to the art of draping. The most common mistakes in draping generally originate with overpinning and working against the nature of the fabric. By understanding the limits as well as the possibilities of the fabric, designers can engineer ways to push the boundaries for each new creation.

Photographs by Tracy Aiguier.

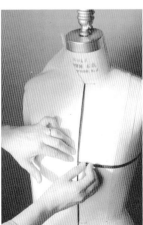
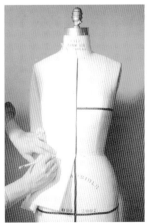

Half   Pinning   Marking

Draping Guidelines

Grainlines: On most woven fabrics the warp is finished with a tighter, denser weave to create the selvage. When draping, it is a good idea to clip the selvage, which creates ease and allows the fabric to hang naturally. The length and cross grains have little or no give. The bias, at a 45-degree angle to the grid of interlocking warp and weft threads, offers the greatest amount of give. It can be employed in areas that need to stretch, conforming to the body without darts, or have a softer, rounder rolling drape, rather than a crisp fold or crease.

Knits: When draping with knit fabrics, a big concern is the degree of stretch and recovery. This will depend on both the tightness of the knit and the properties of the yarns. Another factor is whether a knit is a two-way or four-way stretch, especially important in garments for dancers or athletes who will be extending their bodies beyond normal wear. Like its woven counterpart, the knit used for draping should be similar in gauge to the final fabric.

Blocking: Because muslin is an inexpensive fabric, the grain may have warped on the piece of cloth the designer is draping. Blocking squares the piece of muslin so that the crosswise grain and the lengthwise grain are perpendicular to each other. This often involves pulling on opposite corners of the fabric until it has been manipulated back into the intended shape.

Tearing: With muslin and others fabrics that have a basic weave, the true crosswise grain can be found by clipping into the selvage and tearing. This must be done with conviction, otherwise the tear can deviate from the grain. Designers must be sure of their fabrics, as the technique will not work with complex weaves.

Pressing: Wrinkles in the muslin will affect the final shape of the draped pattern piece. Pressing each square of muslin will avoid discrepancies later in the process. The iron's heat and steam will interact with the sizing and starches often added to muslin and stiffen it. This will make the muslin crisper and easier to handle. If the designer wants the fabric to respond in a softer way, the muslin can be washed first and then pressed.

Half: Unless a design is asymmetrical, most pattern work is done on the half in an attempt to avoid human error. This helps to ensure that both sides are the same and therefore look balanced, although bodies are unbalanced. When cutting the actual sample garment, these pattern pieces are placed on a double ply of fabric that generates two perfectly mirrored sides or on the edge of a lengthwise fold for a single piece.

Pinning: When pinning the muslin onto the dress form and into specific shapes, the fewer pins, the better. Fabric that is pulled too tightly and held with too many pins will often fit poorly. A well-draped pattern will hug the form in areas where it should and skim the body everywhere else. Many designers speak of how the fabric will inform them of what it wants to do. The best designers master the manipulation of fabric but respect its natural properties.

Marking: Cross marks, dots, and corners are the basic markings found on a draped pattern. In areas such as the side seam of a bodice, the designer need only mark the top and the bottom with a corner, knowing that a straight line will connect them. In curved areas, a dot can be placed approximately every half inch (1.3 cm). The apex of a dart should be marked with a cross mark of two pins.

Truing the Pattern: Once all the necessary markings have been made on the draped piece, it is unpinned and laid out flat. At this point, it is trued: All the lines, straight and curved, are clearly drawn on the fabric, ascertaining that corresponding areas match up. During this process, the designer will add the desired amount of ease to areas that allow for greater freedom of movement, such as the armhole, across the upper back and seat, and the center front neck. The "down and out" formula for armholes cuts deeper into the armhole (down) and adds fullness across the torso at this point (out). Squaring corners helps to avoid dips and points where pieces are sewn together.

Positive and Negative Ease: In woven garments, ease involves adding to an area to create more room. Knitted garments can have negative ease as well. This is best illustrated in how a swimsuit will look much smaller than the size of the body for which it has been designed, yet stretches not only to conform to the body but also to support it.

Seam Allowance: All designers establish their own in-house rules for seam allowance. The traditional amount is half an inch (1.3 cm) for most seams, a quarter inch (0.6 cm) at the neck, and two inches (5.1 cm) at the hem. Larger allowances are important when the designer anticipates fluctuations in size, as in the case of a bride who might be putting on pounds due to stress or be dieting before her big day.

Facings: Areas in a pattern piece meant to be finished with a clean edge require facings. Necklines, armholes, center-front lapels, keyhole openings, and other similar features are ideal candidates for facings. These pattern pieces are duplicate reflections of the intended section of the original pattern. Facings may be separate pattern pieces or be designed as a mirrored extension of the original pattern piece and drafted along a fold line. The facings are attached to the designated area, right sides facing, and then turned in to provide the desired finish. Seams that are curved should be clipped for ease so that they lie flat. These facings might remain loose, be tacked down, or be sewn to the lining.

Cutting: Much care should be taken when cutting away the extra fabric that is not a part of the finished pattern. When dealing with an area with darts, close them with a pin at the base and fold the fabric of the darts toward the side seam. Positioning the dart in this manner before cutting will ensure that there is enough fabric at the base of the dart to be caught in the seam when sewn together. This will provide a clean, finished appearance.

OTHER PATTERNMAKING ESSENTIALS

Rub-Offs

The idea behind rub-offs is to develop a pattern directly from a garment. The first step is to align the lengthwise and crosswise grainlines of a piece of muslin with those of each part of the garment (bodice front and back, sleeve, collar, skirt or pant front and back, etc.) and pin into place. Using tailor's wax or chalk, the designer then rubs an impression of each seam and style line for each pattern piece onto the muslin. To obtain the most accurate impression, the section that is being worked on should be laid out as flat as possible. Once a rubbing has been made of each piece, the information needs to be trued in the same manner as a draped pattern would be corrected and refined.

Grading

Most designers work in a sample size. Instead of recreating the pattern for each size they will be producing, they will grade the original pattern. The process increases (when sizing up) and decreases (when sizing down) a pattern. If there is a difference of two inches (5.1 centimeters) in the bust measurement between sizes, that amount is distributed throughout the pattern pieces in such a way that the sizes changes in proportion to the original design. Every company has its own grading standards that relate to the fit the designer is looking to achieve. One method of grading is to cut the pattern piece and spread it to increase the size or overlap it to decrease the size. Grading can also be accomplished by redrawing the shape of the pattern through a series of shifts in its position on the fabric (or paper, if a new pattern is being developed). Grading machines can aid the process, and companies specialize in grading services for designers with smaller operations that don't have the access to computerized grading systems available to larger manufacturers.

Marker Plotting

In marker plotting, all the pattern pieces needed to create the garments designated for production are laid out in a way that conserves the most amount of fabric. The pattern pieces must all be aligned with the grain, direction of print, or nap; whether or not the fabric has a right and wrong side must also be addressed. Markers are made based on the width of the fabric and whether the pieces will be cut with the fabric spread open or on the fold. Even a fraction of an inch (centimeter) saved can make an enormous difference in the amount of waste when production runs are in the hundreds, thousands, or tens of thousands.

Computer-Aided Design

Computer-aided design has helped to establish a global common denominator in patternmaking, grading, and marker plotting. The math of patterns transcends any language barriers, and standardized software takes it a step further. With the design process being parceled out among many individuals and countries, this allows the designer to retain more control over the final product. In some cases, the patternmaking will be draped on a dress form or developed by hand, then digitized so that it can be trued in pattern development software. Some patterns are developed entirely in the digital format.

This technology does speed up the process considerably and creates an environment in which the designer can be painstakingly accurate. But anyone making a pattern with the aid of a computer must first understand fit, ease, seam allowance, notching, and all the other important elements of patternmaking. Gerber Accumark Technology and Lectra are two of the most widely used CAD systems for fashion apparel, and although these and similar software programs each operate a little differently, the goals are the same. Learning how to make good use of their technology becomes a matter of finding out which menus and features will allow the designer to best execute already familiar processes.

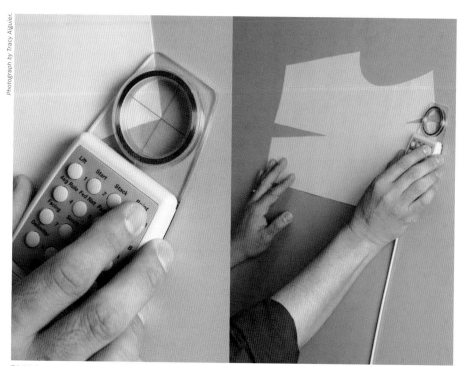

Photograph by Tracy Aiguier.

Digitizing a pattern using a Gerber digitizer

Chapter 16: Stitching

TYPES OF STITCHING

Hand Stitching

They say that "a stitch in time saves nine." Although some designers might opt to skip right to permanent stitches, the temporary hand stitch known as basting proves that the old adage could not be truer. Temporary stitches allow the designer to assemble sections of a garment in a way that can easily be altered. Removing machine stitches will often leave needle marks in, and sometimes destroy, fragile fabrics. Basting seams together before machine stitching can also help avoid slippage when sewing two or more layers of fabrics together. Temporary stitches can be used as well to transfer pattern information, such as the placement of button holes, pockets, and other design details. Not all types of handwork are temporary. Securing buttons, tacking, and finishing touches such as hemming are meant to stand the test of time and repeated use. Besides needles and thread, taking on a sewing task will often require pins, scissors, pinking shears, thread nippers, and every stitcher's best friend, the seam ripper.

Machine Stitching

Designers have several choices when it comes to sewing machines. The basic straight stitch machine allows the sewer to control stitch length, change needle position, and increase or decrease tension as needed. With a well-calibrated machine and the right choice of needle for the job, a designer can sew anything from chiffon to leather. The mechanics of the sewing machine rely on a needle that feeds a loop of the top thread through the fabrics being sewn together and catches the bobbin, a smaller spool of thread situated under the fabric, to create a lock stitch. The presser foot stabilizes the fabric as a feed dog mechanism moves it through the machine at the right pace. The sewer must guide the fabric but never pull or push it through the machine.

Certain types of machine sewing—zigzag, blind hem, button hole, and decorative stitch—can be done on separate specialty machines. In some cases, a regular straight stitch machine can produce these stitches with the change of a presser foot or the attachment of special hardware. A serger, sometimes called an overlock, babylock, or by the brand name Merrow, is a machine that finishes an edge by overcasting it and trimming the excess fabric to prevent fraying.

Machine stitching is employed in making all manner of seams; however, it can be used for more than joining parts of the garment together. Understitching is used on the right side of facings and areas where the designer wishes to avoid rolling. Stitching in the ditch is used when the designer wants the stitching to be inconspicuous. Stay stitches allow the designer to control an area that might stretch out of shape because it is curved or on the bias. Edge stitching and topstitching can be applied decoratively (with thread in a contrasting color) or to reinforce a seam. Zigzag stitches can also be decorative and are helpful when constructing garments with stretch fabrics. Machines can also generate large, loose stitches sometimes referred to as machine basting or gathering stitches. A stronger bobbin thread is used for gathering, because it is the thread that is pulled to make the gathers.

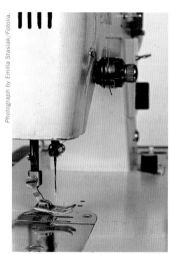

Straight Stitch Machine   Buttonhole Machine

Overlock Machine

SEWING FUNDAMENTALS

Seams

Common garment seams include shoulder seams, bodice side seams, sleeve seams, and skirt or pant seams. Curved seams are usually clipped with small cuts into the seam allowance to prevent puckering or pulling. Which seam technique the designer uses will depend on the desired appearance and the strength required. A plain seam is the easiest way to join two pieces of a garment, by sewing along the stitching line and pressing the seam allowance open. The edges can be left raw or pinked with pinking shears. Tailored seams provide a clean finish because each side of the seam allowance is turned under and edge stitched. Edges in a Hong Kong seam are bound, usually with bias strips, to prevent fraying and provide a professional finish. Using a serger is a quick, cost-effective way to finish the seam allowance.

Fancier seam work can be an important design detail that sets a garment apart from others. A slot seam involves closing a seam with a temporary stitch, then backing it with a strip of the same (or contrasting) fabric, and finally machine stitching along both sides of the temporary seam so that when it is removed a slot is created. Flat felled seams require that the seam be stitched with both wrong sides together. With the seam allowance on the outside of the garment, one side of it is trimmed down, while the other is folded over and stitched down. This type of seam is clean on both sides and can be found on most jeans. A French seam, often used on delicate fabric, is a seam with a seam. It, too, is initially stitched with the wrong sides together so that the seam allowance ends up on the outside, but in this case, all the seam allowance is trimmed down. The garment is then turned inside out so that these seams can be captured within a seam sewn from the inside. Corded seams capture piping, cord, or bias between the layers being sewn together, producing a decorative ridge that shows from the right side.

Corners

Crisp, clean corners are the mark of good workmanship. To give them a perfect point and avoid soft corners, the stitcher must reach the corner with the needle in the fabric, lift the presser foot, and change direction. A miter is required when two sides of a square that meet are being turned up or hemmed. Turning up the seams or hems so that the right sides are facing results in an overlap at the corner; a diagonal line from where they meet to the corner being created by the fold should stitched, trimmed, then turned right side out and pressed.

Darts

Darts should be basted into place because they usually run along the bias of the fabric. Stitching should begin at the base of the dart, being sure to blend the stitch line into the edge by the time it reaches the apex. Most darts are pressed toward the side seam to avoid unnecessary bulk in the front of the garment. Fisheye darts can be found in fitted garments with no waistline, most commonly dresses: The fullness eliminated by a bust dart and hip dart are combined to create one long dart. French darts are curved and begin at the base of the side seam, arching up toward the apex of the bust. Cutaway darts employ seam allowance rather than a fold and are used for bulky fabrics where it is necessary to remove excess material. Pleats and tucks are folds that are stitched down partially or into a seam.

Lining

Coordinating or complementary lining fabric is used to finish the inside of a garment, hiding all the construction details. Soft, silky fabrics give wearers a pleasant experience when the lining comes into contact with their skin and make it easy to slip the garment on and off.

Interlining

Interlining is a layer of fabric between the lining and the fashion fabric. Interlining adds body and resiliency, as in the case of neckties. Thicker flannel-like layers serve as insulation in garments requiring additional warmth. An interlining chosen to provide body will make weaker fabrics more versatile in everything from delicate blouses to evening gowns.

Interfacing

The design of a garment may require that certain parts be reinforced or stiffened or display additional body. Some may need no more than a layer of organza, while others may need the structural integrity of buckram. Collars, cuffs, and plackets on dress shirts are traditional places where a designer will add interfacing. Interfacing is available in a variety of weights and can be applied in several ways. Fusible interfacing is pressed onto the fashion fabric, bonding to it and transforming its body. Nonfusible interfacing can be basted onto the fabric in diagonal rows, as is typical in tailoring, or caught by a stitching line into a seam so that it remains free of the body of the fabric.

Bias

True bias is cut on a 45-degree angle in relation to the lengthwise and crosswise grainlines. Parallel diagonal lines can be drawn onto the fabric and cut to create bias strips of any width. The segments can be joined to create a continuous length of bias, sewn together right sides facing at right angles. Bias can be applied single ply not only to bind seams but also to finish off curved seams like necklines and armholes. When bias is folded and used as a two-ply finish, it is called French bias binding. Bias can also be sewn into tubing for spaghetti straps and ties: right sides together, sewn closed, then turned inside out with a loop turner. When working with bias, it is paramount to prevent the fabric from stretching out unevenly, which reduces its flexibility and effectiveness.

Knits

A certain amount of give should be built into the seams of knit garments. The degree varies and depends on the type of knit. Single knits like jersey have around 25 percent stretch, double knits may reach up to 75 percent stretch, and ribbed knits up to 100 percent. The cut edges of fabrics with less stretch are more apt to curl. Sergers are popular for assembling knits, especially for sportswear, because they have a lot of give and offer a very clean finish. Using a stretch stitch, tricot stitch, or zigzag stitch are options for a conventional machine. Polyester or nylon thread provides greater elasticity, and ballpoint needles are designed to penetrate knits without snagging or breaking threads and causing runs in the fabric.

Knit garments will have areas where stretch is not an asset, such as the neckline, armholes, shoulder seams, waistline and anywhere a zipper is going. Fabrics with little or no stretch can be sewn into these areas to prevent unwanted give. Stay-Tape is a sheer, nonfraying stabilizer used for fine knits. Twill tape, seam or hem binding, and clear plastic are useful alternatives. Topstitching from the right side of the fabric can also prevent curling or stretching.

Zippers

A properly installed zipper is a thing of beauty. Zippers can be sewn into a garment by hand or by machine. The zipper foot attachment for most machines is basically half a presser foot that allows the stitcher to bring the edge of the zipper teeth as close to the needle as possible, while avoiding accidental stitching onto the teeth. With zippers, basting once again is a designer's best friend. Sewers should avoid excess fabric that might catch in the teeth of the zipper; it is also helpful to start with a zipper that is slightly longer than the garment opening. Before inserting the zipper, adding a strip of interfacing along the seam allowance helps to support the zipper's weight and stabilize the fabric.

Zippers come in three basic types: conventional, invisible, and separating. The standard zipper can be intentionally visible, hidden by a flap of fabric on one side, called a fly front, or centered railroad-style with both sides of the seam working to disguise the closure. Invisible zippers are popular because the opening appears to disappear into the seam, but should only be used with the appropriate fabric weights and in areas that do not require great resistance to stress. Separating zippers, commonly used for sportswear and outer garments, are intentionally visible and easy to access.

TAILORING

Good tailoring demands painstaking cutting, fitting, pressing, and finishing. Also referred to as bespoke tailoring, this process eschews preexisting patterns because it starts from scratch for each new customer project. Suits, coats, and trousers are the traditional garments made with tailoring techniques. Expert hand stitching is a key component of tailoring. Both hand and machine stitches should be made secure at the beginning of a stitch as well as at the end of one. Uniform lengths that are both strong and inconspicuous are desired. Using a thimble is helpful when a stitch needs to pierce many layers of fabric. A professional tailored finish is the result of skilled steaming and pressing that shapes and molds fabric to the contours of the body in a way that balances structural integrity with smooth, clean surfaces and seams.

TAILORING STITCHES

Back or Prick Stitches: Used to reinforce an area or to add detail
Buttonhole Stitches: Very strong stitches used to secure fasteners and make buttonholes
Catch Stitches: X-shaped stitches for hemming and joining pieces of interfacing. Also called flat or blind catch stitches
Cross Stitches: X- or cross-shaped stitches used to tack things in place
Diagonal Basting: A longer type of pad stitch
Feather or Briar Stitches: Decorative stitches used to secure appliqués or as embroidery detail
Felling Stitches: Slant stitches used to secure the under collar of a jacket or to close seams
French Tack Stitches: Used to secure segments of a garment together
Overcast Stitches: Used on a seam or edge to prevent raveling
Pad Stitches: Chevron or V-shaped stitches used to provide firmness when attaching interfacing to a garment
Running Stitches: Similar to basting but more permanent; used to create ease, fine gathers, and for darning
Saddle Stitches: Long running stitches used for hand-done topstitching
Slip or Blind Stitches: Sewn under fold lines to give the illusion of being invisible
Slip Basting: Temporary stitch used for matching and securing plaids and other patterns
Stab Stitches: Permanent stitches used in shoulder pads and quilting to secure multiple layers
Whip or Slant Stitches: Used to join seams and finish edges, preventing raveling on hems

PRODUCTION

When the sewing falls to others, designers must carefully supervise the sample-making and production-run processes to guarantee quality control. Companies that specialize in sample making will work closely with the designer to ensure that the garment is executed correctly and according to the designer's specific standards. For a designer who does not have a large staff, sample-making services can greatly help with cutting, stitching, and finishing. Larger scale runs will be done in factories, locally or overseas. In either scenario, the designer should provide as much detailed information as possible—technical or spec sketches, cutting tickets, swatches, photographs—to help avoid miscommunication.

Cutting Tickets

A cutting ticket, or a cutter's must, is record of all pertinent information that goes from the patternmaker to the cutter and eventually the stitcher. Certain basics should appear on all tickets, but they can also be customized to include every component that is to accompany a given garment as it goes through the production cycle.

Chapter 17: Finishing

During the final stages of a garment, the designer has to display a light touch. Any and all details added at this point must be about balance and polish. Finishing also affects the drape and fit. Final work on a garment includes adding closures and decoration, hemming, and pressing. In addition, the designer should check for loose threads, missed stitches, and any other flaws. When making garments for a specific client (or samples that will be worn by a model in photographs or on the runway), a final fitting will ensure a good presentation.

CLOSURES

Buttons

The two basic button types are the sew-thru, which usually has two or four holes for securing it to the fabric, and the shank style, which has a loop. Buttons can be fashioned of practically any material. Special button blanks can be covered in fabric to match the garment. For added strength, a reinforcement button can link to the button from the wrong side. Multi-ply thread chains known as thread loops provide an alternative way to fasten a button. Machines can sew on a button, but this type of procedure is more apt to loosen and come undone with time and wear. Hand-sewn buttons are preferred because of their strength and lifespan.

The placement of any kind of closure needs to be planned out so that both sides align to lie flat and to avoid gaps. Temporary stitches are used as guides for buttonholes, whether they are machine stitched, hand worked, bound, corded, or keyhole. Thread buttonholes usually have bar tacks to reinforce the ends. Correct positioning can be established by using the original pattern piece or a buttonhole template. Buttonholes are usually placed vertically on shirtfronts, with the exception of the collar position where a horizontal buttonhole is preferred. As a rule, suit jackets, waistcoats, outerwear, and waistbands employ horizontal buttonholes.

Hook and Eyes

Fashioned from metal wire, two-sided hook and eyes come in many different sizes and can be painted any color or be covered with thread. They are often used to secure the top of a zipper, close a keyhole opening, or to bustle a fabric train. Flat-back hook and eyes are commonly used for waistbands on skirts and pants for a flush finish. Rows of hook and eyes are found on bras, corsets, and other undergarments. Strips of twill tape equipped with multiple hook and eyes can be machine stitched into garments.

Hook-and-Loop Tape

Hook-and-loop tape is a self-gripping fastener. (Velcro is the brand name.) One side of the tape has rough nylon hooks, the other side has softer loops that are caught when the pieces are pressed against each other. This type of closure can be fixed to the fabric by adhesive or by being stitched into place. Hook-and-loop tape is meant to provide speed and ease in securing or separating two pieces of fabric.

Frogs

Frogs are braid or cord that is manipulated into an ornamental design and include a ball on one side and a loop on the opposite. Although a decorative feature, it does provide a practical method of closure. Frogs can be bought or made by hand.

Snaps

Snaps are two-sided fasteners, one side featuring a stud and the other a socket. When pressed together, they click into place with a snapping sound. The socket is secured to the fabric with a pronged cap or ring, while the stud is secured with a post backing. The procedure can be done by hand using a special pair of pliers or by machine. Snap tape is also available for easy machine installation.

Eyelets

Eyelets are circular metal rings clamped onto fabric to create a finished opening through which cord or ribbon can be laced to draw two sides together. Old-fashioned corsets are secured in this manner.

Buckles

Buckle clasps are used to secure and adjust belts or straps. The traditional buckle engages an independent single, double, or forked tongue to fix the belt into place. Georgia frames commonly feature two stationary tongues that are built into the frame of the buckle. Keepers are bands, usually made of the strap material, that hold the end of the belt strap in place. Ornamental Western-style buckles that hook onto a strap are called plaque buckles. Friction buckles and D-ring buckles, in which the strap fabric double backs on itself to generate resistance, allow the strap to be adjusted to any length. Twist buckles feature two interlocking sides of a clasp that need only be twisted in the opposite direction to be unfastened.

DECORATION

The temptation to embellish is strong for many designers, and it is important to keep in mind that a sparing hand with decoration may produce a greater effect. That being said, embroidery, sequins, rhinestones, jewels, beads, studs, ribbons, bows, silk flowers, appliqué, passementerie braiding or cording, tassels, chains, and fringe are just a few of the bells and whistles that can finish off a garment with a little (or a lot of) flair. In many cases, embroidery, sequins, beads, and appliqués may be applied to sections of the garment before it is assembled; however, small adornments might be planned as a finishing detail, or be necessary when disguising a seam to give the appearance of a continuous pattern.

Photograph by Hubert/Fotolia.

HEMMING

Turning up the hem is, for most designers, the final step of garment assembly. The hem allowance may be a quarter inch (0.6 cm) for a handkerchief-style edge or two to three inches (5–7.6 cm) on average for most skirt or pant hems. Hems can be wired, interfaced, or sewn with horsehair to create the desired amount of body. A hem may also be weighted to define a particular line to the silhouette, as in the iconic Chanel jacket. It is best to measure from the floor up when marking the hemline for a consistent appearance in the length. Hems can be taken up by machine or topstitched, or in the case of bias hems, be tightly serged for a lettuce edge.

Hand hemming uses different types of stitches—pick stitch, catch or cross stitch, slip stitch, blind stitch—to create as indiscernible an appearance as possible. Lace, bias binding, seam tape, or netting can be attached to raw edges to eliminate bulk when turning up the hem. Rolled hems are commonly done by hand, but can also be created by machine with the aid of a rolled-hem presser foot.

PRESSING

Iron pressing and steaming should be done while preparing fabric for cutting and throughout the assembly process, but a garment will require a final pressing or steaming to prepare it for public consumption. When ironing, using a pressing cloth between the iron and the fabric or, when possible, pressing from the inside will prevent shiny unattractive streaks. A hard pressing is recommended when a garment calls for a sharp crease or corner. A tailor's board provides a hard frame that can help keep like areas in the desired shape during the pressing process. The pressing mitt, seam roll, sleeve board, and tailor's ham help press rounded and hard-to-reach areas without running the risk of pressing and creasing adjacent but unintended areas. A needle board prevents crushing fabrics with a pile, such as velvet or corduroy. Steamers are useful when working with softer silhouettes where creases need to be avoided.

FITTINGS AND ALTERATIONS

In the best of situations, a garment has been carefully fitted to the client or model as it is being created. When this is not the case, or when subtle changes have taken place (a client loses or gains weight), new fittings and alterations are necessary. Thinking ahead to this point, a designer might want to add to the amount of seam and hem allowance when initially cutting the garment. It is easy to take in a seam and cut away extra allowances, but having provided them as an insurance policy could save a lot of time when the need to let something out arises. Big changes could require the entire garment be taken apart or a section of it be recut and reintegrated into the piece. To achieve the best fit that satisfies both the client and the designer is a matter of a collaboration among function, comfort, and style.

STORAGE AND TRANSPORTATION

After all the hard work that a designer invests in a beautiful well-crafted garment, it would be a crime not to store and transport it in a way that will retain its shape and polished appearance. Special sculpted or padded hangers, cardboard body frames, and lots of paper tissue are useful tools for providing a safe environment when sending a garment off to the client or to storage. Lightweight, transparent poly garment bags are an easy, fast, and economical way to protect garments from dirt and moisture. Heavier weight zippered nylon garment bags provide a stronger option. A cotton fabric bag is the best choice if the garment needs to breathe or plastic might stick to the finish of the fabric.

Where do you start with the design process when developing a new collection? And why that first?

I start by soaking in the atmosphere. It's very important to have a sense of what's going on in the world that we live in, a keen awareness of what's transpiring, the mood. And that's where I begin. I always try to figure out which moment I am in, and, so, from that, what it is that defines the world of today.

How did you do that in your latest collection?

Well, I did a collection based on counting and on zero waste. I tend to everything at the same time, so there's no separation. The essential thing is to arrive at how you feel about the season and the general mood and how you believe your clients are feeling—they're the people that you dress. And based on that understanding, I do everything: Sometimes I make the pattern, sometimes I drape, sometimes I sketch, sometimes I work with the fabric. Even though by then a lot of the fabric selection has been made, there's still time to tweak it.

Do you consider fashion an art form? A craft? And why?

I consider fashion a design discipline. You take raw materials and you convert them into a finished garment, and the prerequisite, if it's clothing design, is that it be wearable. So it's a design discipline. It's neither an art form nor a craft—you have to design something that has a function.

Did you have a mentor in the fashion industry?

No.

Have you assumed the role of mentor for someone else?

Sometimes, but I don't assume the role. I think that if somebody were to approach me, I would have a conversation with them and try to get a dialogue going about whatever it is that they're interested in discussing. But I don't assume the role because I think that's a little presumptuous.

What brought you into fashion?

Actually, I was always interested in how costume/clothing and headgear affects perception and body movement. You can influence people by what you wear and how you move in it, and I found that aspect fascinating. When I was in school, I did a lot of plays; you had to think about character and about how to assess the character in the costume. Then, too, I was always aware of the supernatural power of a lot of fabric: When you have a lot of fabric it's very imposing—and a tall headdress is dominating.

What should a designer understand about the business of fashion first and foremost?

Make something useful. If you're a clothing designer ("clothing," "fashion," I use the terms interchangeably, so one does not negate the other), if you're a fashion designer, your medium is clothing, right? And if you're going to make clothes, you might as well make clothes that are useful, clothes with a sense of purpose. Why would you do anything other than that? It doesn't make any sense, particularly today when time is of the essence. If your clothes are not functional, you're just wasting everybody's time, including your own.

How important is the world of architecture to your creative process? How do you interpret and apply architectural principles to structures that surround the human body in a more intimate way, to clothing?

Architecture is definitely a source of inspiration. Sometimes it's serendipitous. I was working on my Fall 2005 collection, which had some flourishes and details that I didn't realize were Spanish-influenced. Then I went to Mexico City and saw Luis Barragán's house. And I discovered a real connection between the mood of his house, especially his use of color and shape, to the collection I was already working on. So that happened by chance. On the other hand, I was in L.A. and I visited the Schindler House, which is known architecturally as one of the first modern houses. And the thing that had the most impact on me was the reduction of materials. It was concrete, wood, and glass. I drew upon that simplicity and made a collection for Spring 2007 that was completely reduced. I think I used maybe five different fabrics, the predominant color of which was white. And also Schindler had devised this process of pouring concrete and then having the concrete hoisted up to form the walls. So within the collection I made clothes that were "hoisted" onto the body, resonating with Schindler's construction technique.

What do you think fashion education programs should include in their curriculum to best prepare designers looking to enter the market?

Practical training and good internship programs for credit.

How does the issue of sustainability affect your design process?

Zero waste, absolute economy in fabric and execution, is at the core of my philosophy of the design process.

What role does pop culture and celebrity play in your work if any?

Pop culture and lifestyle trends always have an influence over design decisions. Personally, for my take on celebrity culture please refer to *Galaxy Quest*, which spoofs *Star Trek*. It's hilarious. We're a culture that celebrates people who pretend to be other people who may be far more competent than the people who are doing the pretending. That's what the movie is about and that's what celebrity culture is about. You know you're enamored of the roles they play, not necessarily of the individuals, you know they have a particular skill, but that's about the size of it.

Your clothes have a reputation for being comfortable and low maintenance in addition to being developed in innovative ways. How would you describe how you built that into your brand and in what ways do you connect with your customer through it?

It's a guiding principle. Comfortable and low maintenance, ready for a quick getaway. You really want your clothes to be efficient, to work hard for you. You don't want to have to think a lot when you get up in the morning and get dressed. And yet the women that I dress generally have active working lives and contribute to society with what they do and are decision makers. So I try to support them by making clothes that are efficient, practical, and versatile—in respect of their twenty-first-century lifestyle.

What advice would you give designers starting their career or a business?

Yes, you can.

Have you diversified your design work (costume design, licensing, lifestyle products, etc.)? If so, how?

My design philosophy pervades everything that I do. I use sound as an environment for the collections. I've done a little bit of costume design. I've designed rugs. But my primary focus is clothing.

How would you describe your work?

Clarity and preciseness speak legions about my work. My work is always very spare, very concise, and very to the point. And I try to do things in a way that that becomes a signature.

How do you strike a balance between the theatre of the runway and the reality of retail?

By taking a shot at both. For me, theatrical and functional, it's the same thing. I refuse to make clothes that you cannot wear. The subway is a theatre of everyday life. For the Spring 2005 show, we were literally under the tents at Bryant Park in the metro station. It was September. We had to deal with the station the way it was: The trains were coming and going; there was no lighting, no air conditioning. We staged it at my loft, and I bused over all the models, who were "real people." I had many illustrious women, a very diverse cast, in age and everything else. The MTA had printed one subway ride Metrocard with our invitation on the back. So if you lived in Brooklyn and were coming to my show, you could have taken the train right to it. What we were going to do about the music was really a puzzle. And then one night at the 34th Street station I ran into these guys playing buckets, and they wouldn't stop; I saw a sign—$10 for a CD—I picked it up and called them and they came up and I hired them. The whole experience was amazing, though it was really hot. I remember all my PR people at the end of the show, they were soaked. But each one of them said that they wouldn't have given it up for anything.

Overleaf Left to right, Yeohlee, Spring 2007, inspired by R. M. Schindler's Studio House, West Hollywood; Fall 2007, inspired by the designs of Antoni Gaudí; Fall 2008, inspired by imagining the Shakers in SANAA's New Museum, New York; and Spring 2009, inspired by Bernard Tschumi's Parc de la Villette, Paris. Photographs by Dan Lecca.

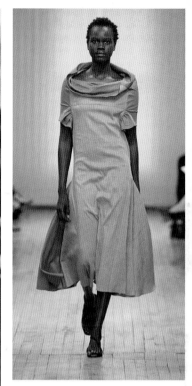

5.

CONNECT

The job of the fashion designer does not end when the garments have been made. Designers must document, display, and promote their collection. Revisiting the processes that resulted in this new body of work can inform how designers choose to present their designs. The research and sources of inspiration that went into building a collection can now inspire the way it is documented in photographs and illustrations. Some portfolios will also incorporate technical drawings, swatches, and mood boards. The appearance of the models or croquis, and how they are accessorized, should reflect a true understanding of the designer's audience. Similarly, the work of identifying their customer base now points to the various avenues by which designers will approach, engage, and expand their clientele. Every interface and experience with the consumer impacts the brand, from logo design to marketing materials to runway show.

Chapter 18: Portfolios

At the beginning of a career, assembling a body of work is about presenting depth and range: The goal is to show how well the designer sketches, styles, and solves design challenges. Talented designers who have already explored many genres of fashion must edit and compartmentalize their work.

PRESENTATION

A master portfolio will archive the complete breadth of the designer's work. It is a good idea to keep quality color reproductions organized into categories. Designers who specialize in custom eveningwear, say, will want to separate their bridal work from formal gowns, dinner suits, and special occasion dresses. Within each category, the designer will want to demonstrate as much variety as possible.

Each segment of the master portfolio can be bound into an independent volume of the portfolio or presentation folder. Designers can work in any size, but traditionally choose 11" × 14" and 14" × 17" (A3 and A2) formats for drawings and photographs. Quality scans, photographs, or copies of the original work can also be reduced to fit in a smaller book that is easier to carry. Hand-held electronic devices like the iTouch or iPhone now make it easy for the designer to have a current portfolio readily available.

Look Book

When this process is undertaken for a specific designer collection, the folio is often called a "look book." The idea is for the pages to be easily perused in the way that a catalogue or magazine might be reviewed. The presentation style is important, because so much fashion content is available to the general public that they are apt to take a certain standard of quality and creativity for granted. When these are lacking, it can undermine the designer's true purpose, which is to focus on the clothes and the ideas behind them. Look books can be made up of sketches, but most big companies produce them with photographs that have been created in a studio or captured on the runway.

Layout

Fashion designers must approach the assemblage of their work into a physical or a virtual presentation with the mindset of a magazine editor. The more thought that goes into the distribution, repetition, scale, and flow of materials in their chosen format, the bigger the impact. Designers need to address a number of questions: What will the content be composed of and how will it be laid out? Which images will be repeated for effect, á la Warhol? Which images will be cropped and resized based on importance and for variety? How will text be handled?

Editor Carmel Snow and fashion editor Diana Vreeland
reviewing layouts at *Harper's Bazaar*, 1952

Will words be manipulated graphically to reinforce an idea? What is the role of black-and-white images versus color? What will be the weight and finish of the paper? How will someone navigate through these images on a computer screen? Will the computer-generated pages flip with a mouse click or slide over with a touch of the screen? Will the viewer require the aid of menus, thumbnails, and links?

Although a portfolio or look book is an artistic archive, ultimately it is a tool for communication. The designer is looking to convey a message, cull critical accolades, and make the sale or get the job. The portfolio exercise should employ the techniques used in good information design. This means that content should deliver something substantial, the layout should take the viewer on an interesting journey, and the artistry with which it is undertaken should captivate. Embellishments should not merely decorate but always inform and amplify the designer's message.

Digital Folio

Any creative content produced today should have a digital counterpart. In this way, it can easily be shared on a CD or be posted to a website. Digital photographs or scans should be cleaned up and enhanced for the screen, where resolution and contrast play different roles from the ones they do in printed materials. Online, thumbnails of the full image or close-ups of one section can be used to link to larger versions of the photograph. Collections can also be presented as slideshows or linked to videos. By such maneuvers, designers can determine how a visitor flips through the images of their work.

APPROACHES

Newsroom

The fast pace of the fashion world places time at a premium. Media runs at an even faster pace. The experienced designer knows that by making readily available anything a journalist might need, they improve their chances of getting coverage—assuming, of course, that the material is also newsworthy. The old-school press kit can seem outdated, if only in that it cannot be accessed instantly the way an online version can. Every designer's website should have an area dedicated to press that the designer has collected and another that provides content that a writer can use to develop a story.

Collateral

Personal designer collateral comprises a résumé or curriculum vitae (CV), a designer's statement of philosophy, a downloadable high-resolution headshot, and a business card. For the design firm, the formula includes a mission statement, press clippings, designer biography and headshot, images that represent the company's work as well as customized letterhead and envelopes. Logos, fonts, and information must be legible and consistent.

Take Away

One way to add value to a portfolio and extend its reach is accomplished with a take away. In the modeling industry, professional models will attend go-sees where they and their portfolios will be reviewed and considered for the job in question. Tucked into a pocket in most portfolios are composite cards that a model can leave behind as a reference and a reminder. These composites are photographic calling cards that will include stats, a headshot, and a variety of photographs that capture the model's range. Fashion designers can create a similar composite that highlights the best of their work.

Online, the take away can be handled with a downloadable image. Designers might even offer (with the permission of the artist) a free MP3 download of music featured in a recent fashion show or played on their website. Even just providing a link to iTunes or Amazon is the sign of a thoughtful online host. A blog is another way for the designer to add distinction. Behind-the-scenes pictures or videos, a journal of the process, rough sketches, and links to the sources of their inspiration help to forge a stronger bond between the designer and their audience.

Virtual Networking

Social networking (Facebook, MySpace, Twitter) and professional networking (LinkedIn) sites have become invaluable tools for building communities and disseminating information. Cautionary tales about a lack of privacy or impropriety aside, when used by fashion professionals with a little common sense, these sites can go a long way toward cultivating, organizing, and maintaining professional relationships. The casual social energy that propels the popularity of these services creates a comfortable environment in which to interact. In many cases, the successful online experience extends into the real world where like minds can meet live.

URL and Email

Securing a unique URL (Uniform Resource Locator) address from a domain registrar is a good idea for any designer who is planning to have a presence on the Web. Yourname.com adds a professional touch to any résumé and provides a memorable, easy-to-access destination for anyone interested in a designer's work. For new design businesses, it has become as fundamental as having a business card. Many registrars also offer emails associated with the URL (you@yourname.com) as well as hosting for web pages or websites. The designer's URL and email address should avoid sounding amateurish, convoluted, or inappropriately provocative.

Chapter 19: Branding

The most common mistake regarding brands is to think that the company name and logo are the brand. They are not. The brand is what the designer or company stands for. Designers that consistently follow through on every endeavor with integrity are building a brand: Anything associated with their design work should ring true, aligning with what the brand has pledged to deliver. Another misconception about brands is that they belong to the designer or company. They do not. The whole idea behind a good brand is that it connects with people, and the moment a customer is let down in any way the brand has suffered a blow. Brands are emotional things in which both the creators and consumers have made an investment. They begin to have significance beyond the actual products. Over time, a brand builds a philosophy and a way of doing business; for the customer, the brand becomes a cultural accessory and a source of inspiration.

A note on the term "luxury brand": Because the idea of luxury has become such a cliché, designers must determine what it means within the context of their own brand. Does it imply a company that produces goods and services to which many consumers would aspire, but because of rarity and restrictive price point are not readily attainable? Or does it mean a company that has used luxurious materials and invested in glamorous advertising and slick packaging, but in essence supplies a basic, albeit desirable, commodity?

BRAND CONSTANTS

Mythology

When a designer has committed to the brand promise, the job at hand is to build a mythology and craft the symbols that make it easy to identify and identify with. The myth is in the message. A myth cuts past rational thought and connects with individuals at a gut level, where they imagine themselves in what they have observed. Chanel is a brand based on the history and vision of Gabrielle Chanel, an embodiment of the thoroughly modern woman. With time, that history has become lore and then legend. The continued success of Chanel is due to innovative of-the-moment interpretations of all the things that she stood for as a designer and as a woman. The Chanel customer knows what she is getting and identifies with the brand because it means something more than just beautiful clothing. Like Chanel, a great design house will always deliver on their promise and manage expectations.

What's in a Name?

A designer's name and variations on it often become the brand name and its offshoots. Coco, Mademoiselle Chanel's nickname, is an extension of the Chanel brand. Similarly, Miu Miu, Miucia Prada's nickname, is an extension of the Prada brand. Developing an original company name involves many considerations. Designers must determine its relevancy and the kind of impact it might have. They must also look at whether the actual structure of the name lends itself favorably to a variety of graphic interpretations: lowercase or capitals, cursive script or block letters, serif or sans serif, color or black and white. Names that imply more than one message or sound like something else are not likely to be memorable or unique.

The Logo

A logo translates a brand name and its message into a graphic representation. It becomes a visual trigger, transcending language to convey everything that the designer has decided is most important. Chanel's design of interlocking Cs is easily one of the most recognizable logos in fashion. It is used in all the traditional ways, but its simplicity also allows it to be worked into the actual design of the products as closures, jewelry, and prints. Designers should be aware that the contemporary fashion consumer is not apt to wear blatant advertising unless it is a rarity, cleverly incorporated into the design, or obviously meant to be ironic.

Photograph by Petit/Hel/Prestige/Newsmakers.

Chanel Fall/Winter 2001/2002 Collection

BRAND DEVELOPMENT

Design Scheme

The message, name, and logo are the constants that will inform a brand's overall design scheme. The checklist of concerns that designers need to address includes color, pattern, texture, font, quality of line, scale, flow, direction, and negative space. Designers must also consider whether there will be one unchanging formula, or whether the design scheme might be periodically reconfigured and recolored. They must ask how the design reads on a business card and on a billboard, even how it looks when reproduced in black and white by an ordinary photocopy or fax machine.

Packaging

The successful packaging of a designer's product should bear a cohesive relationship to the brand. Designers need to decide how the packaging will incorporate the name and logo and how the various packaging elements will interact with each other. Whether color is to be used to stimulate or as a neutral canvas for the product is another consideration. If a designer's packaging does no more than stamp every item with a logo, the overall impact will be clumsy and heavy handed. By contrast, if the designer's shopping bag is printed with a large version of the logo that wraps around the bag, and the gift box inside is sealed with a ribbon and a sticker bearing the embossed logo, then perhaps the tissue paper is printed with a pattern of the full designer name. This example illustrates how the brand can be reinforced using many different methods within a single delivery system.

Lexicon

The language in which a brand message is crafted must be chosen as carefully as any other aspect. All copy should be populated with words pulled from a specific brand lexicon, a vocabulary that will speak in the particular timber and tone the designer wishes to project. For example, is a vibrant pink dress referred to as flirty and playful? Majestic and jewel toned? Or shocking and provocative? Each description could apply to the same dress, but designers must judge which combination of words is most closely aligned with their relationship to the customer. Tag lines are the most economical use of language to deliver the essence and promise of a brand. The phrase "Just do it" is as important a part of the Nike brand as the company name or the swoosh logo.

Brand Profile

Designers who have diligently developed a business plan will have everything they need to create a brand profile. This differs from the company's profile, which concerns facts and figures. The brand profile articulates the essence of the company. By crafting the profile themselves, designers can steer the brand into the areas where it will be perceived in the light they wish to be seen in. They also diminish the chance of being improperly branded by external forces and thus being left at the helm of a brand that, no matter how successful, may not be what they want to pursue.

The Book

In a small operation, the designer and a handful of individuals can easily keep on message. Designers who can conceive of a time when not every decision will come across their desk will see the value of developing a book to serve as a reference guide for the operations and development of the company. This book is more than an employee handbook. It is a compendium of the company's history, implementations of the mission, collections produced, and press clippings that provides the primary source of direction for developing standards, policies, procedural guides, and staff manuals. The "book" can take many different forms: as a set of files, folders, disks, or binders. Designers should make a habit of automatically copying relevant materials and filing them away under the correct designation.

Thirty Seconds

Anyone associated with a designer brand should have a thirty-second pitch at the ready. Sometimes called the elevator speech, this brief snapshot of a company speaks to the brand's mission, its audience, and its future. The more concise, informative, and targeted, the greater the chances of breaking through the clutter of information everyone is inundated with every moment of every day. The sound bite rules television, because airtime is expensive and attention spans are short. Those who are most at ease on camera have prepared to deliver their ideas in condensed form. An individual who has not tends to trail off and is soon interrupted in this fast-paced forum. As helpful as these nuggets of information may be, however, anyone who speaks for the brand still needs to be able to think on their feet. Those who parrot the same responses over and over will be pegged as insincere, if not actually dim.

Advertising Extension

Under certain conditions, advertising offers a powerful tool to the fashion designer. First, the content of the ad or commercial must reflect the spirit of the brand. Second, the designer needs to be clear on the purpose of the advertising. Is it about generating sales? Attempting to align the brand with industry leaders or peers? Part of a philanthropic campaign? Or simply a vanity piece? The intent dictates the correct placement. A full-page, four-color glossy ad in a high-profile national fashion magazine may be impressive, but does not guarantee a single sale for a designer with a limited regional presence. The most important condition for making an investment in advertising is that it be built on something real. When advertising is the natural extension of a brand history and reputation, the return is greater. Design integrity, the right vehicle, and timing add up to results.

Advocates

Assuming that the highest standards of design, quality, and fit have been met and the loyalty of clients secured, consumers can easily be prompted to sing a designer's praises. But only if the designer has provided the tools for them to do so. Designers can engage their clientele, sharing ideas and experiences, through online communications, in-store promotions, and special events. Even their approach to how much designers share about themselves with the press and public will have an impact: Their personal lives might be an open book and a reflection of the brand, or it might be their mystery that captures their customers' imagination. Faithful clients become strong advocates of the brand because they are storytellers, spreading the word.

Additionally, designers might employ a spokesperson who adds to the brand value. This could be someone who is hired to endorse the product or someone already identified as a patron. Designers might also target those who have no practical use for their product, but appreciate the brand for other reasons and count themselves among its most vocal evangelists. For instance, men don't have a personal use for Victoria's Secret lingerie (as a rule) but are a primary focus of the company's public presence via catalogues, advertising, and online or televised fashion shows.

Cult, Attitude, No-Brand, and Lovemarks

Brands can take many forms, and designers must decide which direction is right for them. Cult brands engender loyalty beyond reason; they spend time and money to create magnetic identities and go beyond the sale to strengthen their relationships with customers. Attitude branding revolves less around the product itself than around a feeling to which the customer can relate. As a backlash to brand buzz, some companies embrace a no-brand philosophy that simplifies the shopping experience to deliver goods without a lot of fuss. Generic branding ends up becoming a brand of its own, as in the case of the company American Apparel. Lovemarks, a term coined by ad man Kevin Roberts, are brands that transcend branding. As their name suggests, they connect deeply with the heart of the consumer; they are defined by the mystery of an intriguing mythology, an appeal to all the senses, and an intimacy that comes of the passionate commitment between brand and customer.

Management

In managing a fashion brand, choices must be made regarding what exactly is being branded—the company, the designer, the collection, or a specific product. Any experience around the brand must be designed to be specific and consistent across every point of contact. In the event that a brand partners with another brand, care should be taken to ensure, above all, that the allied brands share a fundamental philosophy. Companies should undergo a regular checkup and be ready to troubleshoot if signs of brand arrogance, greed, complacency, inconsistency, or shortsightedness begin to surface. The proper care and management of a brand will contribute to its success, leading to an increase of value, otherwise known as brand equity.

Chapter 20: Marketing

Most fashion designers that have reached the point where marketing is a concern will have collected a wealth of information about their audience. Developing a marketing strategy entails organizing this data in a way that will determine how best to reach a targeted segment. The message that the designer has so carefully crafted has to be revisited to evaluate how it will be filtered through each media channel. The method of delivery must communicate the essence of the brand and provide both perceived and tangible value. Each part of the plan must have a budget and specific goals and must generate the metrics by which its level of success can be measured and analyzed. All these efforts must be tightly coordinated to have the biggest impact and to build a campaign that will move the designer forward.

Designers must observe and have answers to some basic questions: What is the caliber of customer service? What is the level of customer satisfaction? Have sales shown an increase? Has the press picked up stories? How does the public perceive the brand? More sophisticated research is available as well. Marketing firms specialize in studies of everything from tracking how often a banner ad prompts a website visitor to click through, to tracking the human eye and how it moves when scanning a product. Forecasters are a big part of marketing, always searching for what is cool and which groups empower a product with this distinction. Researchers who study the mapping of the brain and the role of addiction provide an even greater insight into buyers' decision-making processes, helping to predict what they might do next.

MINDING YOUR "P"S

Patterns

The best of marketing plans will fall on deaf ears if designers do not understand the type of customer they are reaching. Designers must establish the buying patterns of their customer base. How loyal are they to the brand? Is their purchase one of passion or just routine? Are they there for a good deal? Do customers resist relying too much on any one product or service because they prefer variety? Or, are they not the actual buyer but the support system for someone who is?

Personalizing

Once customers have been engaged, designers have to give thought to how personal the experience will be. Everyone with whom a client comes into contact at every stage—from the showroom, to the runway, to the salesroom, to the customer service department—must represent how the designer wishes to speak to their customers. So-called mystery shoppers can help establish what is and isn't working throughout the consumer experience.

Personal shopping events are vital tools for introducing prospective customers to a designer's brand. Sales associates that keep up-to-date client books (everything from their purchase history to birthdays) are armed with information that allows them to communicate in a more meaningful way.

Customers can also be given the power to participate in the brand's decision-making process. Offering them a vote in something will appeal to them on many levels, practical and emotional, and provide designers with valuable information about their clientele.

Promotion

Promotion is about information, experience, and a reason to return. These initiatives stimulate interest and action by providing incentives that offer entertainment, such as shows, tie-ins, and exhibitions, or special value, such as contests, coupons, samples, and sales. Designers need to understand which kinds of promotional efforts will grease the wheels of their marketing machine.

Public Relations

Good public relations establish credibility. A designer that moves into a new neighborhood may profess the desire to be a part of that community, but actions speak louder than words. The designer that does not take an active role will never be fully accepted.

Publicity

Publicity stems from human interest and newsworthiness. Thinking like an editor, not just a reporter, will help designers to direct their materials to a specific outlet and its audience. A designer should not be surprised if after pitching a story to a tabloid-style publication, it runs an item slanted toward gossip rather than their work. Designers should offer a combination of the familiar and the unexpected. Repetition will cultivate a level of comfort, dependableness, and intimacy, while innovation will prevent the familiar from becoming stagnant and regularly rekindle interest.

MARKETING TOOLS

Medium	Approach
Film and Video	These media showcase movement and energy. The designer's clothing is featured to full advantage in motion.
Television	This is the arena of buzz—quick, easily digestible and repeatable messages. Editing here is about the clever and the quotable.
Print	Articles, profiles, and photo editorials are story-telling vehicles. The designer provides the substance, direction, and inspiration for journalists to make their own.
Internet	Here content is king. Unlimited space allows for unrestricted sharing and archiving, but the discerning designer will keep a distinctive presence online.
Photography	Photographic images translate the designer's messages into visual cues, styling with light, staging, and décor. They can be an arena for artistic expression.
Graphics	Graphic symbols serve as maps and signposts for a brand. The designer can use them as a visual shortcut into the minds of the public.
Advertising	Ads are a marketing instrument to wield based on budget, timing, and relevance.

AVENUES

Direct

Online marketing and direct-mail pieces can provide the fashion designer with an immediate foot in the door. The danger is always that they will end up filed under junk mail. Standing alone, without a vocal advocate, these pieces must be distinctively designed and engaging. This will mean different things at different times based on the current trends. The online pop-up window is as apt to get the attention of the visitor as it is to annoy them.

Live

Events are wonderful settings for marketing endeavors because they provide environments designed for shared experiences. Lectures, seminars, and workshops build a kind of camaraderie around learning. Trade shows become the marketplace, a town square where the focus is the sale. Fashion shows are entertaining and celebratory rituals that allow designers to take their bow and for their audience to applaud.

Networks

The mere idea of networking can produce anxiety in designers who are shy in social situations. It is also fraught with negative connotations because it is so often undertaken as a contest for the most business cards. When marketing themselves, their company, or their designs, the best plan of action is for designers to focus on building small but powerful relationships. Networks built on this type of connection are strong and act as magnets to others. The concept of six degrees of separation hinges on the links being viable enough to produce actions. Even though online networking services make the process easier, the same consideration should be made regarding quality rather than quantity of connections.

Community and Partnerships

Isolation, self-imposed or otherwise, is a very real trend in society today. Community building offers individuals access to groups of like-minded people. Fashion designers can tap into naturally occurring communities around their products or service and foster their growth. Credible partnerships with businesses, organizations, and institutions that are dedicated to a specific group can extend the reach of a brand. When this interaction begins online, creating opportunities to interact face to face increases its value. Marketing to members of these groups will garner the best results when implemented with respect and authenticity.

Causes

Affiliations with philanthropic organizations are a great way to balance building visibility, strengthening a reputation, and giving something back to the community. A designer can sponsor or underwrite cultural projects or provide educational opportunities and scholarships, whether or not directly related to the field of fashion.

Product Placement

Product placement is generally considered a success when it is seamless and the consumer doesn't realize that something has been placed. Sometimes very obvious, but witty placements can connect with an audience as well. Another form of product placement that fashion designers often try is to send public figures, or their stylists, clothing in the hope that they will wear them where they will be photographed.

Promotional Merchandise

Slapping a logo on a T-shirt is not enough in a marketplace where anyone can do it themselves. Just about anything with a printable surface is fair game in the name of brand marketing. Printing a company logo on someone's forehead or pregnant belly shows just how far "branding" will dare to go. Shock-value aside, well-designed branded items have the potential to become desirable in themselves and even collectable.

Guerilla Marketing

Part of the marketing mix for any brand is about taking it to the street. This marketing approach has its roots in skywriting and blimps. Today the more outrageous and unexpected the better: floor graphics, logo or video projections on public buildings, moving picture ads in train tunnels, even eye-level and urinal cake advertising in men's rooms! In fashion, the concept of the pop-up store has become a great way to infiltrate and capture new audiences; these temporary venues prompt public engagement based on a mix of novelty, convenience, and a sense of immediacy.

Photograph by Sergio Dionsio/Getty Images.

30 Days of Fashion & Beauty, projection on the Intercontinental Hotel Sydney, Australia, 2008

Photograph by Jay Calderin.

Stil Distinctive Clothing, Boston, Massachusetts

Stores

At the retail level, marketing involves the influence a fashion designer has over merchandising and styling. Stores allocate windows, displays, floor space, and placement based on their relationship with the designer and the visibility of the brand. A designer can build this rapport by adding value with trunk shows, special appearances, and exclusivity.

Industry Agents

Within the fashion industry, the specific purpose of delivery channels like showrooms, wholesalers, and trade events is to promote and sell a designer's collection. Although many represent more than one line at a time, these outlets are attractive to buyers because they screen and edit the designers based on the interests of the buyers who use their services. A buyer can also cover more ground, seeing designers that they might not ordinarily come across.

Chapter 21: Shows

The show business side of fashion is a combination of wedding ceremony and rock concert. As theatrical and as fun as this might sound, putting together a full-scale runway show is about impeccable organization and precise follow-through. The culmination of all available research and support systems should be a spectacle that is executed professionally and worth remembering.

COMPONENTS

Intent

What goes into the structure of a show will hinge on who is in the audience. Fashion shows are not one-size-fits-all events. The consumer most often wants to be entertained and swept away into the designer's fantasy. The general press is there to get something newsworthy, a great photograph, or a celebrity sighting. The fashion press and the buyers represent specific publications or retailers and their customer base. They are looking to see how these clothes will fit into their plans for the upcoming season.

Flow

The event must be set up so that everything flows through it by design, including when guests will be given access and be able to interact. The designer should be conscious of removing obstacles and distractions as well as modulating the pace and direction of the experience. Each step of the event should build upon the last, so that the sequence provides pay offs throughout. Balancing the distribution of these rewards with the right amount of downtime will keep the audience engaged and interested.

Illusion Making

Misdirection and sleight of hand are instrumental in helping an audience suspend disbelief and enjoy the experience of illusion making. Light, sound, and visual distractions will build a sensory environment that focuses the minds of the audience, who should pay no attention to the designer behind the curtain—until its time to take a bow. Although a good fashion show is the result of much practice and the mastery of technical details, any suggestion of this effort will result in a heavy-handed, obvious presentation.

Preparing for Mercedes-Benz Fashion Week, Fall 2007, New York

Vogue editor Anna Wintour with designer Karl Lagerfeld before the presentation of Lagerfeld's Spring/Summer 2009 Collection, Paris Fashion Week

Target's model-less fashion show on a video screen in
Grand Central Terminal, 2007

Installations

A popular alternative to fashion shows are exhibits and installations, which might incorporate the actual garments in traditional displays or take shape as digital or video art. To curate this type of presentation, the designer walks a fine line between art and advertising. Collaborations with dedicated artists and filmmakers provide checks and balances to ensure the viability and integrity of the project. Fashion patrons with a penchant for the arts can intellectualize and appreciate a designer's work in an environment rich with the cultural trappings of the art world. Of course, sometimes such installations will appear in less rarified contexts, with an eye to a pop-cultural sensibility. Although live models may not be a component of these productions, the need for spectacle remains part of the equation. Designers must consider how these presentations will be preserved, repeated, reinterpreted, or repurposed.

CHECKLISTS

Like any event the designer undertakes, from product launches to television appearances, the fashion show requires extensive and detailed planning. Live events are also about crowd management, for when dealing with people in numbers the variables increase exponentially. Planning for every contingency requires designers to create, manage, and complete three basic checklists: preshow preparation, showtime, and postshow wrap-up. The items on each of these lists will vary, depending on the scope.

Polaroid wall backstage at Anna Sui, Spring/Summer 2006
Ready-to-Wear, Olympus Fashion Week, New York

Hair prep backstage at Givenchy, Spring/Summer 2009
Ready-to-Wear, Paris Fashion Week

Preshow

The Plan	Timeline—create detailed master schedule
	Lineup—develop show lineup with rotation of models
	Theme—establish central concept to use as guideline
	Budget—estimate overall expenses with line-item breakdown
The Place	Location Scouting—choose and secure venue
	Site Visit—walk through to design event parameters
	Consultations—meet with lighting and sound techs
The Team	Talent—scout models, hair, makeup, stylist, etc.
	Models—audition and cast models
	Hair and Makeup—collaborate on designing the look
	Stylist—select accessories based on concept
	Dressers—find students, volunteers, professionals
	Music Development—select and hire DJ or prerecord soundtrack
The Announcement	Graphic Design—select and hire designer
	Invitation Design—develop and approve graphics
	Save-the-Date or Teaser—choose print and/or email
	Postage and Distribution—select method and budget for delivery
	Email Blast—send e-communications prior to event
	Website Coordination—plan dedicated website or area on established site
	Press Releases— develop newsworthy story angles into releases
	Calendar Listings—submit copy for free listings
	Programs—develop, approve, and print
	Publicity—design media campaign
	Placements—ensure product samples are strategically visible
	Stunts—stage theatrical series of public acts
The Prep	Fittings—ensure proper fitting of models
	Pressing—iron and steam garments
	Packaging—prepare garments for transport
	Inventory—take stock of everything being transported
	Gift Bag—organize and assemble
	Rehearsal—establish choreography at run-throughs

Showtime

Entry Strategy	Delivery and Load-in—transport line and staff
	The Surge—set up backstage and front of house
	Dressing Area—place racks, tables, mirrors, storage
	Hair and Makeup Stations—place mirrors, tables, stools, power source
	Catering—provide food and beverage for staff
	Garment Prep—unpack, inventory, and organize
	Sound Check—test music and microphones
	Rehearsal—run through with models, music, and lighting
Backstage	Designer—ideally free to oversee
	Assistant Designer—execute designer directives
	Production Assistant—act as runners
	Accessory Manager—oversee accessories
	Hair Stylist—prep hair
	Makeup Artist—apply makeup
	Dressers—support models
	Stylist—check models one last time
	Feeder—feed models onto runway
	Models—perform
	Choreographer—block models
Staging	Stage Manager—coordinate all stage needs
	Set—coordinate runway, backdrop, signage, seating
	Décor—set up flowers, table coverings, pipe and drape systems
	Special Effects—produce special lighting, pyrotechnics, videos
Documentation	Photographer(s)—document runway, party, backstage
	Videographer(s)—document runway, party, backstage
Management	House Manager—coordinate designer, venue, and vendors on-site
	Production Staff—provide food and beverage, coat check, and valet services
	Multimedia—oversee lighting and sound tech teams
	Security—protect backstage and front of house
Guest Relations	Greeters—welcome and direct guests
	Ticket Takers—check guest list and act as gatekeepers
	Ushers—escort guests to seats
	VIP Staff—provide special services
	Take-away—store and distribute gift bags
	Food and Beverage—set up and serve
	Entertainment—amuse with pre- and postshow music and visuals
	Transportation and Parking—provide directions, validations, valet

Photograph by China Photos/Getty Images.

Jeanswest Cup Casual Wear Design Contest, China Fashion
Week Spring/Summer 2009, Beijing

Postshow

Exit Strategy	Breakdown Staff—dismantle according to preassigned duties
	Inventory—account for everything
	Guest and Staff Exits—cue guests, schedule staff for departure
	Transportation—arrange for return trip
Postproduction	Pressing and Repairs—refresh garment samples as need
	Photo and Video Editing—process raw footage a.s.a.p.
	Outreach—send video or photo recaps to special clients and press
	Archiving—record and file press clippings, images, video, and memorabilia

Where do you start with the design process when developing a new collection? And why that first?

I work in an almost second-nature kind of process that's both gratifying and mysterious. Sometimes it starts with sketches and sometimes it starts with fabric. And yet it's hard to pinpoint where the process begins because I'm so ingrained in it. I'm always developing fabrics, I'm always developing ideas, so things overlap a great deal. But there's always a moment that catches you, and you say, Oh, this is it.

For example: I was coming home one evening two summers ago and I found a lunar moth on my doorknob. It was the most incredibly ravishing thing I had ever seen in my life, it took my breath away. So I discovered this crazy latent obsession with insects. Even though I don't think I scratched the surface, that's all I thought about and looked at for one year: insects. There's something so classically motivating about insects. Like the way the soft colors of the beating wings, a reflective grey-orange, say, flutter around an intense central color like bright orange. Or the way certain things connect on an insect, it's otherworldly and also very mechanical. So one thought leads to another thought leads to another thought, and my last collection was really about insects.

Of course, I'm obsessed with other things at the moment for my fall collection. I'm always going back to Technicolor. I watch a lot of old movies; I grew up at the Regency Theatre, at the Solaria. There's something about the quality of color when it's projected onto a screen that's impossible to emulate in real life, and yet I keep trying. And every season I discover a way of doing it, one little personal triumph of color that no one else notices.

Do you consider fashion an art form? a craft?

I am an artist, and that's all I have to say about it. I know that my clothes are supposed to sell, as opposed to a painter whose work is almost friggin' not supposed to. As an artist, you're supposed to be dead when your work starts to sell, then you're really considered successful. Whereas for a fashion designer, there's a problem if your clothes don't sell while you're alive. But I do think of myself as an artist. Honestly, I think I could probably do better in the marketplace if I cared less about artistic integrity.

Did you have a mentor or mentors in the fashion industry? What have you taken away from those relationships that serves you today?

The greatest mentor in my life was Perry Ellis. I didn't know it at the time, which is probably why it was so powerful, because it was taking place without my even noticing. When I was emerging as a designer, the person I looked up to most in the world was Geoffrey Beene. I just loved his work. Perry Ellis and Geoffrey Beene were not that different. They both had an off-beat sense of proportion and an exquisite sense of fabric. One was much more sporty, easy, young, and playful; the other was more couture, obsessive, lacey, and fancy. But, in the end, they both had very quirky ways of looking at style, which is what affected me the most. I feel like I learned my sense of grandeur from Ellis—in terms of what he exposed us to and how he took grandeur and made it everyday. With Beene, too, the grandeur is very everyday. It's not Versailles like La Croix (who's also a genius); it's quieter, more intimate, like a beautiful Chinese princess.

Have you assumed the role of mentor for someone else?

I might be a mentor, but we won't know that until twenty, fifty years pass. There's a girl that I work with named Elizabeth, who I think is absolutely wonderful. She has great style, she's a great designer, and she's very devoted. She's absorbing, she's learning.

What books or art are in your reference library?

A great friend of mine, Katell le Bourhis—a fabulous fashion curator, she ran the Met's Costume Institute for a while, years ago—gave me this book about the poet Gabriele D'Annunzio called *Il Guardaroba di Gabriele d'Annunzio* (The Closet of Gabriele D'Annunzio). He was a stylish, stylish man. He was also a huge fascist. But he did have the most gorgeous clothes, the most beautiful uniforms and boots and pajamas and toiletries. That's one book I can't do without. I always was crazy about Cecil Beaton and all of those style books that he wrote, including my bible, *The Glass of Fashion*. I keep all his books close at hand.

I'm mad about Richard Avedon's photographs. His work from the 1950s and 1960s was a big influence when I was in my twenties. I'm still inspired anytime I see them. There are some great contemporary photographers and also a few crazy artists whose work I really love. I'm obsessed with Jim Hodges.

With an industry that is losing skilled craftspeople with every passing generation, what do you think fashion education programs should include in their curriculum to best prepare designers looking to enter the market?

That's such a good question. I'm not an educator, so it's difficult to say. It's more about what's missing altogether. I often mourn the passing of something, like a costume collection that is lost, or a standard that disappears because it's too hard to do something a particular way. I especially mourn the loss of books. People don't buy books anymore, they buy Kindles; they go online to look at pictures. But I treasure my books. There was a kind of rigor about things years ago, a deeper knowledge, and less pop focus. Not that pop's bad—if anyone's responsible for that in fashion it's me.

How does the issue of sustainability affect your design process?

That's a paradigm that is shifting glacially, at least in my world. I'm kind of worshipful of people who can do sustainable design really well. There's a girl in Berkeley, California, who makes only clothes that are sustainable, and I can't believe how great she is. I admire her work to the end of the earth. But, personally, unless I'm really captivated and excited and motivated, it's meaningless. If I work with sustainable materials and integrate them into my process, it can't be a dogma. It has to be, Oh look, we can now do this glamorous thing sustainably, hooray! I won't lose the glamour, the glitter, and the fluff just because it's not sustainable. Reform has to come as part of beautiful design, as part of an organic design process. And by the way, the minute you start recycling something, someone says, No, no, no, that's not the way you do it. There are all kinds of controversies about what is and isn't sustainable. So once everybody knows exactly what's going on, I'm for it. I just don't see it as the be-all and end-all.

You have been very successful at diversifying the Isaac Mizrahi message without diluting it. You've reached customers at Target, at luxury retailers like Bergdorf Goodman, and now at Liz Claiborne with equal power. What does a designer need to do this well?

I can't describe that for anyone else. I swear to God, I don't know how I became who I am. Perry Ellis would take us to Mr. Chow's occasionally and he'd point to Tina Chow and say, She's wearing a Chanel couture skirt with a Hanes T-shirt and she looks amazing. I realized that smart people don't just buy designer clothes and wear them, they actually get involved. They actually think the way I think about clothes: that a beautiful design is more valuable than any so-called luxury label. Luxury is relative. There's nothing more luxurious than a good idea, nothing more luxurious than a good color.

Your diversification goes beyond clothing. You've just written a book, you've created a comic book, a television program, a cabaret act, and an engaging video blog on Facebook. How important is this kind of multifaceted self-expression for a designer today?

All these types of expression are important for me. Whether they're important for other designers, I don't know. There are designers with far more successful design companies than mine because they don't do it. I don't think Miuccia Prada gives a damn about her blog, if you know what I mean. Yet there's Michael Kors, who's been a judge on *Fashion Runway*, or whatever it's called, and he does really well and it's great exposure for him. Those of us who can do these things—hooray for us. But I don't think it's exclusively good to do one thing or another. It's important to make your own way in the world. Really, my best advice to designers is to do what feels good and what they like. Don't be afraid, because you figure it out as you go along.

Overleaf   Spring 2009 and Fall 2009 Collections. Sketches courtesy of Isaac Mizrahi; photographs by Dan Lecca.

Australian
Crochet
Ballgown

FALL 2009

6.

EVOLVE

Never before have fashion designers confronted so much information, so many opportunities, and such a strong cultural impetus to traverse different arenas. The interests, skills, and goals of the contemporary designer can build bridges between different creative disciplines and the world at large. Most important is to achieve a balance and, with that, a sense of well-being. The idea is not to have it all, but rather, to be open to it all.

As the designer grows in the profession, many new possibilities unfold. Designing for celebrities allows for a level of detachment from the everyday world and an exploration of the unattainable. The artistry of a designer's collection, and the critical acclaim it receives, elevates it beyond a simple bundle of goods to something worthy of being collected and shown in the museum. To work with cutting-edge technologies is a direction not every fashion designer will embrace, but all designers should recognize the technological breakthroughs that can serve as a catalyst for solving old design problems in new ways. The designers of the future also need to be good citizens, aware of the impact of their enterprise at a personal and a global level.

Finally, constantly exposing themselves to new avenues of learning, as well as actively participating in all the industry offers, will arm the fashion designer with the most important weapon in a creative arsenal—choice.

Chapter 22: Celebrity

Celebrity has always been a part of the fashion mix, at least by association. Celebrities tend to fall into distinct categories. Royalty, politicians, and other powerful opinion makers serve as public role models. The subjects of scandal and rumor engage the public in a love-to-hate relationship. Entertainers and sports figures allow the public to live vicariously through their roles or their accomplishments. Looking back at the origins of contemporary fashion, one finds the couturier Charles Frederick Worth dressing all three: French Empress Eugénie, famous courtesan Cora Pearl, and actress Sarah Bernhardt. Today celebrities from other fields often try their hand at fashion design, and fashion designers become celebrities in their own right—establishing a new standard for success in the industry.

MODES OF CELEBRITY

Fifteen Minutes

In 1968 Andy Warhol famously declared, "In the future, everyone will be world-famous for 15 minutes." His prediction has come to pass as society's seemingly insatiable appetite for celebrity in any degree, and a general sense of entitlement that demands a moment in the sun for everyone, intersect with new communication technologies that transmit stories and images instantly around the globe.

The producers of reality television have capitalized on the willingness of most people to do just about anything for those fifteen minutes. The Peabody Award–winning series *Project Runway* is the fashion industry's most notable contribution to this phenomenon. From the start, the value of the whole enterprise was increased by being fronted by celebrity supermodel Heidi Klum; in the end, it has made a beloved star of mentor Tim Gunn, now chief creative officer at Liz Claiborne. For the savvy designer, even making it onto the show can be parlayed into press clippings or job offers.

The fascination with celebrity stems from the public's ability to observe, analyze, and critique a polished parallel world. It is a world fabricated on a sense of intimacy, which the consumer enters with the flick of a remote control or the scroll of a mouse. The level of intimacy depends on what any particular celebrity will trigger in a person, be it sexual desire, romantic longing, or a feeling of security. At best, an adoring public uses the connection as a way to bond with their peers, let off a little steam, or simply escape into fantasy and be entertained. At its worst, celebrity worship leads to an unrealistic self-image, issues of esteem, or true obsession. Having even the most basic understanding of the inclination of fans will help designers decide whether or not they wish to tap into the illusions and promises of celebrity.

Editor Bob Colacello, model Jerry Hall, artist/publisher Andy Warhol, singer Debbie Harry, writer Truman Capote, and jewelry designer Paloma Picasso at a Studio 54 party for *Interview* magazine

Tim Gunn and Heidi Klum at the Project Runway Fashion Show, Spring 2009, Mercedes-Benz Fashion Week

Front Row and Red Carpet

The designer with the best front row wins, or so it seems at most major fashion runway presentations—an impression that press coverage does nothing to dispel. Gianni Versace was one of the first designers to line his front row with a virtual who's who of Hollywood and the music world: Paired with his superstar models and rock-concert energy, they helped make every runway show spectacular. Of course, the value can flow both ways: securing an invitation to a high-profile show improves a guest's CQ, or celebrity quotient.

Today very few major events forgo the experience of the red carpet photo-op, where the Hollywood-style set up allows sponsors to position logos behind the parade of guests. The sight has become so commonplace that its absence at a movie premiere, benefit gala, or fashion show might suggest that the event is not newsworthy. In this environment, it is no surprise that designers would vie for the opportunity to dress as many VIP guests as possible. Some designers go out of their way to offer notable guests the loan of their finest frocks to display in front of the paparazzi.

Mary-Kate Olsen and Ashley Olsen at the Chanel Fall/ Winter 2008/2009 Collection, Paris Fashion Week

Actress Sharon Stone wearing Armani on the red carpet at the 57th Berlin International Film Festival, 2007

Crossover

Fame in one field seldom translates into great success in another. Many a movie star, television personality, sports hero, or popular musician has tried to enter the fashion industry, only to end up the subject of ridicule, oversaturation, or sale-rack obscurity. Even celebrities with a passion for fashion and an earnest desire to be involved come face-to-face with the reality of what it takes to be a fashion designer. There have been some notable exceptions, where celebrities have worked with designers to develop successful lines in their own name.

In 1985 Jaclyn Smith of Charlie's Angels fame pioneered the celebrity fashion connection with her women's apparel line for Kmart, a collection that continues to perform well in the market. The small screen also produced one of fashion's most influential style makers, Sarah Jessica Parker of Sex and the City. The company motto of her Bitten line, "Fashion is not a luxury, it's a right" sets the tone for a very accessible and affordable collection based on pieces from her own wardrobe. Mary-Kate and Ashley Olsen were able to cross over into the fashion industry even as child stars, with a teen collection for Wal-Mart. Although the licensing deal was financially successful, the young actresses did not achieve critical success for their contributions to the marketplace until they launched The Row and Elizabeth & James, fashion lines in which they are very involved.

Although first recognized as a supermodel, activist-entrepeneur Christy Turlington has partnered with Puma to produce Nuala, a line of activewear, and Mahanuala, a line of yoga wear. She is also involved in Sundari, an ayurvedic skincare line. Sports stars have been linked to fashion design ever since Jean-René Lacoste, "Le Crocodile," gave his nickname to a tennis shirt in 1929. Since then the line between active sportswear and fashion has continued to blur. World-renowned tennis player and Olympic gold medalist Serena Williams designs a line called Aneres whose focus is fashion rather than sport.

In the field of music, recording artist Gwen Stefani established a reputation for being a trendsetter both as the front person for the band No Doubt and in her solo career. She further demonstrated her fashion acumen as the creator of two successful collections, the fashion-forward L.A.M.B. and Harajuku Lovers, a line of apparel and accessories designed to incorporate the distinctly Japanese aesthetic of kawaii, or cuteness. Rapper and record producer Sean "Diddy" Combs is responsible for the label Sean John, which has retained the respect of its urban customer. His collections have also attracted the attention of the fashion industry, with Combs being nominated for the CFDA Perry Ellis Award for Menswear in his first year in business and the CFDA Menswear Designer of the Year in 2004.

Sarah Jessica Parker unveiling
her clothing line, Bitten, 2007

Celebrity Proxy

The Swedish clothing company H&M has pioneered the concept of collaborations between a mainstream retailer and celebrity designers. Although the company has also drawn on the star power of pop idols like Madonna and Kylie Minogue, their strategy focuses on fashion designers themselves as celebrities. The clout of the guest designer is matched by the power of approximately 1,700 stores in thirty-three countries. This model has succeeded in making high-end designers more accessible through the creation of limited-edition capsule collections available in select cities. The retailer has created a sense of anticipation about who will be the next big celebrity designer, thanks to a string of very prominent associations with Karl Lagerfeld (2004), Stella McCartney (2005), Viktor & Rolf (2006), Roberto Cavalli (2007), Comme des Garçons (2008), Matthew Willamson (2009) and Jimmy Choo (2009). The benefits to the designer and the retailer are obvious, but they are not alone. The press has their celebrity angle and the public has access to a "designer" label.

Industry Celebrity

Naturally, the industry creates its own celebrities. The Fashion Walk of Fame is New York's fashion equivalent of having a star on Hollywood Boulevard. Established in 1999 by the Fashion Center BID, the award honors New York's most influential designers, living and deceased, with plaques embedded in the sidewalk on Seventh Avenue between Thirty-fifth and Forty-first Streets in Manhattan. Each bronze plaque features an original sketch, the designer's signature, and a description of their contributions to the field. Fashion editors, retailers, historians, and museum curators make the selections that are then voted on by more than a hundred industry leaders.

Photograph by Michael Loccisano/FilmMagic.

Gwen Stefani backstage at the L.A.M.B. Spring 2007
show, Olympus Fashion Week, New York

Diane von Furstenberg being inducted into the Fashion Walk of Fame, 2008

New York society photographer Bill Cunningham, 2004

FASHION WALK OF FAME HONOREES

Geoffrey Beene

Bill Blass

Stephen Burrows

Bonnie Cashin

Liz Claiborne

Lilly Daché

Oscar de la Renta

Giorgio di sant' Angelo

Perry Ellis

James Galanos

Rudi Gernreich

Halston

Marc Jacobs

Charles James

Betsey Johnson

Norma Kamali

Donna Karan

Anne Klein

Calvin Klein

Ralph Lauren

Mainbocher

Claire McCardell

Norman Norell

Willi Smith

Pauline Trigére

Diane von Furstenberg

Noncelebrity

The pomp and circumstance of celebrity is not for everyone. Independent fashion design professionals take pride in not having sold out. Often, however, they eventually acquire their own celebrity cult status. The level of anonymity lasts only as long as a subculture stays out of the mainstream, and, in the end, being famous for being an underground talent is still fame. Sometimes the noncelebrity is actually the not-yet celebrity. The industry is always waiting for the opportunity to discover the unproven ingénue. These success stories keep the fashion wheels turning and give established professionals a hand in shaping the future.

Real people can achieve a kind of fashion celebrity, too. Photojournalist Bill Cunningham can be found on the streets of New York City, on the look out for fashion. "On the Street," his column in the Sunday *New York Times*, celebrates extraordinary style on individuals in everyday situations. It has become a popular model for newspapers, magazines, and websites that want to document the frontline of fashion.

The celebration of the ordinary person has become a popular new aesthetic in fashion. "Real people" casting is used to show how accessible a product is to anyone. It is the antithesis of making something desirable by making it virtually unattainable. The makeover concept is also designed to democratize fashion: it shows consumers how to use a product and gives them permission to make it their own.

Chapter 23: Art

The question should not be, Is fashion art? but rather, When is fashion art? Fashion, after all, is a business in which design is responding to a functional challenge. Many will argue that fashion's production of utilitarian items that are not exclusively an artistic expression—meant to stimulate the beholder's thoughts and emotions—disqualifies it as an art form. But there are times when fashion designers take their work to a place that can only be described as art. Intent is at the core of the issue: What drives the designer? The very fact that fashion stirs passionate debate around this question is enough to give it a place at the table. Aesthetic value, it must be also be remembered, is never universal, but always evolving in what it excludes or includes.

IN THE MUSEUM

Garments

Traditionally, museums have collected fashion drawings and garments (as a textile) only for their historic value. The benefits of knowing what people wore within the context of when they wore it slowly gained credibility as a reason for creating fashion archives. These sort of fashion collections can both chronicle an era and document the lives and accomplishments of iconic figures. For example, the John F. Kennedy Presidential Library's 2002 exhibit *Jacqueline Kennedy: The White House Years* examined the First Lady's influence on fashion and style at a time when the world was watching every move she made and everything she wore.

At the same time, museums have put works traditionally categorized as fine arts into context by showing the correlations between them and the design arts, including fashion design. For example, the shift toward Cubism for artists like Pablo Picasso and Georges Braque and their appreciation for clean lines, fragmented angular planes, and a sense of transparency might be displayed in the flapper fashions of Coco Chanel, Madeleine Vionnet, and the Callot Soeurs. Or an exhibit might pair the kinetic canvases of op art painters like Victor Vasarely and Bridget Riley with the mod designs of Rudi Gernreich and Mary Quant.

Only in recent decades has the work of fashion designers been collected, studied, and displayed on its own merit. Museum shows might focus on the artistic contribution of designers and examine their cultural and sociological impact in the twentieth and twenty-first centuries; others shows might focus on innovations in garment making. For example, in 1983 the designs of Issey Miyake, a leader in experimenting with the structure of garments and their relation to the body, began to travel to art museums around the globe in the exhibition *Bodyworks*; his work also appeared on the cover of *Artforum*, the first time clothes were given space in a major art magazine.

Jacqueline Kennedy: The White House Years,
John F. Kennedy Presidential Library and Museum, 2002

Photograph by Christine Liu.

Fashion Show: Paris Collections 2006, Museum of Fine Arts, Boston, 2006–2007

A exhibition installed a few years ago at the Museum of Fine Arts in Boston, Massachusetts, made the case that fashion should be looked at as a fine art. Called *Fashion Show: Paris Collections 2006*, it showcased the then-current work of contemporary designers Azzedine Alaïa, Hussein Chalayan, Karl Lagerfeld for Chanel, John Galliano for Christian Dior, Christian Lacroix, Maison Martin Margiela, Olivier Theyskens for Rochas, Valentino, Viktor & Rolf, and Yohji Yamamoto. That the show was put on by a museum of fine arts and not an institution dedicated to fashion provoked debate, an echo of the grumblings heard in 2000 when the Guggenheim Museum in New York gave over its rotunda to a retrospective of the work of designer Giorgio Armani.

Accessories

The shifts in attitude toward the collection and exhibition of fashion design applies as well to accessory design. Many museums have installed vitrines of jewelry and accessories that tell how cultures have displayed their wealth and status over time. It might be a gold belt of connected lira coins from a Kurdish costume or a collection of cameos from sixth-century B.C. Greece to Victorian England, or the art nouveau finery of René Lalique. Today, accessories are shown as art objects in themselves. Judith Leiber's line of crystal-covered evening bags, for instance, are not just luxury status symbols but little sculptures collected by museums such as the Metropolitan Museum of Art and the Smithsonian Institution.

Other types of accessories are now collected for their artistic value. The London-based milliner Philip Treacy has worked with major fashion houses, including Chanel, Givenchy, Helmut Lang, Alexander McQueen, Anna Molinari, Thierry Mugler, Valentino, and Versace. His fantastical creations are recognized as sculptures in the spirit of Picasso's assemblages. Daniel Storto is a glove artist based in Gloversville, New York (once referred to as the glove-making capital of the world), who has collaborated with Geoffrey Beene, Alexander McQueen, Ralph Rucci, and Dries Van Noten. Breaking with the industry's seasonal schedule, Storto develops series of personally hand-stitched gloves. Signature creations such as his Circle Glove become extraordinary three-dimensional pieces of art when worn fully realized.

Photograph courtesy of Judith Leiber.

Austrian crystal Ganesha minaudière by Judith Leiber

Photograph courtesy of Daniel Storto.

Sculptural gloves by Daniel Storto

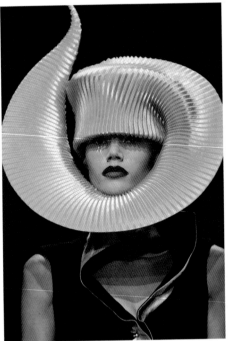

Photographs courtesy of Philip Treacy London Haute Couture.

Hats by Philip Treacy, Fall 2001

Images

Another arena of fashion that has found its home in the museum comprises the images by which designs are conveyed to the public. The history of fashion illustration goes back hundreds of years, and museums worldwide contain extensive collections of beautiful fashion plates from the nineteenth century. In the early twentieth century, illustrated plates by Georges Barbier, Bernard Boutet de Monvel, Pierre Brissaud, Paul Iribe, Georges Lepape, and Charles Martin dominated the fashion scene. The Callot Soeurs, Coco Chanel, Jacques Doucet, Jeanne Lanvin, Jeanne Paquin, and other prominent designers of the day put these artists to work creating glamorous interpretations of their garments. In the 1930s Christian Bérard, a fashion illustrator for Vogue, was sought after for his refined drawings by designers like Coco Chanel, Elsa Schiaparelli, and Nina Ricci. His work as artistic director for the Theatre de la Mode and as production designer for Jean Cocteau's 1946 film *La Belle et la Bête* serve as landmarks in art as well as fashion. For decades, photography relegated fashion drawings to second place. Not until a revival of fashion illustration in the 1980s did such talents as Antonio Lopez, Isao Yajima, and Stephen Stipelman figure prominently on the fashion scene. Today the glamorous works of David Downton and the wit and charm of artists Ruben Toledo, Jason Brooks, and Jordi Labanda hold their own against the photographic image as an artistic format for fashion.

Fashion illustration by Georges Barbier, circa 1922

Christian Bérard sketching a model in the offices of Paris *Vogue*

In the 1920s and 1930s competition between *Vogue* and *Harper's Bazaar* helped to establish fashion photography as an art form, publishing the work of pioneers such as Edward Steichen, George Hoyningen-Huené, Horst P. Horst, and Cecil Beaton. Martin Munkácsi revolutionized the medium by taking fashion outdoors. Old-school fashion photography masters include Erwin Blumenfeld, Louise Dahl-Wolfe, Irving Penn, and Richard Avedon. The next generation of fashion photography saw Melvin Sokolsky's famous bubble series and the edgy expressions of David Bailey. Herb Ritts and Bruce Weber then led the way for the likes of Patrick Demarchelier, Steven Meisel, and Mario Testino. Photographic fashion fantasies have been explored by the provocative Pierre et Gilles, David LaChapelle, and Helmut Newton. Exhibitions of the work of the great fashion photographers continue to draw an audience in galleries and museums.

Photograph by Nick Giordano of an op-art day dress

Chapter 24: Technology

Throughout fashion history, science and technology have been responsible for providing designers with new means for solving design challenges. The industrial revolution mechanized production. The first automobiles popular-ized duster coats, just as motorcycles would later popularize leather jackets: both garments were designed for protection on the road and both became a part of the overall style of the period. In World War II the military's need for an inexpensive alternative to silk for parachutes led to the development of rip-stop nylon, now widely used in sportswear and outerwear. Advancements in environ-mental control through heating, ventilation, and air conditioning freed fashion designers from accountability to natural elements. The aerospace industry put Velcro fasteners to use in space suits; skiers and scuba divers recognized its value and adapted it to their sports; soon after, Velcro appeared in children's clothes, bringing it into the mainstream of clothing design.

Photograph by Douglas J. Eng./DougEngPhoto.com.

Inflatable dress by Diana Eng and Emily Albinski

SCIENCE OF STYLE

Computational Couture

Since 2005 students of technology and fashion from prominent institutions such as the Massachusetts Institute of Technology, Harvard University, New York University, Parsons School of Design, and Rhode Island School of Design have gathered at MIT to explore creative clothing through the lens of technology. "Seamless: Computational Couture" is an event that showcases innovative and experimental works in computational apparel design, interactive clothing, and technology-based fashion. As the name implies, the designs make apparent the seamless relationship between the fashionable and the high-tech. Steps beyond performance fabrics, some of the works featured over the years have included computer-generated knit patterns, boots that change shape based on the speed of the wearer, a shirt with sensors that massage the wearer, and an inflatable dress that establishes personal space boundaries.

Solar Textiles

The fashion techie might be familiar with a futuristic-looking knapsack whose solar photovoltaic panels collect energy to charge personal electronic devices. The development of membrane-like surfaces that function in the same way, but that can be draped like curtains, provides the modern fashion designer with a new way of thinking about energy and style. The nonprofit initiative Portable Light Project has responded to the need in remote communities for dependable, easy-to-use, adaptable materials that are durable enough to serve as renewable energy sources. Their textiles that incorporate flexible solar nanotechnology allow women to weave energy-harvesting bags using a simple backstrap loom. Their work only hints at the possibilities for the two billion people around the world who live without electricity.

Luminex

Luminescent fibers that can be attached to a microchip with a battery source enable designers to add light to their material palette. Originally developed for high-energy physics experiments, the fiber's fineness and flexibility allows it to be easily incorporated into textiles. Luminex fibers can be customized as to shape, size, thickness, finish, density of illumination, color, pattern, and programmability. These light-emitting fabrics have been used in stage costumes for their theatricality and in handbag linings for their practicality, and are being woven into a variety of fashion textiles.

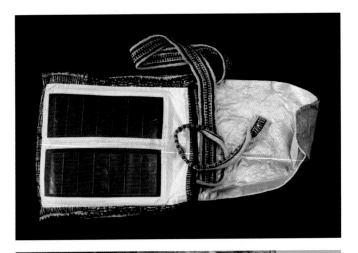

Photographs courtesy of KVA MATx/Kennedy & Violich Architecture.

Portable Light Project by KVA MATx, used by the Huichol
Indians of Sierra Madre, Mexico

Garments made with Luminex fabric

Photograph courtesy of Speedo.

Dava Newman, inventor, science, and engineering; Guillermo Trotti, design; Dainese, S.p.A., fabrication. Photograph by Douglas Sonders.

Michael Phelps in a LZR Racer Suit by Speedo

Dava Newman modeling a Bio-Suit prototype

LZR Racer

The design of Speedo's LZR Racer swimsuit combines the careful placement of seams with a new high-performance fabric to produce a garment that minimizes drag, maximizes muscle support, and does not constrain motion. The TLZR Pulse textile is a high-density weave of very fine nylon and spandex microfibers that is designed to be super-lightweight and water-repellent. Nor has style been forsaken. Speedo collaborated with one of the most forward-looking fashion designers, Rei Kawakubo for Comme des Garçons. She transferred a calligraphic painting by Japanese artist Inoue Yu-ich onto the suit; the graphic print reads *kokoro*, which means "heart, mind, spirit, feeling."

Bio-Suit

Twenty-first-century fashion might need to take a cue from the work of Dr. Dava Newman of the Massachusetts Institute of Technology. Working with Guillermo Trotti and the Italian company Dainese, makers of motorbike and extreme sports apparel, she has created the right balance of biomechanics, human factors engineering, modeling, and design for a Bio-Suit System that hopes to revolutionize human space exploration. Using mechanical counterpressure to establish the necessary internal pressure, Newman's invention replaces bulky, awkward space suits with one designed to behave more like a second skin. The Bio-Suit was honored by NASA and *Time* magazine (Best Inventors 2007) and was included in the Metropolitan Museum of Art's 2008 exhibit *Superheroes: Fashion and Fantasy*—demonstrating that the boundaries between science and style are flexing.

NEW FRONTIERS

No discussion of technology and fashion can exclude the phenomenon of virtual fashion. Virtual fashion can be created for use in computer-simulated environments or developed there with the intention of being worn in the real world. In Second Life and similar interactive online platforms, individuals use avatars that either simulate their own appearance or reflect aspects of their personality in ways that could only be entertained in a virtual world. Everything can be customized, including one's clothes. The technically proficient might undertake this themselves, but many virtual visitors are inclined to take advantage of designers who sell fashions crafted from pixels, not fabric.

Through virtual fashion shows and storefronts, major retailers, indie designers, and fashion students also use this very flexible and accessible new space to display the work that they are doing in the real world. Services such as My Virtual Model provide virtual changing rooms and virtual models that can be personalized to look like the customer and be shared online. From the designer's perspective, such services allow their customers to see themselves in the clothing with a few clicks of the mouse. Some designers that offer virtual residents the opportunity to dress in their fashions also provide a click-through to websites where they can buy the real-world counterparts.

Big-name fashion brands—Adidas, American Apparel, Lacoste, Reebok, Giorgio Armani, Jean-Paul Gaultier, Calvin Klein, and Stella McCartney (who staged an antifur animal rights protest in Second Life)—have all taken advantage of this new frontier to enhance their brands and extend them with actual stores or virtual promotions. Second Life is populated by early adopters, individuals who lead the way in testing and developing new ideas. For fashion designers who become part of the community, this makes it the perfect place to experiment and get feedback on their work. It is an immersive, peer-driven landscape that demands authenticity and innovation.

Second Life Fashion

Chapter 25: Awareness

The world of fashion has begun to recognize many concerns that go beyond perfecting the silhouette of a dress, giving rise to a new generation of conscious designers. Content as well as intent play into the designer's creative process and business strategy. Designers are asked to consider how their daily operations and the imagery they produce affects the environment, fair trade practices, self-esteem, cultural identity, intellectual property, and indeed, the future well-being of their industry.

CONSCIOUS PRODUCTION

Green Design

Green fashion has come to mean something beyond clothing that is more statement than style. Green thinking has become a natural extension of the design process. Leading designers in the market are always ready to shift gears, to map out a place for themselves on the new frontiers of fashion. They see the environmental concerns that have changed the way fashion is approached as opportunities rather than difficulties, for they open up new markets for designers and new kinds of products for the consumer.

The emphasis on organic pesticide-free fibers and production and delivery methods that reduce environmental impact have created new specializations. For example, Massachusetts-based Darn It! Inc. found their niche by helping to maintain the quality of products made overseas by correcting problems and finding solutions to warehousing and distributing goods.

Designers face environmental issues when debating the merits of local or overseas production. Do they go overseas (for large-scale production and speed) or stay local (smaller production runs with reduced environmental impact)? Re-examining the development of a product to identify where processes can be modified to serve a greener standard will vary greatly based on whether their work is exported or kept regional.

Fashion is based on conspicuous consumption and constant change. The designer of the future will embrace alternative practices that still feed the hunger for what is current and exciting. Fashion schools have begun to develop programming that addresses sustainability, generating a new kind of designer who repurposes garments, deconstructing and reassembling them in creative ways to produce entirely new garments. These eco-friendly designers use old clothing, remainders, closeouts, and overstocks—all goods that might otherwise end up in a landfill.

Pablo Cesar Dorado, Eco-friendly Design, Bio-Fashion Show, Cali, Colombia, 2008

Fair Trade

Ethical fashion is produced under decent conditions for fair wages. Disadvantaged communities run the risk of being exploited, making third-party certifiers, for example, the Fair Trade
Federation and Transfair USA, necessary. A transparent supply chain will help to avoid sweatshop situations, with every step along the production path documented and information easily
accessed by everyone from the designer to the consumer.

Fair-trade safeguards also help to create sustainable economies for otherwise disenfran-
chised regions. They are a way for designers to connect with local artisans who would normally
not have a presence in the marketplace. Designers can also be instrumental in popularizing a
local product or service by adopting, protecting, and marketing it.

Those who labor to produce a designer's product constitute the front line of fashion. Equitable
compensation is one more way a designer can do the right thing. In addition to earnings and
hours, many fair trade agreements ensure long-term commitments as well as investments in
the community, such as education and health initiatives.

Caring and Charity

"Animals are not ours to eat, wear, experiment on, or use for entertainment" is the slogan of
PETA, People for the Ethical Treatment of Animals. As it relates to fashion, animal-rights activ-
ism is concerned with the farming of animals for fur, the use of animals in entertainment, and
animal testing. Designers will need to decide to what degree they will embrace or reject the
implications of cruelty to animals for the sake of fashion.

The glamour and excitement of fashion has consistently drawn charities to designers as a way
to build awareness of and raise money for their cause. The Council of Fashion Designers of
America/CFDA Foundation has spearheaded campaigns and events such as Fashion Targets
Breast Cancer and Seventh on Sale (to benefit HIV/AIDS research). These are among the
most visible charities in the fashion industry, but education, poverty, hunger, and many other
causes are worthy beneficiaries. Giving back and showing that fashion cares is an important
part of designers' relationship with the communities they serve. Designers might donate garments for auctions or put on lavish high-ticket fashion shows to benefit their charity of choice.

PROJECTED IMAGES

Sense of Self

Faces with character and bodies with curves need not fall under the category of fashion flaws.
How far has fashion gone when perpetual dieting and plastic surgery remain the only ways to
achieve the latest ideal of beauty? Nor should age be relegated to a second tier in the fashion
hierarchy. The boomer generation represents a gray glamour all its own. Living longer today
also means living better, resulting in vibrant and vital lifestyles—something that designers are
in an ideal position to amplify.

It can be argued that adhering to established standards of beauty (however arbitrary) can contribute to personal and professional success. But when these standards are distorted or out of step with the society that is embracing them, its members are susceptible to poor self-esteem, depression, body dysmorphic disorder, anorexia/bulimia nervosa, or any number of physical and psychological complications that relate to a false self-image. Fashion designers must realize that, one way or another, they are helping to perpetuate or prevent these destructive patterns.

The French fashion industry, supported by the French Minister of Health, has introduced a charter of good conduct that encourages the use of models with diverse body types, in an attempt to avoid potentially dangerous influences on young women. Promoting healthy body sizes instead of idealizing unhealthy ones builds healthier body images. Spain and Italy have also taken steps to ban from fashion shows models whose Body Mass Index falls below the healthy range (18.5–24.9, as classified by the World Health Organization).

The Dove Campaign for Real Beauty is based on awareness and action. Leading by example, the company has produced advertising and programming designed to educate and empower women of all ages, body types, and ethnicities. Integrating all types of beauty sends a message of acceptance to the consumer as well as a challenge to the rest of the fashion and beauty industry.

Ad from Dove Campaign for Real Beauty

Cultural Identity

People from every corner of the globe buy into fashion, and yet there is a disproportionate representation of different ethnicities in the design field as well as among the models on the runways and in the pages of fashion magazines. The perpetuation of a single definition of beauty contributes to racial bias. Moreover, the bottom line has advertisers crafting very culture-specific images designed to harness a particular purchasing power. But how can the fashion industry in the twenty-first century justify this imbalance? As the public becomes more aware of the issue, they realize that if they are being asked to invest in the products, they are entitled to see themselves in the fashion ads, in the editorials, and on the catwalks.

Whatever their background, designers can address the fact that the exclusion of models of color has a detrimental effect on the women of those cultures and limits the potential of fashion. A precedent was set in 2008 when CFDA president Diane von Furstenberg reached out to designers in an effort to encourage them to be diverse in their runway presentations, although many of the shows remained whitewashed. This is not an argument for enforcing multicultural quotas. What is important is that designers expose themselves to many different cultures and recognize how they contribute to the richness and robustness of fashion.

Former model and agency owner Bethann Hardison has initiated a public discussion about the relationship between black models and the fashion industry. History shows that black models have made names for themselves. Dorothea Towles launched her modeling career in the early 1950s working for Christian Dior, Elsa Schiaparelli, and Pierre Balmain. Helen Williams was the first prominent black model in the United States in the 1960s. Mounia was the first black model on the Yves Saint Laurent runway. Naomi Sims appeared on the cover of *Life* magazine in 1969, accompanying an article about new black models. Beverly Johnson was the first black model to appear of the cover of *Vogue*, in August 1974. Pat Cleveland became a 1970s super-model and muse to designer Stephen Burrows. Iman appeared in *Vogue* in 1976, her first job. More recently, Veronica Webb, Naomi Campbell, Tyra Banks, Alek Wek, and Jourdan Dunn have all had a strong presence. Observing the dates associated with each model, though, the question becomes, Does the industry believe there is only room for one model of color at a time?

The current wave of Brazilian models, which include Gisele Bündchen, Adriana Lima, and Alessandra Ambrosio, has taken fashion by storm. Yet they represent only a small fraction of Hispanic beauty when one considers how diverse those origins are: European (Spain), Central American (Belize, Costa Rica, El Salvador, Guatemala, Honduras, Nicaragua, Panama), South America (Argentina, Brazil, Bolivia, Chile, Colombia, Ecuador, Paraguay, Peru, Uruguay, Venezuela), Caribbean (Cuba, Dominican Republic, Puerto Rico), North America (Mexico, United States), Africa (Equatorial Guinea), and Oceania (Easter Island). Asian models have a very low profile in fashion, but the number of new faces is growing: Devon Aoki (Japanese-American), Han Jin (Korean), Yoon Sun Kim (Korea), Lakshmi Menon (Indian), Hye Rim Park (Korean-American), Ling Tan (Malaysian), and Ai Tominaga (Japanese). The launch of *Vogue China* has contributed to the growing awareness of Chinese models, including Xiaoyi Dai, Du Juan, Emma Pei, Audrey Quock, Mo Wandan, Liu Wen, and Sonny Zhou.

DESIGNER ETHNICITIES

Hispanic Designers	African-American Designers	Asian Designers
Cristóbal Balenciaga	Xuly Bet	Michiko Koshino
Mariano Fortuny	Ozwald Boateng	Derek Lam
Carolina Herrera	Sean Combs	Hanae Mori
Paco Rabanne	Duro Olowu	Doo.Ri
Oscar de la Renta	Maurice Malone	Anna Sui
Narciso Rodriguez	Patrick Robinson	Kenzo Takada
Adolfo Sardiña	Tracy Reese	Vivienne Tam
Isabel Toledo	Willi Smith	Vera Wang

Photograph by Andrew H. Walker/Getty Images for IMG.

Designer Isabel Toledo

Photograph by Jeffrey Urberg/WireImage.

Designer Tracy Reese

Photograph by Rob Loud/Getty Images for IMG.

Designer Doo.Ri

INDUSTRY VALUES

Leadership and Legacy

Designers who lead by example make choices that reflect their personal values and those of the brand they've built. Do they run their business with charm, muscle, or a combination of both? How open are they to the experiences and contributions of their team members? What structures have they put in place to interface with the press and the public? There are many strategies for achieving superior results. Integrity of design, authentic relationships, motivation through positive reinforcement, the perception of risk-taking as an investment, the flexibility to easily adapt to change and encourage continued growth, all set an organization apart from the rest. Designers at the helm of healthy, balanced companies never become hostages of fashion. By creating a culture of honor, idealism, and respect they become industry leaders. Successful designers are also charged with preserving the craft and the history of fashion through instruction and mentorship. Preparing the next generation of fashion leaders is a rewarding personal experience and an important part of building a legacy.

Photograph courtesy of Eileen Fisher, Inc.

A crocheting circle at Eileen Fisher, Inc.

Wellness

Designers will define success by what they consider a good quality of life. Fame and money may be two obvious benchmarks, yet some designers reach farther. The "Wholeness Philosophy" at the Eileen Fisher company captures the desire of employees to be whole individuals. Overtime is discouraged in order to prioritize personal and professional time. Company benefits include wellness and education allowances, supporting healthy activities and the development of new skills. Career paths are flexible, allowing any employee to shift gears based on a passion or interest. Ultimately, employers like Eileen Fisher, who support a balanced lifestyle for their employees, can expect to have a loyal and dedicated workforce that brings diversity, enthusiasm, and creativity to their company.

Intellectual Property

Europe, India, and Japan all protect fashion as an intellectual property. Although music, film, and writing are protected in the United States, the merits of the Design Piracy Prohibition Act is still being debated. Introduced in 2006, this legislation is meant to target design piracy, a very important problem facing fashion designers. The bill would go a long way toward balancing the scales for smaller design houses that compete with companies that can knock off designs the moment they are shown on the runway and produce low-cost, low-quality copies before the original designs reach the retail store.

One of the United Nation's specialized agencies, the World Intellectual Property Organization, has called for stricter enforcement of intellectual property safeguards, in the belief that it will encourage healthy competition. Although this legislation would target piracy and is designed to protect designers, some believe that it could undermine an industry that, by its very nature, builds a demand by leveraging trends adopted and interpreted by many designers.

The alternative to copyright legislation does not have to be a matter of anything goes. The nonprofit organization Creative Commons encourages the legal sharing of creative works for the purposes of developing new works. It has released Creative Commons licenses that allow the author of a creative work to identify those rights that they reserve and those that they waive.

Chapter 26: Experience and Education

This book can only begin to suggest what the field of fashion design encompasses. The resources available to the designer are vast. Fertile ground for new ideas can be found in publications and on film, in archives and online. Fashion weeks and trade shows actively engage the designer and offer new sources of stimulation. A fashion designer's education may take many routes, from fashion schools to internships, incubators, professional conferences, workshops, and online classes. In the end, every experience can be mined.

Photograph by Mat Szwajkos/Getty Images for IMG.

Outside the tents at Mercedes-Benz Fashion Week,
Fall 2007

BOOKS

Art of Fashion

A-Poc Making: Issey Miyake and Dai Fujiwara, ed. Mateo Kries and Alexander von Vegesack
Balenciaga Paris, Pamela Golbin and Fabien Baron
Breaking the Mode, Kaye Durland Spilker and Sharon Sadako Takeda
Christian Lacroix on Fashion, Patrick Mauries, Olivier Saillard, and Christian Lacroix
Dior, Farid Chenoune and Laziz Hamani
Fashion in Colors, Cooper-Hewitt National Design Museum
The Fashion of Architecture, Bradley Quinn
Fashion Show, Susan Ward, Pamela A. Parmal, Didier Grumbach, and Lauren Whitley
Madeleine Vionnet, Betty Kirke and Issey Miyake
Ralph Rucci: The Art of Weightlessness, Valerie Steele, Clare Sauro, and Patricia Mears
Rare Bird of Fashion: The Irreverent Iris Apfel, Eric Boman, Iris Apfel, and Harold Koda
Surfers, Soulies, Skinheads and Skaters: Subcultural Style from the Forties to the Nineties,
    Amy de la Haye and Cathie Dingwall

Business, Forecasting, and Strategy

Beautiful Evidence, Edward R. Tufte
Change to Strange: Create a Great Organization by Building a Strange Workforce,
    Daniel M. Cable
The End of Fashion: How Marketing Changed the Clothing Business, Teri Agins
Future Think: How to Think Clearly in a Time of Change, Edie Weiner and Arnold Brown
Good to Great: Why Some Companies Make the Leap ... and Others Don't, Jim Collins
Groundswell: Winning in a World Transformed by Social Technologies, Charlene Li and
    Josh Bernoff
Leading with Kindness, William F. Baker and Michael O'Malley
Made to Stick: Why Some Ideas Survive and Others Die, Chip Heath and Dan Heath
New Media in the White Cube and Beyond: Curatorial Models for Digital Art, Christiane Paul
Predictably Irrational: The Hidden Forces That Shape Our Decisions, Dan Ariely
Purple Cow: Transform Your Business by Being Remarkable, Seth Godin
Remix: Making Art and Commerce Thrive in the Hybrid Economy, Lawrence Lessig
The Long Tail: Why the Future of Business Is Selling Less of More, Chris Anderson
Tribes: We Need You to Lead Us, Seth Godin
T-Shirts and Suits: A Guide to the Business of Creativity, David J. Parrish

Research and History

A Guide to Fashion Sewing, Connie Amaden-Crawford
Costume and Fashion: A Concise History, James Laver
Dictionary of Fashion and Fashion Designers, Georgina O'Hara Callan
Diana Vreeland, Eleanor Dwight
Diana Vreeland: Bazaar Years, John Esten and Katherine Betts
Fashion: A History from the 18th to the 20th Century, Kyoto Costume Institute
Fashion Sketchbook, Bina Abling
Future Fashion White Papers, Earth Pledge
Illustrating Fashion: Concept To Creation, Steven Stipelman

Know Your Fashion Accessories, Celia Stall-Meadows
Survey of Historic Costume, Phyllis G. Tortora and Keith Eubank
Sustainable Fashion, Janet Hethorn and Connie Ulasewicz
Textiles: Concepts and Principles, Virginia Hencken Elsasser
Théâtre de la Mode: Fashion Dolls: The Survival of Haute Couture, Edmond Charles-Roux
The Art of Manipulating Fabric, Colette Wolff
The Collection of the Kyoto Costume Institute, Akiko Fukai and Tamami Suoh
The Complete History of Costume and Fashion, Bronwyn Cosgrave
The Dynamics of Fashion, Elaine Stone
The Fashion Designer Survival Guide, Mary Gehlhar
The Fairchild Dictionary of Fashion, Charlotte Mankey Calasibetta and Phyllis Tortora
The New Complete Guide to Sewing, Reader's Digest
Who's Who in Fashion, Anne Stegemeyer
Writing for the Fashion Business, Kristen K. Swanson and Judith C. Everett

Style

How to Have Style, Isaac Mizrahi
The Little Black Book of Style, Nina Garcia
The Little Dictionary of Fashion: A Guide to Dress Sense for Every Woman, Christian Dior
The One Hundred: A Guide to the Pieces Every Stylish Woman Must Own,
    Nina Garcia and Ruben Toledo
The Lucky Guide to Mastering Any Style: How to Wear Iconic Looks and Make Them Your Own,
    Kim France and Andrea Linett
The Lucky Shopping Manual: Building and Improving Your Wardrobe Piece by Piece,
    Kim France and Andrea Linett
Tim Gunn: A Guide to Quality, Taste and Style, Tim Gunn and Kate Moloney

MAGAZINES

Business

Fast Company www.fastcompany.com
Harvard Business Publishing harvardbusiness.org

Design

Wallpaper www.wallpaper.com
How www.howdesign.com

Fashion and Lifestyle

Elle www.elle.com
Esquire www.esquire.com
Fashion Practice: The Journal of Design, Creative Process, and the Fashion Industry
    www.bergpublishers.com
Fashion Theory: The Journal of Dress, Body and Culture www.bergpublishers.com
Fly www.insidefly.com

GQ (Gentlemen's Quarterly) www.gq.com
Harper's Bazaar www.harpersbazaar.com
In Style www.instyle.com
Lucky www.luckymag.com
Nylon www.nylonmag.com
T Magazine www.tmagazine.com
Threads www.taunton.com/threads
Visionaire www.visionaireworld.com
Vogue www.vogue.com
W www.wmagazine.com

TRADE PAPERS

WWD (Women's Wear Daily) www.wwd.com
DNR (Daily News Report) www.dnrnews.com

FILM

Costumer and Couturier

The Women, 1939, dir. George Cukor (Adrian)
Wizard of Oz, 1939, dir. Victor Fleming (Adrian)
The Philadelphia Story, 1940, dir. George Cukor (Adrian)
Sabrina, 1954, dir. Billy Wilder (Hubert de Givenchy)
Funny Face, 1957, dir. Stanley Donen (Hubert de Givenchy)
Auntie Mame, 1958, dir. Morton DaCosta (Orry-Kelly)
Breakfast at Tiffany's, 1961, dir. Blake Edwards (Hubert de Givenchy and Pauline Trigère)
What a Way to Go!, 1964, dir. J. Lee Thompson (Edith Head)
Belle de Jour, 1967, dir. Luis Buñuel (Yves Saint Laurent)
Great Gatsby, 1974, dir. Jack Clayton (Ralph Lauren)
Annie Hall, 1977, dir. Woody Allen (Ralph Lauren)
American Gigolo, 1980, dir. Paul Schrader (Giorgio Armani)
The Fifth Element, 1997, dir. Luc Besson (Jean-Paul Gaultier)
The Cook, the Thief, His Wife, and Her Lover, 1989, dir. Peter Greenaway (Jean-Paul Gaultier)
Great Expectations, 1998, dir. Alfonso Cuarón (Donna Karan)
Sex and the City, 2008, dir. Michael Patrick King (Patricia Field)

Documentaries

11 Minutes, 2008, dir. Michael Selditch and Rob Tate
Arimatsu-Narumi Shibori: Celebrating 400 Years of Japanese Artisan Design, 2007, dir. Andrew Galli
Because We're Worth It!, Viktor & Rolf, 2004, dir. Femke Wolting
Catwalk, 1996, dir. Robert Leacock
Chanel, Chanel, 1986, dir. Eila Hershon and Rberto Guerra
Chop Suey, 2001, dir. Bruce Weber
Galanos on Galanos: America's King of High Fashion, 1996, Films for the Humanities & Sciences

In and Out of Fashion, 1998, dir. William Klein
Issey Miyake Moves, 1996, Films for the Humanities & Sciences
Lagerfeld Confidentiel, 2006, dir. Rodolphe Marconi
Marc Jacobs and Louis Vuitton, 2007, dir. Loic Prigent
Mastering Fashion Design: Studying with Vivienne Westwood, 2000, Films for the Humanities
  & Sciences
Mode, 1984, dir. William Klein
Model, 1980, dir. Fred Wiseman
Notebooks on Cities and Clothes: Yohji Yamamoto, 1989, dir. Wim Wenders
Seamless, 2005, dir. Douglas Keeve
Secret World of Haute Couture, 2007, dir. Margy Kinmonth
The September Issue, 2009, dir. R. J. Cutler
Signé Chanel (House of Chanel), 2007, dir. Loïc Prigent
Unzipped, 1995, dir. Douglas Keeve
Valentino: The Last Emperor, 2008, dir. Matt Tyrnauer
Yves St. Laurent: His Life and Times/5 Avenue Marceau 75116 Paris, 2007, dir. David Teboul

Biography.com (Documentaries on Giorgio Armani, Halston, Edith Head, Donna Karan,
Calvin Klein, Gloria Vanderbilt, Gianni Versace, Vera Wang)

Fashion Industry

The Fashion Model, 1945, dir. William Beaudine
Qui êtes-vous, Polly Maggoo?, 1966, dir. William Klein
Prêt-à-Porter/Ready to Wear, 1994, dir. Robert Altman
The Devil Wears Prada, 2006, dir. David Frankel

TELEVISION

The Fashion Show (2009–)
Project Runway (2004–)
Sex and the City (1998–2004)

MUSEUMS

Belgium

Mode Museum www.momu.be

Canada

Bata Shoe Museum www.batashoemuseum.ca
Costume Museum of Canada www.costumemuseum.com
Textile Museum of Canada www.textilemuseum.ca/index.cfm

France

Louvre Costume Museum www.louvre.fr
Musée de la Mode et du Costume www.galliera.paris.fr
Musée des Arts Décoratifs, Mode et Textile www.lesartsdecoratifs.fr/francais/mode-et-textile

Japan

Kobe Fashion Museum www.fashionmuseum.or.jp
Kyoto Costume Institute www.kci.or.jp

Netherlands

Gemeentemuseum Den Haag www.gemeentemuseum.nl/index.php?id=031814

Spain

Museo de Traje museodeltraje.mcu.es

United Kingdom

Design Museum www.designmuseum.org
Fashion and Textile Museum www.ftmlondon.org
Fashion Museum, Bath www.fashionmuseum.co.uk
Museum of Costume www.museumofcostume.co.uk
Museum of London
    www.museumoflondon.org.uk/English/Collections/1700Today/Dress-fashion.htm
Victoria and Albert Museum   www.vam.ac.uk

United States

American Textile History Museum www.athm.org
FIDM Museum and Galleries, Hollywood Costume Collection
    fidm.edu/resources/museum+galleries/index.html
Hollywood Museum www.thehollywoodmuseum.com
Los Angeles County Museum of Art www.lacma.org
Kent State University Museum dept.kent.edu/museum/collection/coll.html
Maryhill Museum of Art www.maryhillmuseum.org
Metropolitan Museum of Art, Costume Institute
    www.metmuseum.org/works_of_Art/the_costume_institute
Museum of the City of New York, Costumes and Textiles Collection www.mcny.org
Museum of Fine Arts, Boston www.mfa.org/collections/index.asp?key=31
Museum at the FIT www.fitnyc.edu/museum
Smithsonian National Museum of Natural History americanhistory.si.edu/collections/costume
The Textile Museum www.textilemuseum.org

FASHION WEEKS

Beijing, China www.china.org.cn/english/features/cfwc/203783.htm
Berlin, Germany www.mercedes-benzfashionweek.com
Boston, Massachusetts, USA www.bostonfashionweek.com
Copenhagen, Denmark www.copenhagenfashionweek.com
Chicago, Illinois, USA www.chicagofashionweek.com
Dallas, Texas, USA dallasfashionweek.elle.com/schedule.html
London, UK www.londonfashionweek.co.uk
Los Angeles, California, USA www.fashionweekla.com
Madrid, Spain www.semanamoda.ifema.es
Melbourne, Australia www.lmff.com.au
Miami, Florida, USA www.mercedesbenzfashionweek.com/miami
Milan, Italy www.milanfashionshows.com
Moscow, Russia www.fashionweekinmoscow.com
Mumbai, India www.indiafashionweek.com
New York, New York, USA www.mercedesbenzfashionweek.com
Paris, France www.modeaparis.com
Sydney, Australia www.rafw.com.au
Tokyo, Japan www.jfw.jp/en/index.html

TRADE SHOWS

The Accessories Show (New York/Las Vegas, USA) www.accessoriestheshow.com
Action Sports Retailer (San Diego, USA) www.asrbiz.com
Americasmart (Atlanta, USA) www.americasmart.com
Atelier (New York, USA) www.atelierdesigners.com
Copenhagen International Fashion Fair (Copenhagen, Denmark) www.ciff.dk
Curve (New York/Los Vegas, USA) www.curvexpo.com
Dallas Apparel and Accessories Mart (Dallas, USA) www.dallasmarketcenter.com
Designers and Agents Show (New York, USA) www.designersandagents.com
Ebony Fashion Fair USA www.ebonyfashionfair.com
Enk International Tradeshows (New York, USA) www.enkshows.com
Fame (Fashion Avenue Market Expo) (New York, USA) www.fameshows.com
Florida Fashion Focus (Miami, USA) www.floridafashionfocus.com
Garment Technology Expo (New Delhi, India) www.garmenttechnologyexpo.com
Global Eco Apparel Trade and Fashion Show (Los Vegas, USA) www.globalecoshow.com
Hong Kong Fashion Week (Hong Kong, China) hkfashionweekfw.hktdc.com
Interfilière (Paris, France) www.interfiliere.com
Intermoda (Guadalajara, Mexico) www.intermoda.com.mx
International Istanbul Fashion Fair (Istanbul, Turkey) www.cnr-if.com
Interselection (Paris, France) www.interselection.net
Le Showroom (Paris, France) www.leshowroom.fr
Link It Fashion Trade Show (Bologna, Italy) www.linkitbologna.com
Magic (Las Vegas, USA) www.magiconline.com
Moda Manhattan (New York, USA) www.modamanhattan.com
Moda Salonica (Salonica, Greece) www.moda-salonica.gr
Mode City Show (Paris, France) www.mode-city.com
Modefabriek (Amsterdam, Netherlands) www.modefabriek.nl

Mom2B Maternity Trade Show (Los Angeles, USA) www.mom2btradeshow.com
Motexha Exhibitions Series (Dubai, United Arab Emirates) www.motexhaonline.com
New England Apparel Club (Marlboro, Massachusetts, USA) www.neacshow.com
Nouveau Collective (New York, USA) www.nouveaucollectivetradeshows.com
The Train New York (New York, USA) www.thetrainnewyork.com
Pacific Northwest Apparel Association, NW Trend Show (Seattle, USA) www.nwtrendshow.com
Peru Moda (Lima, Peru) www.perumoda.com
Pitti Immagine (Milan, Italy) www.pittimmagine.com
The Prestige Show (New York, USA) www.theprestigeshow.com
Prêt-à-Porter (Paris, France) www.pretparis.com
Project Global Tradeshow (New York/Las Vegas, USA) www.projectshow.com
Pure (London, UK) www.purewomenswear.co.uk
Stylemax (Chicago, USA) www.stylemaxonline.com
Vendôme Luxury Trade Show (Paris, France) www.vendomeluxurytradeshow.com
White Show (Milan, Italy) www.whiteshow.it
Women's and Children's Chicago Apparel Market (Chicago, USA) www.merchandisemart.com

BRIDAL

Bridal Bazaar (USA) www.bridalbazaar.com
Brides and Beaus (USA) www.bridesandbeaus.com
Dream Wedding Fairs (UK) www.dreamweddingfairs.com
Gateway Bridal Show (USA) www.gatewaycenter.com
The Great Bridal Expo (USA) www.greatbridalexpo.com
Springfield Bridal Show (USA) www.osbornejenks.com
Weddex Korea (Korea) www.weddex.com
Worcester Bridal Expo (USA) www.originalweddingexpo.com

TEXTILES

Asian Pacific Leather Fair (Hong Kong, China/New Delhi, India) www.aplf.com
Direction by Indigo (New York, USA) www.directionshow.com
Expofil (Paris, France) www.expofil.com
Munich Fabric Start (Munich, Germany) www.munichfabricstart.com
Prefab (New York, USA) www.premiumfabricshow.com
Première Vision (Paris, France) www.premierevision.fr

ECOFASHION AND FAIR TRADE

Center for Sustainable Fashion www.sustainable-fashion.com
Ethical Fashion Show www.ethicalfashionshow.com
Fair Trade Federation www.fairtradefederation.org
People Tree www.peopletree.co.uk
TransFair USA www.transfairusa.org
World of Good worldofgood.ebay.com

DIY

DIYStyle www.diystyle.net
Etsy www.etsy.com
Studio 28 Couture www.studio28couture.com
StyleShake www.styleshake.com
Threadbanger www.threadbanger.com

VIRTUAL

Entropia Universe www.entropiauniverse.com
My Virtual Model www.mvm.com
Second Life www.secondlife.com
Second Style www.secondstyle.com
Virtual Fashion www.virtual-fashion.com
Virtual Fashion Technology www.fashiontech.wordpress.com

FORECASTING

The Color Association www.colorassociation.com
Pantone www.pantone.com
Peclers Paris www.peclersparis.com
Permière Vision www.premierevision.fr
Springwise www.springwise.com
Trendwatching.com www.trendwatching.com
WGSN Creative Intelligence www.wgsn.com

CAD/CAM

Artlandia www.artlandia.com
Assyst Bullmer www.assyst-us.com
Clicdesign www.clicdesign.com
Colour Matters www.colourmatters.com
Daz 3D www.daz3d.com/i/software/studio
Gerber Technology www.gerbertechnology.com
Lectra www.lectra.com
OptiTex www.optitex.com
Pointcarré www.pointcarre.com
SnapFashun www.snapfashun.com
Unique Solutions www.uniquescan.com

PRINTING AND PROMOTIONALS

CafePress www.cafepress.com
Modern Postcard www.modernpostcard.com
MOO www.moo.com
Vistaprint www.vistaprint.com

OTHER ONLINE SOURCES

2121 www.2121vision.com
Apparel Search www.apparelsearch.com
Costumer's Manifesto www.costumes.org
Creative Commons www.creativecommons.org
Daily Candy www.dailycandy.com
Danish Fashion Institute www.danishfashioninstitute.dk
David Parrish www.davidparrish.com
Fabric.com www.fabric.com
Fashion Calendar www.fashioncalendar.net
The Fashion Center www.fashioncenter.com
Fashion-Era www.fashion-era.com
Fashion Illustration Gallery www.fashionillustrationgallery.com
Fashion-Incubator www.fashion-incubator.com
Fashion Showroom www.fashionshowroom.com
Fashion Television www.fashiontelevision.com
Fashion Week Daily www.fashionweekdaily.com
Fashion Wire Daily www.fashionwiredaily.com
Fern Mitchell www.fernmitchell.com
Infomat www.infomat.com
Le Book www.lebook.com
Le Couturière Parisienne www.marquise.de
MyStyle www.mystyle.com
Nuno www.nuno.com
Seamless seamless.sigtronica.org
Showroomaccess.com www.showroomaccess.com
Style.Com www.style.com
Textile Affairs www.textileaffairs.com
The Fashion Spot www.thefashionspot.com
Fashion Scholarship Fund www.the-yma.com
Whiting Davis www.whitinganddavis.com

SCHOOLS

Australia

Australian Institute of Fashion Design www.aifd.com.au
Elizabeth Bence Fashion School www.thefashionschool.com.au
RMIT School of Fashion and Textiles www.rmit.edu.au/fashiontech
Whitehouse Institue of Design whitehouse-design.edu.au

Belgium

Royal Academy of Fine Arts, Antwerp www.antwerp-fashion.be

Canada

MONTREAL

Lasalle College Montreal www.collegelasalle.com

TORONTO

Ontario College of Art & Design, Fibre Design Program www.ocad.ca
Ryerson University www.ryerson.ca/fashion

VANCOUVER

Lasalle College Vancouver www.lasallecollegevancouver.com

China

Hong Kong Polytechnic University, Institute of Textiles and Clothing www.itc.polyu.edu.hk

Denmark

Danish Design School www.dkds.dk
Margrethe-Skolen Scandanavian Academy of International Fashion and Design
    www.margrethe-skolen.dk/

France

Les Ecoles de la Chambre Syndicale Parisienne
    www.modeaparis.com/va/ecoles/index.html
ESMOD International www.esmod.com/en/index.html

Germany

Akademie Mode und Design www.amdnet.de
Akademie JAK Modedesign neu.jak-network.de

India

National Institute of Fashion Technology www.niftindia.com

Italy

Istituto di Moda Burgo www.imb.it
Istituto Marangoni www.istitutomarangoni.com
Koefia International Academy of Haute Couture and Art of Costume www.koefia.com

Japan

Bunka Fashion College www.bunka-fc.ac.jp/en/history.html

Kobe Design University www.kobe-du.ac.jp/english/menu/menu.html

Mexico

Instituto Modstil www.modstil.com/instituto.asp

Pakistan

Pakistan School of Fashion Design www.psfd.edu.pk/about.htm

Russia

Moscow Industrial College www.muctr.ru/en/08-hobbies.htm

Spain

Escola Disseny i Moda Gemma www.edimoda.es
Escuela Superior de Moda y Empresa www.esme.es
Estudos Superiores en Deseño Téxtil e Moda de Galiza, Universidade de Vigo
   www.esdemga.uvigo.es

Sweden

Beckmans College of Design www.beckmans.se

United Kingdom

ENGLAND

Central Saint Martins College of Art and Design www.csm.arts.ac.uk
London College of Fashion www.fashion.arts.ac.uk
The Royal College of Arts www.rca.ac.uk
University of Westminster www.wmin.ac.uk
University for the Creative Arts www.ucreative.ac.uk

IRELAND

Limerick Institute of Technology www.lit.ie/Deparments/artdesign.html

SCOTLAND

Edinburgh College of Art www.eca.ac.uk
Heriot-Watt University www.hw.ac.uk
Glasgow School of Art www.gsa.ac.uk
Cardonald College Glasgow www.cardonald.ac.uk

United States

CALIFORNIA

Academy of Art University www.academyart.edu
FIDM/The Fashion Institute of Design & Merchandising www.fidm.edu

FLORIDA

Miami International University of Art & Design www.artinstitutes.edu/miami

GEORGIA

American InterContinental University
    drf.fashionschools.com/American-Intercontinental-University-Buckhead
Savannah College of Art And Design www.scad.edu/fashion/index.cfm

ILLINOIS

School of the Art Institute of Chicago www.artic.edu
Columbia College www.colum.edu/Academics/Art_and_Design/Programs/fashion

MASSACHUSETTS

Bay State College www.BayState.edu
Fisher College www.Fisher.edu
Lasell College www.Lasell.edu
Massachusetts College of Art and Design www.MassArt.edu
Mount Ida College www.MountIda.edu
School of Fashion Design www.schooloffashiondesign.org

NEW YORK

Parsons the New School for Design www.parsons.newschool.edu
Fashion Institute of Technology www.fitnyc.edu
Pratt Institute www.pratt.edu

PENNSYLVANIA

Drexel University www.drexel.edu
Moore College www.moore.edu

PUERTO RICO

Lisa Thon School of Design www.lisathon.com

RHODE ISLAND

Rhode Island School of Design www.risd.edu

INCUBATORS

Australia

Fashion Incubator Melbourne www.fashionincubator.com.au

Canada

Toronto Fashion Incubator www.fashionincubator.com

United Kingdom

Center for Fashion Enterprise www.fashion-enterprise.com
Fashion Fringe www.fashionfringe.co.uk

United States

Garment Industry Development Corporation www.gidc.org
The Fashion Business Inc. www.fashionbizinc.org
Texas' Next Top Designer texasnexttopdesigner.org
U.S. Small Business Administration www.sba.gov

CAREER

24Seven www.24seveninc.com
Fashion Jobs Central www.creativejobscentral.com/fashion-jobs
Enternships www.enternships.com
Fashion Career Center www.fashioncareercenter.com
Fashion Career Expo www.fashioncareerexpo.com
Freelancers Union www.freelancersunion.org
Mayor of the Mall www.mayorofthemall.com
Style Careers www.stylecareers.com
Style Portfolios www.styleportfolios.com
WWDCareers www.wwd.com/wwdcareers

PROFESSIONAL ORGANIZATIONS

Chambre Syndicale Fédération Française de la Couture www.modeaparis.com
Fashion Group International www.fgi.org
Costume Society of Great Britain www.costumesociety.org.uk
Costume Society of America www.costumesocietyamerica.com
Costume Society of Ontario www.costumesociety.ca
Council of Fashion Designers of America (CFDA) www.cfda.com
Fashion Fringe www.fashionfringe.co.uk
Gen Art www.genart.org/fashion
Textile Society of America textilesociety.org
Vintage Fashion Guild www.vintagefashionguild.org

Where do you start with the design process (research, sketching, sculpting) when developing a new collection?

I sketch to begin with, then when the ideas start flowing I'll get started on the collection. Once you have something formed, it's much easier to see the collection coming together.

What drew you to millinery?

I believe in beauty and elegance and communicating thoughts and dreams in a visual way. I started designing hats fifteen years ago while a student at the Royal College of Art. At the time, hats were perceived publicly as something worn by ladies of a certain age and as something from a bygone era. I thought this was totally ridiculous and simply believed that since we all have a head, anyone can wear a hat. I love to work with my hands making something from nothing. Turning two-dimensional materials into a three-dimensional object is the ultimate moment of creativity of my craft.

How have you developed successful partnerships with fashion designers?

It's exciting to work with strong designers because they let you interpret their style. Some designers are specific, but many designers that I have worked with for a long time give me free rein to design with their collections in mind. I am not trying to be diplomatic, but I've worked with so many that I really can't choose one designer above another. It was fun to work with Valentino, because there's only one Valentino. The same holds true for Karl Lagerfeld or Alexander McQueen.

Did you have a mentor in the fashion industry? What did you take away from that relationship that serves you today?

Isabella Blow was the first extraordinary person I met in this country when I moved here from Ireland. Isabella had something common to all of us, but unusual in fashion: a big heart. Her dilemma was that she worked in the fashion business, but was more interested in the fashion than the business. She lived for the art and drama of fashion. She would attend a show with six hundred people dressed in black, and she'd be wearing a lobster hat and a Nell Gwyn–inspired gown. Everyone would sit there all serious, she would be the only one to woo-hoo and clap. She didn't care!

I was so inspired by how she wore my hats. She wore them like she was not wearing them, like they happened to be there. She gave me my first commission while I was still a student at the Royal College of Art. I remember someone said to Isabella, Why is this student making your wedding hat when you could have anyone in the world make it? She didn't give a f*** what they thought. Her focus was creativity. When you were in her focus—and this includes Alexander McQueen, Stella Tennant, and Sophie Dahl, whom she also discovered—it was like being in the middle of a love affair. She was never a snob; she believed in talent, no matter where you came from. I'm a baker's son, Alexander McQueen is a cabdriver's son.

Everybody loved Issy, but she didn't always love herself. She had ovarian cancer and she suffered with depression—it was all too much for her. In twenty years I have met all of my heroes, and nobody in my honest estimation has surpassed her. She was incredible. I used to think there must be others like her, but there weren't; everyone was boring in comparison. I will miss her laugh, her passion, and her humanity. I went to my studio today and Isabella is everywhere. In every hat I've made, every corner I turn, she is there.

How important is the history of fashion to your creative process? What are your references?

People always ask me if I would have preferred to live in a more "hat" era, such as the 1920s or 1940s. But I think it is much more exciting to work today. I use contemporary influences, be it sculpture, or art, or whatever is going in the world at the moment.

Philip Treacy

So many designers dream of showing in the tents during New York's biannual Fashion Week. What would you include on a must-do checklist for designers who want to participate?

Designers must have a complete collection, be tied in with a showroom, and be able to sell the collection. They need a good PR firm to get the right guests invited and in their seats. They should also have a vision and a talent that "deserves" to be seen on the runway. Finally, they have be properly financed, so that the runway show becomes a part of their marketing budget and expenses.

Fashion is by definition about change, so what do you see as the future of Fashion Week? Does that direction include technology? What part do industry publications like fashionweekdaily.com play?

Fashion is always changing, and technology makes the images available instantly all over the world through a wide variety of devices, from computers to phones to Blackberries. At the same time, nothing replaces seeing the clothes in person on models on a runway, seeing them move, and seeing how a professional audience responds to them. Technology will, of course, continue to play an evermore important role, as will fashion websites, blogs, and publications like www.fashionweekdaily.com that have a unique point of view and audience allegiance.

Based on your experience, what advice would you give designers about standing out in the crowded roster of shows during Fashion Week? How important is the buzz around celebrity associations for a designer?

Be true to your own spirit, work hard, and put the very best effort forward. You have a quick shot—maybe fifteen minutes—to make an impression, to give the audience a sense of your vision, a sense that this is a collection, and that there are many more ideas in your head to pursue in future seasons. Don't try to shock to get gratuitous media coverage. Celebrities are great for exposure if they make sense, if the designer knows them, and they are, or potentially would be, the right type of customer for the clothes.

As a global leader in fashion event production, what does IMG look for in someone interested in pursuing a career in fashion show/event production?

We look for someone who is bright, eager, and passionate, and able to convey all that. Someone who will be the first to arrive and the last to leave. Someone who comes dressed appropriately for a job in fashion (and is never chewing gum). Someone resourceful who can research and write. Not someone who sits at the computer all day, checking his/her Facebook pages or shopping online.

Photograph by Shawn Ehlers/WireImage.

Fern Mallis

What advice can you give a designer about reaching out to the press?

Reach out when you have a collection that's constructed in a professional and polished manner (seams finished, fit appropriate) and when you truly understand the story you mean to tell in your collection. Your inspirations will vary, but you should have an overarching vision of who would wear your clothes that's consistent from season to season. In terms of a how-to on contacting the press: Mail or e-mail a short bio (two to three paragraphs, max, should suffice) and a look book or website link. Afterward, follow up with a call. Even if an editor doesn't immediately respond (and that's pretty common), politely keep in touch. A good way to do it is by updating publications each season with five or six images from your latest collection. Edit it down to the best pieces rather than sending everything. Choose images, too, that would be most relevant to the publication—take into account whether the fashion they feature is edgy or mainstream and whether they need to stay under a certain retail price. Editors will also want to know where you sell your goods. If they are a city-specific or regional publication, they will want you to have a store, or a website at least, where readers can go to purchase your designs.

What makes a designer newsworthy?

A designer can be newsworthy for a number of reasons: they're getting buzz from influential retailers who sell their goods, they've developed a taste-making clientele that's seen or photographed regularly in their outfits, or simply because they have a dynamic vision for dressing that they're presenting in a fresh and relevant way. Writers are interested, as well, in collections that are unusual in concept or trying to reach new niches. An eco-friendly prom dress collection, for example, would be more newsworthy than a beaded earring collection or contemporary denim line. Fashion press will also consider whom a designer has worked with (on any level—even an internship counts) in the past when considering whether the person merits coverage.

What are some of the most important things to consider when writing about fashion?

It's important to describe the overall mood of the collection, rather than just a string of individual pieces. It might be "washed cotton pieces with a gentle, beachy mood" or "structured cocktail dresses with an emphasis on asymmetry, knife-edged pleats, and stiff, ornate fabrics." Tell readers about the strongest pieces, who might wear such garments and on what occasions. Both consumers and retailers who might wish to carry a collection will want information on pricing (for example, "T-shirts start at $35") and where the pieces are currently sold. As in all writing of any kind, avoid clichés! Lots of aspiring designers dressed dolls—Barbie, paper, or otherwise—as kids, so strive to understand more specifically how they've developed their taste, their fit, and what they want to convey about modern dressing. Not every shift dress should be described as á la Jackie Kennedy, but it is important to understand some of the basic lingo, some of the hallmarks of each design era, and the notable women who best exemplified the look. To that end, legendary *Vogue* editor Diana Vreeland's memoir, *D.V.*, is a terrific read and an example of fashion writing at its best. And don't overlook movies for getting good fashion background: Tippi Hedren in *The Birds*, Audrey Hepburn in *Breakfast at Tiffany's* or *Charade*, Ali MacGraw in *Love Story*, Winona Ryder in *Heathers* in the 1980s or *Reality Bites* in the grungy 1990s, Kate Hudson in *Almost Famous*. I could go on, but I'll spare you.

Which magazines, newspapers, and websites would you recommend that designers read to stay up-to-date and informed about fashion?

For a great take on the contemporary zeitgeist, I love *Lucky* magazine and their website, which features a number of great blogs. *Lucky* excels at the kind of "high-low" dressing that's driving a lot of today's fashion. They were one of the first publications to intensively cover the contemporary price point, which has been one of the strongest markets of the last decade. The trade newspaper *Women's Wear Daily* is also a must-read for anyone seriously interested in fashion. It has been called the Bible of the fashion industry because it covers the business and culture of the industry—everything from fiber and fabric to what the socialites and street kids are wearing. Style.com does a terrific job of covering the runway collections. I'd pay particular attention to leading-edge designers such as Marc Jacobs, Miuccia Prada, Alexander McQueen, and Nicholas Ghesquiere at Balenciaga, whose brainstorms each season ripple down to a wave of interpretations. Then there is just being curious and looking at lots of people wherever you can—in airports and cafés, in *US Weekly* and on You Tube—keeping your eyes as open as you can.

Photograph by Meghan Jones Colangelo.

Katherine Bowers

How do you successfully tune in to what your retail customers or television audience are looking for?

In the store, it's great because the best information doesn't come from trend reporting, magazines, or hired services; it comes direct from your customer. We listen to our clients each season, then go back, and try to find the looks. Many times, it isn't me bringing new lines into the store, it's the client.

For the TV shows, we do use data. I get to know the audiences for *Tim Gunn's Guide to Style* and *The Rachael Ray Show*. The greatest tool today is the blog, so that we can actually speak to the consumer. When I read people's blogs and they tell me what they like or dislike, I absolutely apply that information. The same goes for QVC: I asked the audience to vote on different looks and we were inundated with people expressing what style they liked best. We're lucky that we can gather that info for free and simultaneously can fine-tune that relationship.

As a retailer, what are you looking for from a designer?

I'm looking for quality, craftsmanship, and uniqueness in design. The designer needs to be a good partner to me and my clients, offering special events, trunk shows, etc. These initiatives truly give clients a deeper understanding of what they're investing in.

What advice could you give to designers about working with stylists?

Designers should be open to working with stylists and specifically listen to their feedback on the function of the design. Stylists deal on a personal level with the customers and get a real sense of what they want. Sometimes designs become limiting even though they're beautiful. People need design to be more functional. Designers should know how to make things work from dawn to dusk. Today, I'm trying to figure out what can I wear to both an afternoon meeting and an evening event because I have no time to change in between. If designers want to remain successful, they need to stay focused on everyday apparel.

Working with celebrities should be a collaboration. We stylists are the middleman, we act as the matchmaker. The service needs to be there from the designer. The designer has to be flexible and be committed to the relationship. Sometimes that means tweaking concepts or coming up with a new idea. I work closely with designers who will do that because I need to please my customer. Even if I love the design, I won't refer designers if they aren't committed.

How important are associations with celebrities for the designer? And what's the best way to cultivate those relationships?

Today, these relationships are critical. Celebs are marketing tools for the brand. They can also create the image. You're getting a free editorial ad every time that person walks on the red carpet in your creation. Weeklies cover this constantly. When you're starting out, it really puts you on a very different level to have that relationship. It needs to be a focused effort. You have to matchmake your design philosophy with the right people; it's valuable when they strike the right chord.

Photograph courtesy of Gretta Monahan.

Gretta Monahan

So many companies seem to have adopted the word "luxury" in some way or another. How would you define what a luxury brand really is?

A true luxury brand features products representing the highest level of quality obtainable within a given category. Fabrication and manufacturing detail are of particular importance, whether the design is classic or more adventurous.

At one time, "Made in Italy" or "Made in France" designated luxury; however, luxury products are now manufactured worldwide.

As a retailer, what are you looking for from a designer?

I'm looking for quality, craftsmanship, and uniqueness in design. The designer needs to be a good partner to me and my clients, offering special events, trunk shows, etc. These initiatives truly give clients a deeper understanding of what they're investing in.

You saw something in designer Tom Ford that proved to be exactly what Gucci needed to be repositioned as a luxury brand. What advice would you give designers interested in pursuing a successful career with a major fashion house?

Tom Ford, whose previous job was at Perry Ellis Jeans, was one of several designers hired by Gucci in 1990. He initially reported to the design director of apparel, who, in turn, reported to the creative director. Tom's exceptional talents were apparent early on, and when the design director left the company, he was the natural successor for the job, supervising the design of all product categories. Having grown in that position, he was a natural candidate to lead the company as creative director four years later. Tom's success took place over a period of years as part of a natural growth process: He learned step by step, and his talents were recognized along the way.

What should a new designer be aware of regarding manufacturing luxury goods today?

Do not expect overnight success in the industry. Experience is integral to a growth strategy that will ultimately lead to success.

From the perspective of someone who has been at the helm of high-end retailers such as Bergdorf Goodman, what makes a new designer stand out as an attractive investment?

In my experience, it has been designers who think out of the box—but not too far out. Hard work and talent are a prerequisite, with a little bit of luck added to the equation.

Photograph by Ted Thai/Time Life Pictures/Getty Images.

Dawn Mello

You are the head of the textile and fashion arts department at the Museum of Fine Arts, Boston. What makes fashion collectible?

Museum curators acquire works for their collections based on the collecting policy of that institution. An art museum might focus on works that are examples of good design, reflect important trends in design and society, or are key examples of a specific designer's work. A historical society might focus on costume and textiles that were worn, used, or made in the specific community. Each museum will have different criteria for collecting; however, all acquisitions should be in good condition and be exhibitable.

What advice would you give a designer about researching and using museum collections?

Be specific. Know what you want to look at and why. Don't be afraid to contact the curator and discuss your project. If the curator is a good one, they will be the person most knowledgeable about the collection and be able to assist you in selecting the most appropriate pieces. And maybe they will introduce you to objects in the collection you didn't know you wanted to see.

Why do you believe that collectors and museums are now taking fashion more seriously?

There is a growing understanding in academia that fashion, clothing, and textiles were and continue to be important forces in society. More scholars are examining the social, cultural, economic, and historic roles of these objects. As the understanding of textiles and dress increases, so, too, does the appreciation of these collections. They will play increasingly important roles within museums and academia.

Which resources should be a part of every designer's reference library?

Anything that you find inspiring.

Pamela Parmal

Index

Acknowledgments

Special thanks are due to the designers and fashion professionals interviewed here: Joseph Abboud, Katherine Bowers, Carla Fernández, Fern Mallis, Dawn Mello, Isaac Mizrahi, Gretta Monahan, Pam Parmal, Ralph Rucci, Yeohlee Teng, and Philip Treacy.

And to Alicia Kennedy, my editor, Chris Grimley and Kelly Smith, our graphic designers, and Justin Cote and Victoria Dominguez, my assistants.

Thanks to Robert Frye, Viola Gonzalez, Tina Calderin, Jorden Irizarry, Rebecca Gonzalez, Kilsy Curiel, Rafael Villalona, Fred Rogers, Jake and Ena Calderin, Jennifer Hudson, Jaycey Wetherington, Jaclyn McGeehan, Jamie Mendoza, Kathleen Pilarski, Patricia & Wallace Frye, Richard Brooks, Mary Garthe, Louis Selvitella, Javier Berdecia, Tracy Aiguier, Lisa Baker, Cynthia, Alex and Zak Atkinson, Jacobo and Edith Calderin, Fructuoso, Gloria and Leslie Gonzalez, Carmen Rita Gonzalez, James Hannon, Sondra Grace, Richard Bath, Cheryl Richardson, Richard Ventura, Mariclaire Hession, Cloud Devine, Laura Soelter, Doreen Mendez, Meredith Byam-Miller, Dianna Matherly, Mary Higgins, Bethany Van Delft, Gina Fox, Mike and Rosita Boudjouk, Forough Vaziri, Pedro Miranda, Shirley Sweet, Anita Trottman, Mrs. Garofalo, Mrs. Walsh, Betty Riaz, Christine Liu, Donna Rice, Robert Birnbaum, Maggie Trichon, Alfred Fiandaca, Frank Xavier, Katherine Dibble, Jess Meyer, Haven Tyler, Beate Becker, Jim Goshen, Ray Cadrin, Lois Ingledew, Tania Haddad, Rachael Lahren, Rosina Rucci, Jennifer Lurie, Nina Tryon, Laurie Austin, Ian Wagasky, Myra Hackel, Brianne Carmody, Anne Vanderheyden, Christina Ramirez.

And to the faculty, administration, and students, past and present, at the School of Fashion Design in Boston, Massachusetts.

About the Author

Jay Calderin was born and raised in New York City. He teaches a wide variety of fashion and professional development courses at the School of Fashion Design in Boston, where he is also the Director of Creative Marketing. He founded and serves as Executive Director of Boston Fashion Week and is the Regional Director of Fashion Group International of Boston. Calderin's designs have appeared in the pages of *Vogue* and *Elle* magazines. On a personal note, he has been involved with the Big Brothers Big Sisters organization as a mentor since 2001 and was named Big Brother of the Year in 2009.